DIRECTIONS IN MUSIC CATALOGING

Music Library Association
Technical Reports Series
Mark McKnight, Series Editor

1. *SLACC: The Partial Use of the Shelf List as a Classed Catalog,* by Donald Siebert (1973)
2. *Directory of Music Library Automation Projects,* by Garrett Bowles (1979)
3. *Proceedings of the Institute on Library of Congress Music Cataloging Policies and Procedures,* ed. by David Sommerfield (1975)
4. *The Classification and Cataloging of Sound Recordings: An Annotated Bibliography,* by Barbara Knisely Gaeddert (1977) 2nd Edition (1981)
5. *Recordings of Non-Western Music, Subject and Added Entry Access,* by Judith Kaufman (1977)
6. *Index to Audio Equipment Reviews, 1978,* by Arne Jon Arneson and Stuart Milligan (1979)
7. *Shelving Capacity in the Music Library,* by R. Michael Fling (1981)
8. *Index to Audio Equipment Reviews, 1979,* by Arne Jon Arneson and Stuart Milligan (1980)
9. *Shelflisting Music: Guidelines for Use with the Library of Congress Classification, M,* by Richard P. Smiraglia (1981)
10. *Index to Audio Equipment Reviews, 1980,* by Arne Jon Arneson and Stuart Milligan (1981)
11. *The Acquisition and Cataloging of Music and Sound Recordings: A Glossary,* by Suzanne Thorin and Carole Franklin Vidali (1984)
12. *Index to Audio Equipment Reviews, 1981,* by Arne Jon Arneson and Stuart Milligan (1982)
13. *The MARC Music Format: From Inception to Publication,* by Donald Seibert (1982)
14. *Library of Congress Subject Headings for Recordings of Western Non-Classical Music,* by Judith Kaufman (1983)
15. *Sheet Music Cataloging and Processing,* by Sarah Jean Shaw and Lauralee Shiere (1984)
16. *Authority Control in Music Libraries: Proceedings of the Music Library Association Preconference, March 5, 1985,* ed. by Ruth Tucker (1989)
17. *Planning and Caring for Library Audio Facilities,* by James P. Cassaro (1989)
18. *Careers in Music Librarianship: Perspectives from the Field,* ed. by Carol Tatian (1991)
19. *In Celebration of Revised 780: Music in the Dewey Decimal Classification,* by Richard Bruce Wursten (1990)
20. *Space Utilization in Music Libraries,* ed. by James P. Cassaro (1992)
21. *Archival Information Processing for Sound Recordings,* by David H. Thomas (1992)
22. *Collection Assessment in Music Libraries,* by Jane Gottlieb (1994)
23. *Knowing the Score: Preserving Collections of Music,* ed. by Mark Roosa and Jane Gottlieb (1994)
24. *World Music in Music Libraries,* by Carl Rahkonen (1994)
25. *Cataloging Musical Moving Image Material,* by Lowell E. Ashley (1996)
26. *Guide to Writing Collection Development Policies for Music,* by Amanda Maple and Jean Morrow (2001)
27. *Music Librarianship at the Turn of the Century,* ed. by Richard Griscom and Amanda Maple (2000)
28. *Cataloging Sheet Music: Guidelines for Use with AACR2 and the MARC Format,* ed. by Lois Schultz (2003)
29. *Careers in Music Librarianship II: Traditions and Transitions,* ed. by Paula Elliot and Linda Blair (2004)
30. *Shelflisting Music: Guidelines for Use with the Library of Congress Classification, M,* 2nd Edition, by Richard P. Smiraglia (2008)
31. *Uniform Titles for Music,* by Michelle S. Koth (2008)
32. *Directions in Music Cataloging,* ed. by Peter H. Lisius and Richard Griscom (2012)

DIRECTIONS IN MUSIC CATALOGING

Edited by

Peter H. Lisius and Richard Griscom

Co-published by

 Music Library Association

and

 A-R Editions, Inc.
Middleton, Wisconsin

To the memory of Arsen Ralph Papakhian:
teacher, mentor, colleague, and friend

Arsen Ralph Papakhian (1948–2010)

Library of Congress Cataloging-in-Publication Data

Directions in music cataloging / edited by Peter H. Lisius and Richard Griscom.
   p. cm. — (Music Library Association technical reports ; 32)
  Includes bibliographical references and index.
  ISBN 978-0-89579-719-3 (alk. paper)
 1. Cataloging of music. 2. Papakhian, A. Ralph (Arsen Ralph), 1948–2010—Influence.
I. Lisius, Peter H. II. Griscom, Richard.
  ML111.D43 2012
  025.3'48—dc23
                                                      2011032299

ISBN 978-0-89579-719-3

A-R Editions, Inc., Middleton, Wisconsin 53562
© 2012 All rights reserved.
Printed in the United States of America
1 3 5 7 9 10 8 6 4 2

TABLE OF CONTENTS

Introduction ... vii
    H. Stephen Wright

Part 1: The Foundations of Music Cataloging Today ... 1
Music in the OCLC WorldCat: A Replication ... 3
    The Students of UWM LIS 791 Summer 2010 and Richard P. Smiraglia
Theoretical Implications Arising from the Study of Personal Name Headings in the Indiana University Music Library Card Catalogs ... 15
    Richard P. Smiraglia
Furthering Access to Music: A History of the Music OCLC Users Group ... 27
    Jay Weitz

Part 2: Cataloging Theory in Transition ... 41
Works and Expressions in RDA: Problems and Solutions ... 43
    Damian Iseminger
The Music Genre/Form Project: History, Accomplishments, and Future Directions ... 63
    Beth Iseminger
Dreams from My Library ... 79
    Michelle Hahn

Part 3: Current and Emerging Standards in Practice ... 87
Cataloging Ethnographic Audiovisual Field Collections ... 89
    Suzanne Mudge

Square Pegs in Round Holes: Adapting Cataloging Metadata Standards for
    Use with Digital Media Files   111
    Peter H. Lisius

The FRBR Models: Thinking More Deeply about Library Metadata   139
    Jenn Riley

Epilogue: Arsen Ralph Papakhian   155

Ralph: A Remembrance   157
    Sue Ellen Stancu

About the Contributors   165

Index   169

INTRODUCTION

H. Stephen Wright

"Why?"

This simple, direct question encapsulates Ralph Papakhian's influence on me, and perhaps it characterizes Ralph's influence on the world of music librarianship and on so many of my colleagues and friends. Delivered in a flat monotone (in fact, a more accurate transcription would omit the question mark), it was not so much a question as a challenge—a challenge to one's assumptions about cataloging, librarianship, politics, philosophy, or anything else you might be discussing with him. When talking to Ralph, I often found myself explaining ideas that I believed were self-evident and defending ideas that I thought required no defense.

I entered the library profession, and received my training as a music cataloger from Ralph and his colleague Sue Stancu, during an era that a younger generation of librarians would hardly recognize. Of course, there was no Internet and most libraries still depended on card catalogs, but it would be simplistic to make the comparison in technological terms alone. The most profound distinction is that the American library world of that era was a hierarchical universe, as rigid as the Elizabethan "Great Chain of Being," and the Library of Congress occupied the pinnacle of that cosmos. Cataloging produced by LC was the gold standard; its quality was simply above question. Catalogers who found themselves obliged to produce original bibliographic records did their best to replicate what they believed LC would have done with the item; if they followed idiosyncratic local policies, they did so secure in the knowledge that this deviant cataloging would remain safely buried in their local catalog. When music catalogers first began tentatively adding score and sound recording information to the OCLC database, they did so under the considerable disadvantage of having no LC-generated MARC records available for music materials.

Ralph, as I quickly learned, respected LC's lofty position in the music library world but was hardly awed into passive acceptance. I recall one summer afternoon when he was guiding me through the cataloging of a Prokofiev work, and I ventured the opinion that LC's uniform title for that work didn't seem right. I expected Ralph to shrug indifferently and say that LC had decided the matter, and that was that. To my astonishment, he suggested I write a letter to LC questioning their decision and explaining what I thought the title should be. I felt a bit like Dorothy being sent to confront the Great Oz, but I wrote the letter and was stunned to receive a reply a few weeks later from an LC librarian, who thanked me and promised that they would correct the uniform title. It was my first lesson from Ralph on the power of *why*.

One should not infer from this anecdote that Ralph was contemptuous of cataloging rules or slapdash in his work. He frequently questioned the underlying assumptions of what catalogers did, but he was acutely aware of the importance of consistency and accuracy in cataloging and pursued those ideals with intensity and passion. During that same summer I had the opportunity to watch Ralph add an original bibliographic record to OCLC; although we had reviewed it together and it looked perfect to me, he proceeded to move the cursor through the entire record, tapping the right arrow key in a slow, deliberate tempo as he checked every single character. "My rep is on the line here," he muttered when I questioned the need for this microscopic examination.

I met Ralph the year after he and Richard Smiraglia published their celebrated study, "Music in the OCLC Online Union Catalog: A Review," in *Notes*.[1] At a time when music catalogers were still struggling to assimilate this new technology, Ralph clearly saw the implications of a world of shared cataloging newly unmoored from the isolation of card catalogs and the comforting leadership of the Library of Congress. For this volume, Richard Smiraglia and his students have replicated the original study, and we can now clearly see what was perhaps inevitable when Ralph and his colleagues began typing the first original records on the glowing green screens of their OCLC terminals: the explosion of the OCLC database into a resource with vast coverage—and vast variations in quality and style as bibliographic records emanate from an ever-growing multiplicity of sources. In contrast to the rigid, LC-centered cataloging world of the 1970s, cataloging is on its way to becoming a fungible commodity for which the original source is increasingly irrelevant.

Ralph's long career spanned multiples eras of cataloging; as Sue Stancu's delightful biographical sketch tells us, he began his professional career in 1973 and arrived at Indiana University in 1975, just a few years before the second edition of *Anglo-American Cataloguing Rules* was published. The impact of AACR2 on libraries—particularly music libraries—was almost astronomical in scope. A seemingly innocuous phrase in the rules for formulating personal name headings—"the name by which he or she is commonly known"—obliged catalogers to alter or replace an unimaginable number of physical cards, at a cost that has never been fully calculated. Yet, during this time of upheaval, notable people in the library profession were openly dismissive of the impact of this crucial element of AACR2, citing the oft-repeated truism (known as Lotka's Law) that most authors write only one book.

It was Ralph Papakhian who stepped forward to articulate why this facile perception—which persists today—was utterly, disastrously wrong for music collections. Here, Richard Smiraglia recounts the remarkable story of Ralph's 1985 study of personal name headings in the Indiana University Music Library's catalogs;[2] Smiraglia correctly identifies Ralph's work as a political gesture as well as a scholarly achievement. Anyone who knew Ralph knows that he was an intensely political person, unafraid of taking bold and counter-intuitive positions; although I have always considered myself a liberal, I always felt oddly conventional when discussing politics with Ralph (who generally supported obscure third-party candidates I had never heard of). If Ralph had not published that powerful article, it is difficult to imagine who else would have, or could have. Although most music librarians intuitively know that music libraries are intrinsically different from general libraries, making this point so decisively on the national stage required the intellectual acuity and political boldness of Ralph Papakhian.

Throughout his career, Ralph was also deeply involved with the Music OCLC Users Group, an organization whose history mirrors the evolution of music cataloging in the digital era. Jay Weitz's crisp and concise history of MOUG (in which Jay typically minimizes his own significant role) demonstrates how far our field has progressed from its early struggles with the new and unfamiliar MARC music format. Now, the OCLC database—with its current and quite apt name, WorldCat—is a vast bibliographic organism that has long since transcended its role as a tool for sharing the work of cataloging, and MOUG is still playing a critical role in insuring that the idiosyncrasies of music materials are acknowledged, understood, and accounted for by OCLC. Ralph, of course, was a fixture at MOUG conferences for more than three decades and served a distinguished term as chair. Jay's history takes note of Ralph's satirical essay on "cataloger envy," which he wrote for the *MOUG Newsletter*; never has the peculiar and sometimes strained relationship between catalogers and other librarians been so vividly depicted.

Ralph's career, which began with the birth of OCLC and AACR2, extended well into the transitional era that is upon us now. The FRBR (Functional Requirements for Bibliographic Records) conceptual model suggests a bold new path toward ending the "format chauvinism" of AACR2 and previous cataloging schemes that are fixated on describing physical objects. FRBR may allow librarians to make the crucial distinction between the objects they collect and their underlying intellectual entities, a distinction once evoked by Arthur C. Clarke's haunting description of a Bach recording as "the frozen thoughts of a brain that had been dust for twice a hundred years."[3] Yet making this model a practical reality is not unproblematic. Damien Iseminger offers an incisive critique of how a new cataloging code, *Resource Description & Access* (RDA), approaches works and their expressions, and he suggests ways to ameliorate the problems they identify.

Yet it would be remiss to characterize music cataloging as an endeavor that seeks only to collocate names and works within the Western canon. In a clear and practical explanation of how ethnographic audio and visual recordings are cataloged at Indiana University's Archives of Traditional Music, Suzanne Mudge reminds us that not all materials fit the comforting and familiar patterns that AACR2 and RDA are designed to address. Beth Iseminger examines the Music Genre/Form Project, a commendable effort to release music catalogers from the stodgy confinement of subject headings that frequently—and awkwardly—conflate musical genres and performance media. The significance of this project cannot be understated; it is incredible to realize that when users of our sophisticated online catalogs choose a subject search, they are searching the phrases once intended to be typed in red ink in the top margins of catalog cards. A rebuilding of our entire concept of subject access to music is long overdue.

Ralph Papakhian was intimately involved in early attempts to implement online public access library catalogs. I recall many discussions with Ralph of the strengths and manifold weaknesses of the primitive online catalogs that proliferated during the 1980s and early 1990s. Ralph was especially disturbed by online catalogs that could not be used effectively without training. He once declared that a good catalog should be "self-revelatory" and not require users to think like catalogers. I particularly recall Ralph bringing a thick computer printout to one conference;

it was a list of all searches input into Indiana University's online catalog over a period of several days. Reading this printout was a stunning experience; there were many searches typed as questions in natural language, as if the computer was some kind of oracle. Almost none of the searches obeyed the patterns that bibliographic instruction librarians implore students to use. Of course, online catalogs have improved considerably since then, but we still have a long way to go in realizing the full potential of the technology available to us. In a meditation on the state of library catalog technology, Michelle Hahn reflects on the disturbing gap between our lofty dreams of a FRBR-based catalog and the reality of online catalog systems produced by commercial vendors.

Ralph left our world in 2010, but he lived long enough to see the beginning of trends that will absorb the attention of music catalogers for decades to come. Of course, Ralph realized that libraries were inevitably moving away from collecting physical carriers for sound recordings, as Indiana University pioneered this approach in their renowned Variations digital music project. Yet while libraries were puzzling over how to deploy digital music in their own collections, the rest of the world went about assimilating digital music in their own way. The overwhelming popularity of the iPod and other digital music players, and the advent of the MP3 audio file format, has led to some unintended consequences, which Peter Lisius examines in his essay. Unsurprisingly, the metadata embedded in MP3 files does not conform to library cataloging codes; Lisius discusses the feasibility of reconciling that data with AACR2 and RDA.

Ralph Papakhian was no Luddite and had no fear of innovation; he was the first person I knew who utilized electronic mail and one of the first people I knew who owned a computer. But he did not embrace anything simply because it was new, and he disdained the fads that are endemic in the library profession. As Jenn Riley points out in her essay on the potential of the FRBR conceptual model, Ralph was somewhat skeptical of RDA. In particular, Ralph recognized that implementing this vastly new and more sophisticated approach to cataloging and authority control would have political and economic implications. Ralph was keenly aware of the hidden costs of many mundane activities in libraries; I recall him describing how he determined the cost of a particularly onerous committee meeting by calculating what each person in attendance earned per hour. Ralph was acutely cognizant of the politics in the library world that militated against anything that increased the scope of authority work. His landmark 1985 study of personal name headings was a counterweight against a tide of library administrators who breezily insisted (and continue to insist) that "authority control doesn't matter."

The implementation of RDA, pointing to the future FRBRization of the bibliographic universe, is both a turning point and a grave risk. As comfortable and reassuring as AACR2 and MARC and Library of Congress Subject Headings may be, they are all rooted in a reality that is disappearing around us: a world of card catalogs, of libraries as walled gardens and librarians as gatekeepers. We cannot continue to use these increasingly obsolete tools to catalog a digital world that refuses to conform to our rules. Yet the risk is that the colossal effort and the equally colossal cost of this paradigm shift will be viewed as pointless and unnecessary by the world at large. We live in a society where even people of power and influence assume that all human knowledge is freely available on the Internet, that Google is the only intermediary required, and that libraries will disappear within our lifetimes.

Librarians are fond of complaining about these misguided perceptions, but too often they ignore the political realities lurking behind them. Just a few decades ago, at the beginning of Ralph Papakhian's career, the Library of Congress was our primary provider of cataloging—and this role was never questioned. It was a public good that we expected government to provide, like interstate highways or a safe food supply. Now, consider the shift in our nation's politics in the last thirty years; increasingly, government is viewed as malevolent and incompetent. Many of our political leaders are trapped in an Ayn Rand fever dream in which the private sector will meet all of society's needs, and government has no duty except to remove any impediments to business—or annihilate itself. In this political environment, should libraries embark on an immense and costly restructuring of the bibliographic edifice, particularly when much of that cost will be borne by public institutions?

Ralph Papakhian was a realist; he dealt in what was possible and practical. He did not tilt at windmills. Yet he believed passionately in the importance of cataloging as a public good. He is not here for us to consult, but I strongly suspect that given the choices we are faced with—cling to the past, or move ahead—he would advise us to move ahead. Not long before I wrote this introduction, President Barack Obama proposed an ambitious, far-reaching plan to rebuild America's decaying infrastructure. Of course, his plan addresses things like bridges and highways, not cataloging. But what is cataloging if not the infrastructure of our intellectual world?

In the conclusion of her essay, Jenn Riley suggests that as we continue to develop new models for metadata, we continue to ask "why" as Ralph often did. This, I believe, is Ralph's legacy to the music cataloging world: to move forward, while never ceasing to question our own assumptions and conclusions. Music cataloging has a future—perhaps not the most comfortable future, and certainly not a perfect, untroubled future—but a future nevertheless, and it is incumbent on us to plan for it. The essays in this volume offer the signposts; let us follow them, without falling under the spell of fads or lofty fantasies—and, like Ralph, always asking ourselves *why*.

NOTES

[1] Richard P. Smiraglia and Arsen R. Papakhian, "Music in the OCLC Online Union Catalog: A Review," *Notes* 38, no. 2 (December 1981): 257–74.

[2] Arsen R. Papakhian, "The Frequency of Personal Name Headings in the Indiana University Music Library Card Catalogs," *Library Resources & Technical Services* 29, no. 3 (July/September 1985): 273–85.

[3] Arthur C. Clarke. *2001: A Space Odyssey* (New York: Roc, 2000), 230.

PART 1

The Foundations of Music Cataloging Today

The cataloging environment in the early 1980s was in a period of tumultuous change. AACR2 had been implemented in January 1981, and the era of the online public access catalog (OPAC) was about to begin. As technological innovations in OCLC and other bibliographic utilities increased, and the transition from printed card catalogs to OPACs gained speed, the unique challenges in providing access to music materials came to the forefront. These challenges manifested themselves in ways that demanded not only technological innovations that met these unique needs, but also a shift of thinking about access to musical works—a shift that clearly differentiated the issues surrounding access to musical works from those surrounding access to other formats.

Several important studies were done by Ralph Papakhian during this time: one, with Richard Smiraglia, examining holdings of musical works in the OCLC database, the other examining the frequency of name headings in the Indiana University Music Library. In the second article, within the context of a catalog containing musical works, Papakhian challenged the widely held assumptions articulated by Lotka's Law of author productivity, predicated on the belief that most authors write (or "compose") only one work. As Papakhian would examine in his article, Lotka's Law did not account for the fact that most composers "write" multiple works, nor did it, as Smiraglia writes in the present volume, account for multiple iterations of works—a situation that is much more prevalent among musical works than works in other formats. Papakhian's findings influenced the way AACR2 was used and affected the music cataloging landscape in the late 1980s.

The 1980s also saw the rise of the Music OCLC User's Group (MOUG), which had and continues to have a significant impact on the way in which musical works are accessed in OPACs everywhere. MOUG was originally a task force that worked with OCLC on the implementation of the MARC music format, and after soon after its founding, MOUG organized the Retrospective Music Project (REMUS), which evolved into the first NACO "funnel" project, the NACO Music Project (NMP). Many of the authors in this volume have served in some leadership capacity in MOUG.

The theoretical studies and technological innovations that manifested themselves in the 1980s built the foundation on which current music cataloging is based. As will be seen in the following articles, Ralph Papakhian was at the center of these early theories and innovations. It is within this context that the volume begins.

MUSIC IN THE OCLC WORLDCAT
A Replication

THE STUDENTS OF UWM LIS 791 SUMMER 2010 AND RICHARD P. SMIRAGLIA

Abstract: In 1981, Ralph Papakhian and Richard Smiraglia published the study "Music in the OCLC Online Union Catalog: A Review" in *Notes*. The paper reported on the nascent music cataloging situation in what was to become WorldCat at a time when coverage was spotty, there was little cataloging contributed by the Library of Congress, and major music libraries were struggling to make good use of the OCLC utility. The study won an award from the Music Library Association and served as an opening manifesto for what became the Music OCLC Users Group (MOUG). To honor Papakhian, Smiraglia and students in his 2010 summer session LIS 791 Music Cataloging course at the University of Wisconsin–Milwaukee replicated the study. Students assessed currency by checking lists of music, books, and recordings recently issued to see how quickly they become part of WorldCat. Using a random sample of score and musical sound bibliographic records contributed by the OCLC Office of Research, students assessed the accuracy and quality of cataloging for scores and recordings in WorldCat.

MUSIC, MARC, OCLC AND THE 1980S

Music cataloging in the 1980s seemed like something of a brave new world, at least when it came to the shift from manual systems to automated cataloging. The MARC (MAchine Readable Cataloging) format for monographs had been published in 1968[1] and implemented on a large scale by the Library of Congress (LC) for card production. The MARC music format, however, was not published until 1976,[2] despite a very rich history of research and development in automated music cataloging.[3] Automated cataloging support and offline card production for monographs and serials was available from the mid-1960s through the precursor of the world's now sole bibliographic utility, OCLC, which was then called the Ohio College Library Center. Created in 1965 and incorporated in 1967, OCLC quickly became a leading purveyor of MARC-based cataloging services, but not for music. It was not until 1978 that the music format was implemented by OCLC, not until 1980 by the research library service then called RLIN (Research Libraries Information Network), and not until 1985 by LC on a large scale. So, for active catalogers of music in the early 1980s, cataloging online had a sort of thrill attached, because there were few or no precedents. Meetings of the Music Library Association Cataloging Committee were always exciting, and there was frequent interaction among heads of major music cataloging centers, such as those in the largest research libraries. For example, the Sibley Library (Eastman School of Music) and the music library at Northwestern University come to mind, along with, of course, the libraries at Indiana University Bloomington (IU) and the University of Illinois at Urbana-Champaign (UIUC). It was not unusual in those days to phone a cataloger in another institution to inquire about a record one had seen online in OCLC (this was before the Internet—there was no email). And it was also fairly routine to call for advice before inputting a controversial record. The Music OCLC Users Group was established in 1977[4] to provide a venue for consultation and also for research and development among librarians at participating institutions.

It was in this exciting time that Arsen Ralph Papakhian, then head of music technical services at IU, and Richard Smiraglia, then head of music cataloging at UIUC, decided to conduct a study to gather empirical data about the coverage and quality of cataloging for music and sound recordings in OCLC. The study was published in *Notes* in 1981.[5] At that time, OCLC had 2,500 member libraries, 7.4 million bibliographic records, and of those, 141,143 were scores and 118,041 were musical recordings.

To analyze coverage, we searched the entire *Basic Music Library*[6] to see whether a small music library on opening day could expect to find cataloging for its holdings in OCLC. Interestingly and importantly, even at that time 91.5% of the publications included in *A Basic Music Library* were located in OCLC. Furthermore, all of the specific publications not located were represented by other editions, meaning that the entire essential collection could have been searched and cataloged using OCLC. This remarkable result was also consistent with results cited by Robert Michael Fling.[7] To analyze currency we searched the "Books Received" and "Music Received" columns published in *Notes* in December 1979 and September 1980, and "New Listings" from the same issues of the *Schwann-1 Record and Tape Guide*. Virtually all books were found—98.42% of December 1979 books and 94.78% of September 1980 books. Much lower proportions of scores were found—60.71% and 31.05%, respectively. And the same was true for sound recordings—58.7% and 22.7% respectively. The disparity was likely a reflection of the influence of LC's MARC Distribution Service, which was already covering most book production at the time, but had little impact on scores and recordings. Note, however, that for both scores and recordings the proportions roughly doubled during the seven-month interval.

To analyze the utility of bibliographic data, samples of bibliographic records for all three media were compiled using all catalog records from both libraries during July and September 1980. The sample could be criticized because it was not drawn at random. But, in each case, the entire population of bibliographic records was analyzed, so one could say that the results were representative of the cataloging being used at IU and UIUC in the specific period of analysis. To the extent these two libraries were cataloging materials similar to those being acquired by other libraries, the results might also have been representative. On average, 6 changes were being made to monographic records, 10.5 to records for scores and 15.9 to records for sound recordings. For all three categories, most changes were made to descriptive data—probably reflecting shifting cataloging rules at the time (ISBD revision of AACR1 was implemented in 1974; AACR2 had not yet been implemented widely, but was in use at UIUC),[8] and for the sound recordings almost certainly reflecting expanded contents notes. Analysis of the sources of cataloging showed that 58 percent of the cataloging for monographs was from LC, but only 30 percent of the cataloging for scores and recordings was from LC, with the clear majority of the copy coming from OCLC member libraries. A comparison of changes required for bibliographic records plotted alongside dates of entry in OCLC showed there had been a rapid rise in the number of changes required since the beginning of music implementation in September 1976, but they had fallen off by the time of the study.

REPLICATING THE STUDY THIRTY YEARS HENCE

To honor Ralph Papakhian, we decided to try to replicate the study, and in particular we decided to incorporate the study as a class project for the students enrolled in Music Cataloging for the summer 2010 term. The idea was to provide an opportunity for these students to become acquainted with Papakhian's contributions to research about music cataloging as well as his reputation as an educator and mentor of young catalogers. But also it was pedagogical, to help the students assess the actual impact of their cataloging on the bibliographic apparatus in general—that is, how the quality of the copy one generates influences its use in other libraries—and in the OCLC WorldCat in particular. On the other hand, there was no need to replicate the search of *A Basic Music Library,* because it was clear that essential coverage was now available in WorldCat. When the present study was designed, in May 2010, OCLC had 72,000 member libraries and 183,028,917 bibliographic records, of which the OCLC Office of Research estimated 4,000,000 were for musical recordings and 3,400,000 were for scores.

We decided to attempt to replicate the check for timeliness of coverage, albeit in a slightly different way. (The *Schwann* guide had long since ceased publication, and the influence of the World Wide Web had to be taken into account). Therefore, students searched:

• The "Music Received" columns published in the December 2009 and March 2010 issues of *Notes*; each had six pages of approximately twenty entries.
• The "Books Recently Published" columns published in the December 2009 and March 2010 issues of *Notes*; each had twenty pages of approximately twenty entries.
• *Billboard* "New Releases" (http://www.billboard.com/new-releases#/new-releases); we searched two hundred albums under "New Music Releases" from June 2010, in reverse, through December 2009 (twenty screens, each with ten albums).
• *Classical Music Sentinel* (http://www.classicmusicsentinel.com/gates.html); using the site's navigation tools to locate the latest releases for June 2010, approximately twenty-four albums.

Students worked together in groups of three or four: one group was assigned to scores, two groups split the books recently published, and two more groups split the sound recording searches. Bibliographic records were located using the OCLC Connexion cataloging interface; results of the searches were entered on Excel spreadsheets, and each group was encouraged to contribute a narrative of any interesting results.

To analyze the part of the study focused on the quality of bibliographic data, a random sample of bibliographic records for scores and sound recordings was constituted. Sample size calculations were made based on the proportion of LC copy in the original study, which was 30 percent, and the mean number of changes made to bibliographic records for sound recordings (the larger figure), which was 11. It was determined that with 95 percent confidence and an acceptable error of 5 percent, a sample of 322 bibliographic records each for scores and recordings would yield generalizable results. The OCLC Office of Research provided a random sample of 323 bibliographic records for scores and 309 bibliographic records for sound recordings. Students were once again assigned to small groups of three or four (in different combinations) and each was assigned a segment of each sample. Students were asked to find each bibliographic record by record number in WorldCat and to record for each:

- date entered and the latest date replaced
- inputting library symbol
- all other symbols in field 040
- cataloging rules used
- encoding level

As before, groups were asked to provide brief narratives of interesting observations.

RESULTS

Coverage

Coverage was nearly universal for books and "popular" sound recordings. That is to say, OCLC contains bibliographic records for 99 percent of the resources our groups searched. For books the figure was 99.6 percent, for sound recordings listed in *Billboard* it was 95.27 percent. Table 1 contains comparative figures.

The figure was much lower, however, for recently released classical recordings and for scores. Table 2 has comparative figures.

What is going on here? It seems likely there is some disparity between coverage and recency for resources that are in the higher end of the economic demand stream, and coverage is a bit slower for other resources, including Western art music, but there is evidence of increased coverage over time. Table 3 contains the comparative data from both studies.

Coverage for monographs and popular sound recordings clearly is not at issue. Coverage for scores has improved but still lags far behind coverage for monographs. And coverage for recently released classical recordings is at about the same level as that for scores. Thus it is interesting to note that three decades after the first study there still is some lag in the bibliographic coverage of music scores and newly released classical sound recordings. Does this reflect somehow the relationship between music schools and their libraries, on the one hand, and the commercial sector, on the other? Or is it a reflection of the contents of the "Music Received" lists in *Notes*? We have no data available to answer either question, but both are surely provocative questions for further research.

Books December 2009	99.5%
Books September 2009	99.7%
Billboard February 2010	98.8%
Billboard May 2010	99.1%

Table 1. Coverage of monographs and sound recordings in OCLC.

Classical Music Sentinel	67.8%
"Music Received" December 2009	73.1%
"Music Received" March 2010	64.7%

Table 2. Coverage of newly released classical sound recordings and musical scores in OCLC.

Narrative Comments from the Researchers about Coverage
Students were encouraged, as researchers usually are, to make notes as they went along, and each small group was encouraged, in kind, to discuss these notes and report observations along with their data. Probably the most frequent observation concerned the duplication of coverage. Many, if not most, resources had multiple records. This is a result of the several recent mergers of online systems into OCLC, such that it is now possible to find bibliographic records from several national libraries alongside contributed records for almost every resource. Duplication is now a problem in OCLC. The students noted that many of the titles they searched under the category of "books recently published" included electronic resources—CDs, CD-ROMs, and DVDs. Thus the list of "books" is really more a list of "not music," and there is much diversity among the media represented.

Students who searched *Classical Music Sentinel* reported the majority of bibliographic records found were from Baker & Taylor, a vendor, and had minimal descriptive cataloging. For several sound recordings, multiple records were present with conflicting MARC 100 fields (composer vs. performer). Many of the recordings were quite difficult to find using name-title searches, possibly because of incomplete cataloging. Most often the Universal Product Code was used to locate the actual bibliographic record—something of a sad state of affairs for the world's single bibliographic utility. Students who searched *Billboard* reported similar problems and also found it difficult to decide whether divergent bibliographic records actually represented the same resource. Students also had some difficulty distinguishing cases of multiple records (minimal, and full, for example) from cases of multiple instantiations (deluxe editions, imports,

1981 Study	
Recordings Dec. 1979	58.7%
Recordings Sept. 1980	22.7%
Scores Dec. 1979	60.71%
Scores Sept. 1980	31.05%
Monographs Dec. 1979	98.42%
Monographs Sept. 1980	94.78%
2010 Study	
Recordings *Billboard* Feb. 2010	98.8%
Recordings *Billboard* May 2010	99.1%
Recordings *CMS* June 2010	73.1%
Scores Dec. 2009	73.1%
Scores March 2010	64.7%
Monographs Dec. 2009	99.5%
Monographs March 2010	99.7%

Table 3. Coverage over time.

etc.). This is of interest for this study, because our students—future librarians—are fairly sophisticated users of bibliographic systems. If they are confused, what will happen to real users encountering this plethora of undisambiguated instantiation networks?

There was confusion as well with the titles listed in "Music Received," again because most bibliographic records found were vendor-supplied minimal records. There was, therefore, frequently insufficient detail for the students to decide whether the record they found online actually represented the resource for which they were searching, even when composer, title, and publisher all seemed to match, more or less. One group noted a tendency for sacred music to be less available in OCLC than secular.

ANALYSIS OF BIBLIOGRAPHIC RECORDS

A major limitation of this replication clearly was the time available for the students to search OCLC. While it was considered pedagogically useful to have them manually data-mining WorldCat, it also was necessary to limit this analysis to simple measures of quality. Groups were asked to retrieve bibliographic records by record number and to record specific data from the individual records. Because our sample was drawn at random, we can say with 95 percent confidence that what we report here is generalizable to the population of all bibliographic records for scores and musical recordings ±5 percent. These data reveal some interesting facts about the content of music and sound recording cataloging in WorldCat. But a full analysis of bibliographic record quality will have to await a follow-up study.

Our initial measure was date of entry and latest date revised. The earliest date of entry for a score was 13 December 1972 and the latest date was 14 December 2009. Table 4 contains the distribution of scores by date of entry. What we see is consistent entry over time, with slight bumps due to the scatter of the random sample. (For instance, there are no records in the sample entered in 1982.) The critical chronological points are represented—a bump in 1976 when the MARC music format was published, again in 1978 when it was implemented in OCLC, and again in 1985 when LC implemented it. The largest jump occurs in 2009—most likely with the tape loading of records from the former RLIN database.

The earliest date of entry for a sound recording in the sample was 16 March 1975, and the latest date was 19 December 2009. Table 5 contains the distribution over time of dates entered for sound recordings in the sample.

Dates of entry for sound recording bibliographic records reveal rather a different picture from those for scores. The key dates that were important bumps for scores are irrelevant this time. Instead, 1990–91 and 2009 seem to show the most significant increases. One supposes these dates correspond to times of various tape-loads into WorldCat. Prior to 1990, input is steady but at a pretty low level. The widespread adoption of the compact disc dates from about 1985; it is possible that the switchover in the marketplace from LP to CD is reflected here as well. Figure 1 plots the growth of both formats in WorldCat, nicely demonstrating the steadiness of input of bibliographic records over time, but also visualizing the occasionally divergent growth trends.

In addition to the date the record was entered, we also recorded the date of replacement, which is a system-generated date added whenever the record is altered. It can be an indication of revision, correction, or update, but it can also simply mean a batch-load process took place that overwrote the original record. Thus it is only a minor indicator of record quality. For scores, the mean length to time of replacement was 10 years, with a range from 1 to 38 years, and with 22 percent of the records unchanged over time. For recordings the mean length to time of replacement was 10.1 years (more or less the same as scores) with a range from 1 to 28 years, and with 29 percent of the records unchanged. For both scores and recordings, most of the unchanged records were entered into the system in the 2009 spike.

We also recorded descriptive cataloging rules, encoding level, and cataloging source, which can be summarized simply. For scores, 44 percent had AACR2 descriptions, 10 percent had pre-AACR2 ISBD descriptions, 24 percent were full level, 50 percent were M level (less than full, from batch loading), and 94 percent were not LC records. For sound recordings,

Year	Number Entered	Percentage
2009	62	20%
2008	13	5%
2007	16	4%
2006	6	4%
2005	12	4%
2004	9	4%
2003	7	4%
2002	13	4%
2001	12	4%
2000	12	3%
1999	8	3%
1998	4	3%
1997	8	3%
1996	12	3%
1995	5	2%
1994	7	2%
1993	12	2%
1992	5	2%
1991	7	2%
1990	6	2%
1989	6	2%
1988	6	2%
1987	5	2%
1986	4	2%
1985	10	2%
1984	7	2%
1983	8	1%
1981	2	1%
1980	4	1%
1979	3	1%
1978	5	1%
1977	2	1%
1976	3	1%
1975	1	0%
1974	1	0%
1972	1	0%

Table 4. Bibliographic records for scores by date of entry.

Year	Number Entered	Percentage
2010	1	0%
2009	49	15%
2008	12	4%
2007	17	5%
2006	11	3%
2005	11	3%
2004	7	2%
2003	28	8%
2002	23	7%
2001	15	4%
2000	7	2%
1999	4	1%
1998	8	2%
1997	8	2%
1996	4	1%
1995	7	2%
1994	15	4%
1993	9	3%
1992	5	1%
1991	32	9%
1990	15	4%
1989	8	2%
1988	5	1%
1987	6	2%
1986	3	1%
1985	5	1%
1984	3	1%
1983	2	1%
1982	2	1%
1981	4	1%
1980	3	1%
1979	1	0%
1978	3	1%
1977	1	0%
1976	1	0%
1975	1	0%
1973	1	0%

Table 5. Bibliographic records for recordings by date of entry.

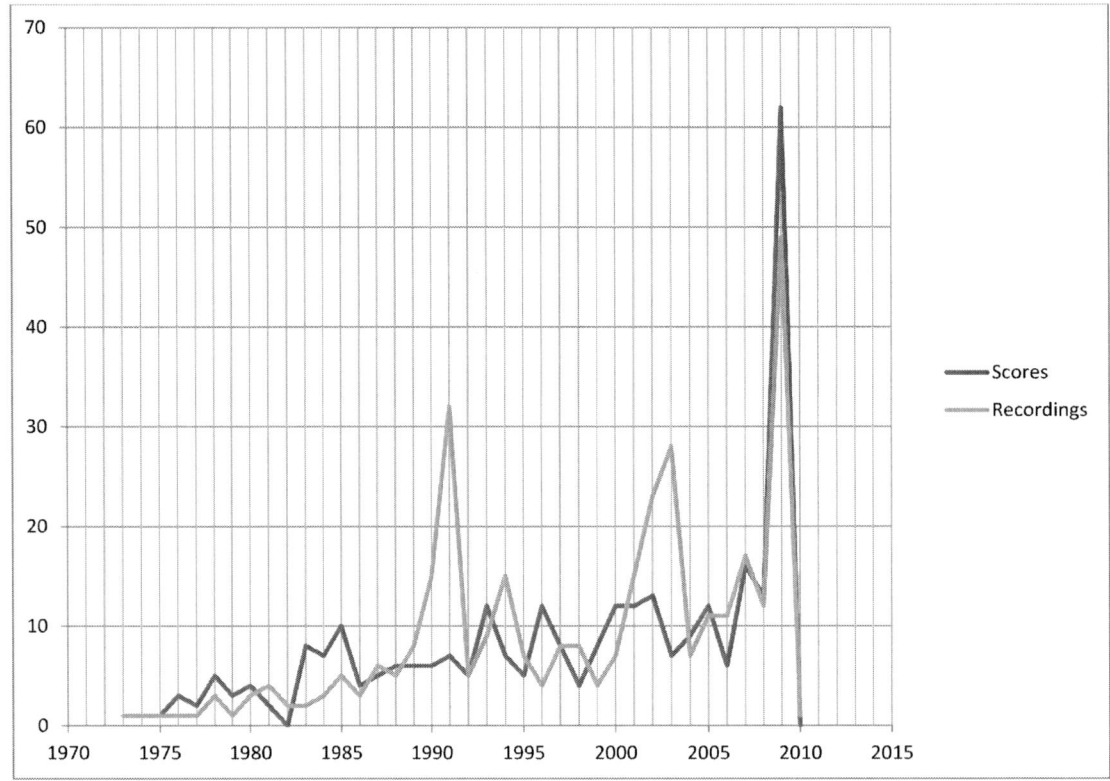

Figure 1. Growth of music and sound recordings in WorldCat.

19 percent were full level, 48 percent were M level, and 87 percent were not LC records. Most of the bibliographic records, in other words, were not from LC, and about half were batch-loaded minimal records, which likely were vendor records. That is, only about 20 to 25 percent seem to have been contributed by member libraries. (These variables were cross-tabulated using SPSS; Chi-square showed statistical significance for the figures reported here, which means they are not the result of chance. It is probably important to note that there was too little LC-contributed cataloging for which to generate statistically significant associations.)

Students were again regrouped, and each group was assigned three bibliographic records for analysis. In general, students found few errors other than punctuation or typographical errors in bibliographic records. There was confusion among them about the presence of obsolete fields and subfield indicators. Merged records also presented some anomalous data.

CONCLUSIONS

Our replication was undertaken in the spirit of Ralph Papakhian's own quest for facts as a means of honoring his memory and promoting his legacy. Our findings demonstrate the value of continuous replication of research for theory building, as well as the need for further detailed research into the content and quality of OCLC's WorldCat, in particular for music and musical sound recordings. We were not surprised to discover the ubiquity of national-library cataloging copy for monographs, and we were gratified to find the extensive coverage for sound recordings, most of which is contributed, much of it by vendors. We were a bit surprised to find the gap between coverage in WorldCat and the contents of the *Notes* "Music Received" column. An interesting question would be whether the list contains material that is not essentially collected by libraries. Further analysis over time is clearly warranted.

The analysis of sources of cataloging and dates entered and replaced has been most useful for helping us visualize the growth of the music and recordings database. We see that much of the bibliographic data entered is not coming from library catalogers, although accuracy is not so much a problem as is completeness of bibliographic data. In this we see perhaps the major difference between the 1981 study and the present analysis: today's OCLC WorldCat is a different entity than the OCLC Online Union Catalog of the 1980s. Rather than a collective source of library cataloging data, carefully monitored and built one record at a time, WorldCat is truly a global bibliographic utility, built with diverse sources of bibliographic data for essential, extant bibliographic items. This is not a criticism, but rather an observation of the changing nature of OCLC as a utility, and of WorldCat as a database that supports cataloging, but is not essentially just a catalog.

The pedagogical value of the study had sufficient impact that it is a success as a tribute to Papakhian's role as educator. For these students of music cataloging, encountering the bowels of the beast, to borrow a phrase, was enlightening from day one. The course ended not only with their own complete original bibliographic and authority records due, but alongside those, their qualitative analyses of specific records from the sample. Many of the students commented on the value of this intimate look inside the details of WorldCat for music. Future students of music cataloging are encouraged to continue in this tradition, by continuing to study and analyze the bibliographic reality of the immense utility that WorldCat has become.

NOTES

[1] Henriette D. Avram, John F. Knapp, and Lucia J. Rather, *The MARC II Format: A Communications Format for Bibliographic Data* (Washington, D.C.: Information Systems Office, Library of Congress, 1968).

[2] Library of Congress, MARC Development Office, *Music, a MARC Format: Specifications for Magnetic Tapes Containing Catalog Records for Music Scores and Musical and Nonmusical Sound Recordings* (Washington, D.C.: Library of Congress, 1976).

[3] See Richard P. Smiraglia, *Music Cataloging: The Bibliographic Control of Printed and Recorded Music in Libraries* (Englewood, Colo.: Libraries Unlimited, 1989), 121–22.

[4] Music OCLC Users Group, "About MOUG," revised 21 January 2010, http://www.musicoclcusers.org/aboutmoug.htm.

[5] Richard P. Smiraglia and Arsen R. Papakhian, "Music in the OCLC Online Union Catalog: A Review," *Notes* 38, no. 2 (December 1981): 257–74.

[6] Pauline Shaw Bayne, ed., *A Basic Music Library: Essential Scores and Books*, comp. the Music Library Association, Subcommittee on Basic Music Collection (Chicago: American Library Assoc., 1978).

[7] Robert Michael Fling, "Reference Uses of OCLC in the Music Library," *Music OCLC Users Group Newsletter*, no. 11 (1981): 7–8.

[8] International Federation of Library Associations and Institutions, *International Standard Bibliographic Description: For Single Volume and Multi-Volume Monographic Publications* (London: IFLA Committee on Cataloguing, 1971). (See also subsequent ISBD standards published for monographic publications [rev. 1978], nonbook materials [1977], and printed music [1980].) C. Sumner Spalding, ed., *Anglo-American Cataloging Rules* (Chicago: American Library Assoc., 1967). Joint Steering Committee for the Revision of AACR, *Anglo-American Cataloguing Rules*, 2nd ed., ed. Michael Gorman and Paul L. Winkler (Chicago: American Library Association, 1978).

THEORETICAL IMPLICATIONS ARISING FROM THE STUDY OF PERSONAL NAME HEADINGS IN THE INDIANA UNIVERSITY MUSIC LIBRARY CARD CATALOGS

RICHARD P. SMIRAGLIA

Abstract: In 1985, Ralph Papakhian published a study of the frequency of name headings in the music and sound recording catalogs at Indiana University. The study, published in *Library Resources & Technical Services*, constituted a major theoretical contribution to the understanding of the distribution of works and names in library catalogs. This paper is a review of the evidence in Papakhian's 1985 study, compared to evidence from other, similar studies, to demonstrate the theoretical significance of Papakhian's contribution.

MUSIC CATALOGING IN THE 1980S

In the 1980s, music cataloging—like all parts of library technical services—was undergoing a series of shifts that would prove to be essential epistemologically. The aura of constant change and constantly changing technology was pervasive, but so too was the influence of new communities of mutual shared responsibility for bibliographic control that arose from the evolution of bibliographic utilities (such as the RLIN, the Research Libraries Information Network, and OCLC, the Online Computer Library Center) and from the rapid evolution of automated cataloging technologies. Simultaneously, the world was growing smaller, as international developments in resource description evolved and overtook everyday cataloging practice. The imposition of the second edition of the *Anglo-American Cataloguing Rules*[1] (AACR2) from 1981 onward in libraries in the English-speaking world went hand-in-hand with the growth of the International Standards for Bibliographic Description (ISBD).[2] In turn, the music and sound recordings components of ISBD and hence also AACR2 were influenced greatly by the discussions of the International Association of Music Libraries (IAML), which had developed its own extensive cataloging code in the same period. (Actually in rough parallel to the ISBD movement, the IAML code appeared in parts between 1957 and 1983.)[3]

The shifting parameters of music cataloging moved from a base of pragmatic local solutions enacted by catalogers working essentially in isolation in their own institutions, to a much more imposing universe of rational practice undertaken according to ever-changing and ever-growing codes of cataloging practice implemented by national and international teams in the glare of universal witness in the OCLC Online Union Catalog, RLIN, and other large-scale bibliographic utilities. Gone were the days of typed cards reflecting eccentric local practices. Cards were now printed by the computers of the bibliographic utilities and shipped to the library in boxes. Right around the corner was to be the age of the online public access catalog (OPAC). But in the early 1980s it was important to comprehend the vast apparatus not only of AACR2 and the Library of Congress (LC) MARC (MAchine Readable Cataloging) formats, but also the imposing volume of LC rule interpretations (LCRIs) that governed actual practice.

This shift, like any epistemological shift, was jarring for the cataloging community. The implementation of AACR2—published in 1978 but not implemented by the Library of Congress until 1981—had been delayed by serious squabbling among major academic and research libraries and in the very politicized arenas of national library association governing bodies, such as the American Library Association's Committee on Cataloging: Description and Access (CCDA), the supranational Joint Steering Committee for the Revision of the Anglo-American Cataloguing Rules (JSC), the Association of Research Libraries, and others. Fundamental changes to be implemented in AACR2, especially a change in the rules governing the representation of name headings, presented a potential economic catastrophe for libraries still reliant on card technology. The essence of this simple rule change was a shift from using an author's full name as found in reference sources to using whatever popularized form was found in the person's works. The change had actually been introduced in the first edition of AACR in 1967 but had never been implemented.[4] There was fear that thousands of cards would have to be pulled and retyped in order to integrate new cataloging into old catalogs. While the Library of Congress planned to close its card catalogs and implement the changed rules in its automated OPAC, it was among only a very few very large libraries that could afford such a plan.

Many alternatives were considered—eventually a system of declaring old headings "compatible" so they could be ignored was used—and much research was conducted to discover empirical evidence about the potential impact of the rule changes. Major studies were published by Potter, McCallum and Godwin, and Taylor Dowell, all of which promised limited impact would come from the rule change.[5] The reason was the effect of a power-law distribution, known as Lotka's Law of author productivity,[6] which, among other things, demonstrates a simple fact that most authors (Lotka posited the figure at 60.79 percent)[7] write only one work and only a very few authors write a large number of works. (The effect of quantities of editions of a creator's works also conforms to Lotka's Law, as it turns out, but this was not demonstrated until much later by Smiraglia.)[8] Ultimately, as Taylor Dowell especially pointed out in her extensive review of small, medium, and large academic libraries, most new cataloging would add unique headings to the catalog, only a few older headings would require change, and using LC's compatibility interpretation would limit even those. Taylor Dowell demonstrated convincingly that after five years the impact of the change would have come to an end; she later provided evidence that her projections had, in fact, been correct.[9]

Nonetheless, all of these changes took place in large general academic catalogs. The impact in music catalogs, where most works are new editions or performances of core repertory, seemed likely to be much more serious. Evidence from the University of Illinois's music library indicated the consequences on authority control that had been the result of Illinois' early implementation of AACR2.[10] As Smiraglia would indicate[11] and Vellucci would demonstrate beyond a shadow of a doubt,[12] catalogs of music libraries were quite different from those of their generalist colleagues. The distributions of works—and therefore name headings—was entirely dependent on the aforementioned core repertory, and thus did not conform to Lotka's Law. However, the critical study that pointed the direction for this research was published by Papakhian in 1985.[13] "The Frequency of Personal Name Headings in the Indiana University Music Library Card Catalogs" was Papakhian's attempt to refute the generalist's findings about the impact of AACR2 in music catalogs. The article had wide impact because it was published in 1985 in *Library Resources & Technical Services*, in those days an influential journal of research published by the American Library Association's division now known as ALCTS (Association for Library Collections and Technical Services). Papakhian's perhaps not-so-subtle political agenda was well served by publishing his results, which essentially refuted earlier results, in a major journal that Potter, McCallum, and Taylor Dowell all also published in and would read. Designed for high impact, the study was methodologically flawless, as it neatly demonstrated empirically—perhaps for the first time—the essential difference between a collection of musical documents and a general library.

Now, more than a quarter century later, the article's impact can be seen as even more critical to theoretical understanding in the field of knowledge organization, of which music cataloging must be considered an adjacent component. Cited by Smiraglia not only in his analysis of works[14] but also in two theoretical papers,[15] Papakhian's contribution continues to lend empirical evidence to theory concerning the bibliographic and bibliometric contents of music collections, the distribution of author productivity and therefore of name headings in bibliographic resources, and perhaps by far most importantly, the grounds for external validity in research concerning all of the above. A search of the *ISI Web of Knowledge* shows there are four indexed citations to this paper; aside from Smiraglia,[16] there are citations from Petek's 2008 article on Lotka's Law,[17] Borgman and Siegfried's 1992 article about applications of personal name matching,[18] and Weintraub's 1991 paper about personal name variations in rare books catalogs.[19]

Interestingly, *Web of Knowledge* picks up only one Petek citation, although this article is derived from her 2003 Ph.D. dissertation.[20] The dissertation replicates Smiraglia's,[21] examining the derivative bibliographic relationship in a Slovenian bibliographic utility, and reporting comparable results.

SUMMARY OF THE ARTICLE

Papakhian's article, of course, is available to today's searchers in digital format through standard information-science databases, and readers are encouraged to read it with care. For the purpose of the present paper we want to focus on some of the unique features of the article. To begin, Papakhian situated his work by describing the Indiana University music library's holdings in some detail—for example, 661 catalog drawers representing 129,000 musical resources.

Sampling

The sampling technique employed was a replication of the method used in Potter's study. Catalog drawers were selected at random, and every name heading in each selected drawer was recorded together with the extent of repetition of names; names at the front of a drawer that continued from the previous drawer were omitted. This is a form of systematic sample, in essence using clusters of randomly selected names. Thus, the results are generalizable to other clusters within the same catalog, which, given the state of cataloging research in 1985, was a remarkably resilient approach. It seems clear from the text that Papakhian was trying to exactly replicate Potter's study so as to have directly comparable results.

An alternative, which might have been considered (we cannot know from the article) but rejected because of time and cost implications, would have been to generate random number pairs so as to select a random drawer number and then a random position within the drawer. Usually in card catalog research this would send one to a specific position—say five inches into drawer 230. On arrival, one would select the card behind the designated location so as to control for cards thickened from use,[22] thus equalizing the probability of the selection of any particular card. Then, the technique Papakhian reports would also have had to have been employed by discarding any selection that was not the first card with a particular name heading. It is easy to see that it would likely have required many more random pairs to achieve an eventual sample of 2,400 headings in each catalog, and this might be why the technique was not used.

Of course, today, in the online environment, it is pretty simple to generate a random sample of bibliographic records using record numbers. Because individual bibliographic records carry multiple name headings, it would be a multi-step process to generate a sample of names from bibliographic records chosen at random. Alternatives would be to sample from an authority file, or to sample from a fixed snapshot of a flat-file name index—this would be the closest we could come in the online environment to replicating Papakhian's technique.

Lotka's Law

The proportion of names occurring only once in the printed materials catalog was 61.22%,[23] which pretty closely conforms to Lotka's Law, but the proportion in the sound recordings catalog was 47.64%,[24] which does not. At the top of the productivity distribution, Papakhian reported the proportions of names that occurred more than three times in each catalog and drew again a comparison with Potter. These proportions all conform to Lotka's prediction, because we understand that only a small number of authors in the distribution will be highly productive. Papakhian found that 16.4% of the headings in the printed materials catalog occurred more than three times, but the figure was 26.4% in the sound recordings catalog. (Potter had reported 15.05% in the comparable general catalog at Illinois.)[25] The importance of this finding is twofold: first, the music library catalog that mixes scores and books has the characteristics of a general academic library catalog—at 95% confidence, 15% and 16% are not statistically significantly different; and, second, the catalog that contains only sound recordings does not conform to the same parameters as the others. Establishing this distinction empirically for the first time is one of the most important contributions of Papakhian's article.

THEORETICAL INDICATIONS

CHARACTERISTICS OF COLLECTIONS

Any research that uses sampling techniques must include a report about the discovered demographics of the sampled subjects in order to properly situate the results. In cataloging research, this usually means reporting the bibliographic characteristics of the titles sampled and relating these figures to what is known about the collection in general. To make good predictions based on available evidence, research relies on compounded data and replicated studies that demonstrate statistical norms within a given domain. This is a complicated way of saying that a weather forecast in the year 2011 is likely to be accurate because it is based on centuries of observations (replications) and data (in this case, meteorological data). A problem that has plagued research in cataloging has been the absence of such theoretical data. We do not have sufficient evidence to know clearly how one library is like another in terms of its critical bibliographic parameters. The result of the Papakhian study—that sound recording catalogs are not like other kinds of catalogs—was among the first empirical evidence that there might be a good reason to collect more detailed data, because there might be important consequences to the differentials. Smiraglia used meta-analytical techniques to draw together bibliographical data from several studies,[26] demonstrating for the first time the potential for what is called "external validity" in cataloging or bibliographic research. That is, there is some reason to begin to generalize results from one library to another insofar as we know that the bibliographic characteristics of their collections are similar.

As was alluded to earlier, there is only one published study that reports any bibliographic characteristics concerning music collections—Vellucci.[27] Papakhian's data, therefore, are quite limited; we learn only the quantities of media in the music library collection at one point in time. Still, his evidence that sound recording collections are different in bibliographic terms from those of general media or even printed music and books is important. Vellucci reports more detail—for instance, that in the collection of scores from which she sampled, 32.8% of titles were published in the United States, 55% were published after 1951 but only 80% had specific dates present.[28] We draw these few proportions simply to contrast them with the characteristics of general collections analyzed in Smiraglia's meta-analysis—roughly 60%–80% U.S. imprints, 70%–80% after 1960.[29] In other words, the contrasting proportions confirm Papakhian's observation that the contents of sound recording catalogs are bibliographically fundamentally different from those of general catalogs, and that the inclusion of sound recordings in general catalogs might alter otherwise normative distributions.

OCCURRENCE OF NAME HEADINGS

Also in Smiraglia's meta-analytical review is an analysis of the frequency of occurrence of name headings, and conformance of that frequency to power-law distributions. The immediate importance of these findings was to tell us how to predict the impact of changes AACR2 would introduce in the early 1980s, or, theoretically speaking, future changes in name-heading structure as well. But the impact of these findings goes much farther, which Smiraglia and Taylor demonstrated in 2009 by accurately predicting the frequency of occurrence of names derived from metadata stored in MINDS@UW.[30] Table 1 contains the meta-analytical results reported in all of the studies that have been cited here.

Notice that these figures are from different studies that used varying methodologies. The role of meta-analysis is to pull common theoretical understanding from such diverse data sources. Most of these studies involved random samples of bibliographic records, but from different sampling frames. All of the figures in the right-hand column except those from Taylor Dowell report the proportion of name headings in the sample that was unique; the Taylor Dowell figures tell us, instead, the proportion of headings caused to change by AACR2 that

Study	Proportion of Unique Name Headings
Potter – small academic library	69.33%
Potter – large academic library	63.5%
McCallum and Godwin – Library of Congress	65.65%
Taylor Dowell – small academic library*	51.6%
Taylor Dowell – medium academic library*	50%
Taylor Dowell – large academic library*	29.7%
Papakhian – scores and books	61.22%
Papakhian – sound recordings	47.64%
Fuller – large academic library	61%
Weintraub – special collections	36.7%
Smiraglia and Taylor – MINDS@UW	71%

*Headings that changed form with AACR2 but are unique in the catalog

Table 1. Meta-analytical comparison of unique name headings.

were unique—essentially an unknown proportion of all unique headings. Still, if we compare the methodologies, Taylor Dowell's sampling technique is similar enough to the others to allow us to proceed with comparison.

We can better understand the theoretical dimensions of this analysis by highlighting different segments of the table. For instance, if we compare the figures from general collections including books, serials, and music, we see an interesting trend emerge. Table 2 contains only those rows, to which an estimated confidence interval has been added.

What we can see in this table is that the estimated confidence intervals converge toward a central point at approximately 60%—in other words, in conformance with Lotka's Law. Figure 1 is a graphic illustration of this effect.

Study	Proportion of Unique Name Headings	Estimated 95% Confidence Interval ± 5%
Potter – small academic library	69.33%	64.3% – 73.3%
Potter – large academic library	63.5%	59.5% – 68.5%
McCallum and Godwin – Library of Congress	65.65%	60.65% – 70.65%
Taylor Dowell – small academic library*	51.6%	46.6% – 56.6%
Taylor Dowell – medium academic library*	50%	45% – 55%
Taylor Dowell – large academic library*	29.7%	24.7% – 34.7%
Papakhian – scores and books	61.22%	56.22% – 66.22%
Fuller – large academic library	61%	56% – 66%
Smiraglia and Taylor – MINDS@UW	71%	65% – 76%
*Headings that changed form with AACR2 but are unique in the catalog		

Table 2. Meta-analytical comparison of unique name headings in general collections.

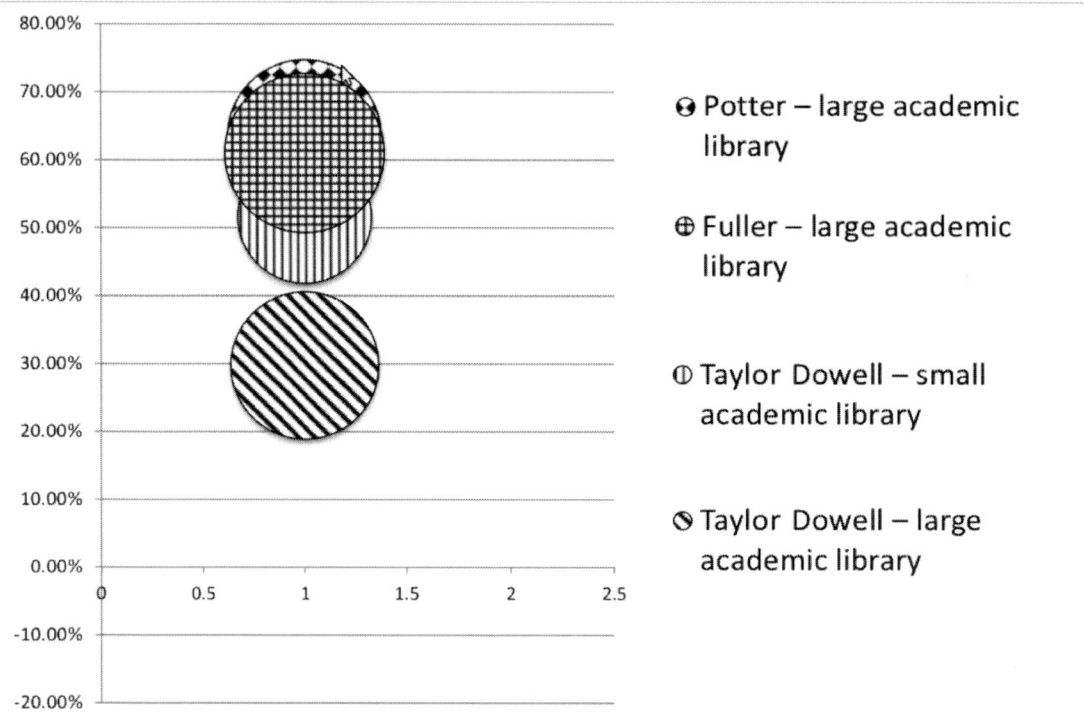

Figure 1. Bubble diagram of the central convergence of proportionate confidence intervals.

There is considerable variation, and there is considerable distance from Taylor Dowell's large library at about 24% to the remaining clusters. Taylor Dowell was measuring headings that required changes under AACR2, but they still hover near Lotka's predicted 60%. So we see clearly the strength of this distribution in academic libraries, in a music library printed materials catalog, and in an online metadata repository.

But we also can look at the anomalous results. Table 3 presents those proportions that do not seem to conform to Lotka's Law.

Now we have three divergent findings. Taylor Dowell's large academic library had a very low proportion of changed name headings that were unique. We have to assume that the collection represented by that particular library (the University of North Carolina at Chapel Hill) contained a broad array of materials other than the liberal arts and sciences academic core. And Papakhian and Weintraub's results offer the explanation. Papakhian's reported proportion shows that collections of musical sound recordings in academic libraries have very few unique name headings. In other words, most names in that catalog are the names of the standard composers

Study	Proportion of Unique Name Headings
Taylor Dowell – large academic library*	29.7%
Papakhian – sound recordings	47.64%
Weintraub – special collections	36.7%

*Headings that changed form with AACR2 but are unique in the catalog

Table 3. Anomalous meta-analytical comparisons.

and performers of the Western art music core, and most of the names are repeated many times, as the library's collection policy dictates collection of comparatively different recordings of specific works. Weintraub's reported proportion reflects the presence of rare books in a special collections library (at the University of California, San Diego)—once again, a collection in which collection policy dictates the acquisition of not only many editions of all of the works of featured authors, but also—and particularly—many copies of those editions with different physical features (particularly with marginalia, bindings, illustrations, etc.). According to Taylor Dowell, the UNC library catalog contained entries from many disciplinary branch libraries as well as the entire rare books collection, but not musical scores and recordings.[31] Lotka's Law holds in normally distributed bibliographic populations but does not predict the instance of multiple iterations of works (compositions, performances, editions, etc.) of the same named creator.

CONCLUSION

So we have seen in this brief paper the simple power of empirical observation. Arsen Ralph Papakhian was a keen observer, and he knew from what was going across his desk that the results reported by Potter, McCallum and Godwin, and others was not in accordance with his own observations. An epistemological shift had visited the desk of the average music cataloger and it was going to require empirical evidence to join the rising tide in the new automated scientific information-retrieval domain. Fortunately, Ralph Papakhian knew how to turn his everyday observations into science. This brief exposition is just one demonstration of the power of Papakhian's simple, precise observations. Also, we have considered where his observations might have generated more powerful theoretical statements. Music librarians reading this ought to be motivated to replicate this work, to do so with more carefully controlled samples, in a variety of different institutional contexts, and to report their results in peer-reviewed journals in our discipline. And music librarians also ought to be motivated not to ever make critical decisions again without empirical evidence.

The final piece of commentary comes from a close reading of Papakhian's article. It is no mean simple research report. Rather, it is a deliberate attempt to politically turn back the tide unleashed by Potter's naïve work. "Little is known," "the peculiarity of the distribution," "substantially different," "obviously." Ralph was a keen intellectual observer and also a keen user of language; he chose this very cautious presentation format for maximum impact, he chose this publishing venue so his results would be seen by those whose prior results had almost carelessly had such immense and costly impact on music libraries, and he peppered the paper with these words to drive his point home. Music librarians of future generations would do well to mold their own work in this pattern.

NOTES

[1] Joint Steering Committee for the Revision of AACR, *Anglo-American Cataloguing Rules*, 2nd ed., ed. Michael Gorman and Paul L. Winkler (Chicago: American Library Association, 1978).

[2] The standards for various formats that were issued beginning in the early 1970s have been compiled as International Federation of Library Associations and Institutions, ISBD Review Group, *International Standard Bibliographic Description (ISBD)*, prelim. consolidated ed., IFLA Series on Bibliographic Control, vol. 31 (Munich: K. G. Saur, 2007).

[3] Richard P. Smiraglia, *Music Cataloging: The Bibliographic Control of Printed and Recorded Music in Libraries* (Englewood, Colo.: Libraries Unlimited, 1989), 17.

[4] *Anglo-American Cataloging Rules* (Chicago: American Library Association, 1967).

[5] William Gray Potter, "When Names Collide: Conflict in the Catalog and AACR2," *Library Resources & Technical Services* 24, no. 1 (Winter 1980): 3–16; Sally H. McCallum and James L. Godwin, "Statistics on Headings in the MARC File," *Journal of Library Automation* 14, no. 3 (September 1981): 194–201; Arlene Taylor Dowell, *AACR 2 Headings: A Five-Year Projection of Their Impact on Catalogs* (Littleton, Colo.: Libraries Unlimited, 1982).

[6] Alfred J. Lotka, "The Frequency Distribution of Scientific Productivity," *Journal of the Washington Academy of Sciences* 16, no. 12 (1926): 317–23.

[7] Ibid., 320.

[8] Richard P. Smiraglia, "Uniform Titles for Music: An Exercise in Collocating Works," *Cataloging & Classification Quarterly* 9, no. 3 (1989): 97–114; Richard P. Smiraglia, "Authority Control and the Extent of Derivative Bibliographic Relationships" (Ph.D. diss., University of Chicago, 1992), summarized in Richard P. Smiraglia, *The Nature of "A Work": Implications for the Organization of Knowledge* (Lanham, Md.: Scarecrow Press, 2001).

[9] Arlene G. Taylor and Barbara Paff, "Looking Back: Implementation of AACR 2," *Library Quarterly* 56, no. 3 (July 1986): 272–85.

[10] Robin Fradenburgh, "AACR2 at Illinois," *Music OCLC Users Group Newsletter*, no. 8 (1980): 2–3.

[11] Smiraglia, "Uniform Titles" and Smiraglia, "Authority Control."

[12] Sherry L. Vellucci, *Bibliographic Relationships in Music Catalogs* (Lanham, Md.: Scarecrow, 1997).

[13] Arsen R. Papakhian, "The Frequency of Personal Name Headings in the Indiana University Music Library Card Catalogs," *Library Resources & Technical Services* 29, no. 3 (July/September 1985): 273–85.

[14] Smiraglia, *Nature of "A Work."*

[15] Richard P. Smiraglia, "The Progress of Theory in Knowledge Organization," *Library Trends* 50, no. 3 (Winter 2002): 300–49; Richard P. Smiraglia, "Further Progress toward Theory in Knowledge Organization," *Canadian Journal of Information and Library Science* 26, no. 2/3 (June/September 2001): 31–50.

[16] Smiraglia, "Progress of Theory."

[17] Marija Petek, "Personal Name Headings in COBIB: Testing Lotka's Law," *Scientometrics* 75, no. 1 (April 2008): 175–88.

[18] C. L. Borgman and S. L. Siegfried, "Getty's SYNONAME™ and Its Cousins: A Survey of Applications of Personal Name-matching Algorithms," *Journal of the American Society for Information Science* 43, no. 7 (August 1992): 459–76.

[19] Tamara S. Weintraub, "Personal Name Variations: Implications for Authority Control in Computerized Catalogs," *Library Resources & Technical Services* 35, no. 2 (April 1991): 217–28.

[20] Marija Petek, "Odnosi med bibliografskimi zapisi, ki predstavljajo dela s skupnim predhodnikom, v slovenskem vzajemnem katalogu COBIB" (PhD diss., Department of Library and Information Science and Book Studies, University of Ljubljana, 2003).

[21] Smiraglia, "Authority control."

[22] Abraham Bookstein, "Sampling from Card Files," *Library Quarterly* 53, no. 3 (July 1983): 307–12.

[23] Papakhian, "Frequency," 276.

[24] Ibid., 277.

[25] Ibid., 282–83.

[26] Smiraglia, "Further progress."

[27] Vellucci, *Bibliographic relationships.*

[28] Ibid., 51, 53, 56.

[29] Smiraglia, "Further progress," 42–43.

[30] Richard P. Smiraglia and Arlene G. Taylor, "Letter to the Editor," *Cataloging & Classification Quarterly* 47, no. 8 (2009): 760–63.

[31] Taylor Dowell, "AACR 2 headings," 40.

FURTHERING ACCESS TO MUSIC
A History of the Music OCLC Users Group

Jay Weitz

Abstract: Born out of a task group that was assembled in the late 1970s to advise OCLC on the implementation of the MARC music format, the Music OCLC Users Group was the first such group, and more than three decades later remains the most influential. This essay traces the history of MOUG and the impact it has had on OCLC products and services.

Since it first went online on 26 August 1971, OCLC's WorldCat has grown to become the largest bibliographic database in the world, built record-by-record by the now over 72,000 institutions in 171 countries and territories that have contributed to the cooperative effort. When Frederick G. Kilgour founded OCLC as the Ohio College Library Center in 1967, *he* may have envisioned such an eventuality, but that doesn't make it any less of an achievement. In fact, it is an *ongoing* achievement, as a new record is added to WorldCat roughly every ten seconds.

Although nearly 85 percent of the more than 200 million bibliographic records in WorldCat are in the books format, there are nearly 5.6 million records for sound recordings (2.83%) and over 4.7 million for scores (2.4%). That translates into what is likely the world's largest existing bibliographic database of mostly music materials, numbering over 10.3 million records (5.23%). Again, it is OCLC users who have built this extraordinary resource. In the case of music materials, there is a group that has been instrumental in that development for more than three decades, the Music OCLC Users Group, affectionately known as MOUG.

When the OCLC system came up in 1971, there was no MARC format for scores or sound recordings, and there would not be until the publication of *Music, a MARC Format: Specifications for Magnetic Tapes Containing Catalog Records for Music Scores and Musical and Nonmusical Sound Recordings* by the Library of Congress (LC) MARC Development Office in 1976.[1] But as early as 24 October 1975, representatives of the Music Library Association (MLA) and OCLC had met in Columbus, Ohio, to begin plans for the implementation of the format. MLA President Clara Steuermann (University of Southern California) and MARC/MLA committee members Walter Gerboth (Brooklyn College), Mary Lou Little (Harvard University), and Donald Seibert (Syracuse University) began drawing up plans in anticipation of being able to input scores and sound recordings using the MARC format in late spring 1976, with card production to follow that summer.

Out of that meeting came the MLA proposal for the establishment of a permanent joint advisory committee for music to establish priorities and access points. In November 1975, OCLC instead proposed that an MLA interest group be created. Rather than a working committee, a task force based on MLA recommendations and with strong Ohio representation would be constituted to serve until the MARC format was "settled in." Discussions focused on the most efficient means of establishing priorities and deciding on such questions as indexing, display, and card printing.

These discussions resulted in the formation of the OCLC Task Force on the Cataloging of Music Scores and Sound Recordings. The task force met several times throughout 1976 and made valuable recommendations about these questions and others in preparation for the implementation of the MARC music format. At its first meeting in Columbus on 10 February 1976, the task force was charged with advising the OCLC Advisory Committee on Cataloging about implementing the format, including screen workforms, searching, and the need for quality control. Attendees included Olga Buth (Ohio State University), Barbara Denison (Cleveland Public Library), David "Jack" Knapp (Oberlin College), Mary Lou Little, Myrtle Nim (Carnegie-Mellon University), Donald Robbins (Cornell University), William Shurk (Bowling Green State University), Karl Van Ausdal (SUNY College at Purchase), and Margaret Wilson (University of Cincinnati). As a result of this meeting, OCLC announced that all fields in the MARC music format would be validated and that OCLC would adopt all Anglo-American Cataloguing Rules changes in tandem with LC.

Following the second task force meeting in Columbus on 12 April 1976, OCLC announced a revamping of current indexes to accommodate field 240 (Uniform Title), a delay in the card print program rewrite until December 1976 or later, and the possibility of converting correctly entered records for scores and sound recordings when the MARC music format was finally implemented. The task force met only briefly at the MLA/ALA meeting in Chicago that July. The formal third meeting took place on 11 October 1976, in Columbus, at which time OCLC announced that card production for scores and sound recordings would be available in December 1976. The task force was asked to recommend six libraries that would be able to upgrade records in the two formats, choosing Bowling Green, Cornell, Harvard, North Carolina, Oberlin, and Ohio State.

In September 1976, OCLC published *On-line Cataloging of Sound Recordings* and *On-line Cataloging of Scores*.[2] The task force's fourth Columbus meeting, on 17 and 18 November, resulted in recommendations on searching, Encoding Level "I" input requirements, and quality control. On 24 November 1976, OCLC implemented both the Scores and Sound Recordings formats, and the Audiovisual Materials, Manuscripts, and Maps formats. On 7 December, the OCLC Advisory Committee on Cataloging accepted the task force recommendations for fixed field requirements.

At the MLA meeting in Nashville, 31 January–5 February 1977, Karl Van Ausdal, representing the OCLC Music Task Force, reported on the task force's two short-term goals: music cataloging input standards for OCLC and interpretation of the MARC music format. At that same MLA meeting in Nashville, "concerned music users of the OCLC system" met to discuss the need for a Music OCLC Users Group. A core group consisting of Lenore Coral (University of Wisconsin–Madison), Karen A. Hagberg (Eastman School of Music), David Knapp, Mary

Lou Little, and Karl Van Ausdal, volunteered to draft bylaws, compile a mailing list, and start planning a first official meeting.

Discussions among the MLA Automation Committee, LC's MARC Development Office, and the OCLC Music Task Force resulted in the publication of "Guidelines for Subfielding Music Uniform Titles" in the *Music Cataloging Bulletin* in May 1977.[3] That October, the premiere issue of the *Music OCLC Users Group Newsletter* was published. It included an announcement of the first MOUG meeting to be held in Boston in conjunction with the annual meeting of MLA in February 1978, a draft of the MOUG bylaws, and a list of nominees for MOUG's first election. Curiously enough, the candidates list did not indicate who might be running for which office. That oversight must have been cleared up, because in November, MOUG's first Executive Board was elected: Chair Karen Hagberg, Vice Chair Olga Buth, Secretary/Newsletter Editor Pamela F. Starr (University of Wisconsin–Madison), Treasurer Ann E. Hess (University of Cincinnati), and Continuing Education Coordinator Karl Van Ausdal.

MOUG's first annual meeting was held in Boston on 26 February 1978. By all accounts, it was a great success and remains the best-attended MOUG meeting to this day, with some 250 registrants. Sessions included Jamie Levine on the structure and role of the New England Library Information Network (NELINET), Sharon Walbridge on quality control at OCLC, newly appointed MOUG/OCLC Liaison Helen Hughes on the OCLC Users Service Division, a business meeting, and a question-and-answer session that might be seen as the first of many "Ask MOUG" forums. Issue number two of the *MOUG Newsletter* was published in September 1978 and briefly inaugurated what would later become another long MOUG tradition, a question-and-answer column from Continuing Education Coordinator Karl Van Ausdal.

On 31 October 1978, MOUG suffered what would turn out to be the first of a series of leadership crises in its early years. Chair Karen Hagberg resigned both from Eastman's Sibley Music Library and from MOUG to become co-publisher and co-editor of *New Women's Times*. Olga Buth, now at the University of Texas at Austin, stepped up to become MOUG chair and appointed A. Ralph Papakhian (Indiana University) to be vice chair.

MOUG held its second annual meeting in Columbus on 26–27 March 1979, with a session on authority work, tagging workshops on sound recordings and music manuscripts, and an open forum. A particular highlight of the meeting was OCLC President Fred Kilgour's address to the MOUG banquet. MOUG also began exploring the possibility of an official relationship with MLA. During its 4–5 June 1979 meeting, the OCLC Users Council, with significant encouragement from MOUG, passed a resolution urging LC to implement the MARC music format.

Later in 1979, Robert Cunningham left Smith College to become the music specialist quality control librarian at OCLC, where he remained for two years before leaving OCLC for NELINET. During his tenure at OCLC, Cunningham was a strong advocate for MOUG.

With issue number four (September 1979) of the *MOUG Newsletter*, Ralph Papakhian became the editor, getting considerable help from his Indiana University colleague Sue Stancu. In that issue, Papakhian and Richard Smiraglia (University of Illinois at Urbana-Champaign) published their "OCLC Music Cataloging Survey," the results of which would appear in issue number seven (May 1980).

One of MOUG's early successful projects was the OCLC Musical Recordings Analytics Consortium (OMRAC), coordinated by Richard E. Jones of the University of Wisconsin–Milwaukee. MOUG members would do the authority work for the addition of composer/uniform title added entries to records for musical sound recordings, reporting the additions to OCLC via change requests. OCLC Quality Control staff would actually add the fields to the records. This effort was aided immensely by the 29 January 1980 implementation by OCLC of its copy of the LC authority file.

When MOUG held its third annual meeting in conjunction with MLA in San Antonio, February 1980, Michael Gorman (University of Illinois), coeditor of the new second edition of the *Anglo-American Cataloguing Rules* (AACR2),[4] spoke to the membership. OCLC's Cunningham and Glenn Patton (Illinois Wesleyan University) presented a tagging workshop for music catalogers. At that meeting, Patton became MOUG chair, with Vice Chair Ruth W. Tucker (Cornell University), Secretary/Newsletter Editor Ralph Papakhian, Treasurer Richard Smiraglia, and Continuing Education Officer Christina McCawley (West Chester University). Also in San Antonio, MOUG formed the Retrospective Music project, REMUS. This new committee was intended as an organized means by which to create MARC records for scores and sound recordings that had been cataloged prior to the implementation of the MARC music format. It was seen as a sort of unofficial musical counterpart to the CONSER program for serials.

Those two MOUG initiatives, OMRAC and REMUS, helped inspire OCLC to look for ways to empower its cataloging users with new capabilities that would allow them to share even more directly in the growth and maintenance of the bibliographic database. In November 1982, MOUG participated in the Oglebay Institute on Quality Control, which brought together representatives of OCLC, its regional networks, the Health Sciences OCLC User Group (HSOCLCUG), and others to discuss database-quality issues. At this three-day conference in Wheeling, West Virginia, OMRAC, REMUS, and other grassroots quality efforts were discussed, and OCLC spoke about its plans for the future.

Just over a year later, in December 1983, OCLC's Enhance capability was installed, and by June 1984, the first twenty Enhance participants (including four in the Scores format and three for Sound Recordings) had been chosen and trained. The Enhance Program allows specially authorized OCLC users to lock and replace certain categories of records in WorldCat, correcting or adding data. It is interesting to note that to this day, Enhance participants authorized for either of these music formats constitute a disproportionately large number when compared to the relatively small percentage of music records in WorldCat. Score and sound recording records combined are approximately 5.23 percent of the database, but of the roughly 340 institution code/bibliographic format combinations authorized for Enhance, about 29 percent of them are for scores and sound recordings. This speaks volumes about the music community's deep and abiding concern for database quality.

In the meanwhile, however, in June 1980 MOUG had experienced its second leadership crisis when Chair Glenn Patton joined the OCLC staff as an instructional coordinator. Compounding the situation around the same time, Cornell University withdrew from OCLC to become a member of the Research Libraries Group (RLG) and its Research Libraries Information Network (RLIN). With Cornell went MOUG Vice Chair Ruth Tucker, who would otherwise have taken Patton's place as chair. On 1 September 1980, David Knapp of Oberlin College was appointed the new MOUG chair. Also in 1980, *The Music OCLC Users Group Tagging Workbook and Reference Manual* by Ruth Patterson Funabiki and Karl Van Ausdal was published by NELINET.[5]

Momentous changes were also afoot within the larger world of cataloging. In December 1980, the first large conversion of headings in the OCLC database to conform to AACR2 took place. This required taking the OCLC system down for several weeks. Then on 1 January 1981, OCLC users were officially allowed to begin cataloging according to the new rules. When MOUG met 9–10 February 1981 in New Haven, Connecticut, Glenn Patton presented a workshop on how AACR2 changes affected the music formats. Robert Cunningham regaled catalogers with a session on the new standards for retrospective input. Catherine Garland (Library of Congress) reported on LC's plans for the MARC music format, and other meetings concerned reference use of the OCLC bibliographic database and use of the OCLC authority file. Before the end of 1981, Patton had taken over from Helen Hughes as the second MOUG/OCLC liaison and Cunningham had left OCLC to rejoin NELINET as a network coordinator.

MOUG met in Santa Monica, California, in February 1982 for updates on REMUS and OMRAC, music use of the OCLC Union Listing capability, a session on paraprofessionals, and a tagging workshop. Richard Smiraglia took office as MOUG chair, Joan Swanekamp (Eastman School of Music) as vice chair, Sue Stancu as secretary/newsletter editor, Joseph W. Scott (University of Connecticut) as treasurer, and Tim Robson (Case Western Reserve University) as continuing education coordinator. On 28 June 1982, Jay Weitz (Capital University) replaced Robert Cunningham as the quality control librarian specializing in the music formats at OCLC. Before the end of the year, Weitz was working with Philip Youngholm (Connecticut College) on the Vivaldi Project, updating uniform titles for works by Antonio Vivaldi to conform to AACR2.

Not long after MOUG's meeting, 28 February–1 March 1983, in Philadelphia, the search key for Johann Sebastian Bach became the first to exceed the OCLC system limit of 256 records retrieved in the OCLC authority file. At MOUG's insistence, the OCLC Users Council adopted a resolution at its May 1983 meeting urging that OCLC work to solve the Name Authority File searching problem. Although Bach's name was the first, it would be far from the last to become inaccessible without the implementation of an author/title or other alternative search capability. In anticipation of Mozart crossing the same searching threshold, a list of Mozart uniform titles and their authority record numbers compiled by Dean Corwin (Trenton State College) appeared in *MOUG Newsletter* no. 22, June 1984. A similar list of authority records for Johann Sebastian Bach, compiled by Indiana University's Anne McGreer, was published in *MOUG Newsletter* no. 23 (September 1984).

Updated versions of these two lists, plus three others, would serve as the basis of the first edition of *The Best of MOUG*, edited by Ann McCollough (Eastman School of Music) and published in early 1987.[6] McCollough compiled an expanded second edition in 1988. A third edition of *The Best of MOUG*, the first of five editions to be edited by Judy Weidow (University of Texas at Austin) appeared in 1989. Each edition expanded significantly on the one before. Unfortunately, it took until the May 1992 installation of authority-file search enhancements for OCLC to completely solve those authority indexing problems. Contrary to the expectations of many, however, *The Best of MOUG* continued to thrive long after the indexing issues were remedied. When the two-volume eighth edition, edited by Margaret Kaus (Kansas State University), was released in 2008, it covered thirty composers. Both catalogers and public service librarians have continued to find it invaluable in aiding access to many of the prolific composers who are most difficult to search.

Joan Swanekamp became MOUG chair, Joan Schuitema (Southern Methodist University) became vice chair, Judy Weidow became treasurer, and Don Hixon (University of California, Irvine) became continuing education coordinator in 1984. LC began creating MARC records for scores and sound recordings for the first time in March 1984, although it was not until Beethoven's 215th birthday on 16 December 1985 that OCLC was able to load them.

MOUG and the Online Audiovisual Catalogers (OLAC), which had been founded in June 1980 with Nancy B. Olson (Mankato State University) as its first president, held their first joint conference at OCLC headquarters in the Columbus suburb of Dublin, Ohio, 30 April–1 May 1984. The MLA meeting in Austin earlier that year was the first and only one where MOUG did not also meet. In July and September 1984, the Council on Library Resources sponsored a pair of "Music Recon Conferences" with MOUG participation that included Richard E. Jones and Ralph Papakhian. The purpose was to begin development of a nationally coordinated music retrospective conversion effort. "The National Plan for Retrospective Conversion in Music" was published for comment in the *MOUG Newsletter* no. 27 (September 1985).

One of the big topics at the MOUG meeting in Louisville in March 1985 was the proposal to create a union list of serials for music, an effort spearheaded by Ellen Rappaport of the SUNY/OCLC Network. In June 1985, MOUG suffered its third leadership crisis when Vice Chair/Chair Elect Joan Schuitema joined the OCLC staff as a System Support and Training Specialist. Once at OCLC, however, Schuitema was instrumental in helping to implement the authorities phase of the Linked Systems Project, which allowed online exchange of authority data among LC and the three bibliographic utilities, the Western Library Network (WLN), RLG, and OCLC. At the MOUG meeting in Milwaukee in February 1986, Schuitema took over as MOUG/OCLC liaison from Glenn Patton. Timothy Robson took over as chair,

Don Hixon as vice-chair, Ann McCollough as secretary/newsletter editor, Pam Juengling (University of Massachusetts at Amherst) as treasurer, and Dean Corwin as continuing education coordinator.

On 29 December 1986, the second AACR2 conversion of the bibliographic database began, but this time system functions were not interrupted. The conversion ran through 17 July 1987 and touched about 36 percent of the bibliographic records in WorldCat. Soon thereafter, in August 1987, all MARC bibliographic fields 705 and 715, designating the personal and corporate names of performers on sound recording records, were converted to 700 and 710, respectively, in accordance with changes to the MARC format. At the February 1987 MOUG meeting in Eugene, Oregon, one piece of big news was OCLC's proposed score and sound recording subset of the bibliographic database to be issued on compact disc, helping libraries save telecommunications costs.

During 1988, the REMUS Project evolved into the first of the Name Authority Cooperative (NACO) "funnel projects," with the NACO-Music Project (NMP) under the coordination of Ralph Papakhian. As a result, Indiana contributed the first non-LC records to the LC authority file through the Linked Systems Project. At the time of this writing, the NMP had grown to more than sixty-five institutional contributors and had been responsible for more than 280,000 new or changed authority records. Among the many headings added and altered over the years were several "composer projects" organized by the NMP, systematically adding composer/uniform title headings for as many of an individual composer's works as possible. The first of these was the "Prokofiev Project" completed in 1990 by Linda Barnhart (University of California, San Diego). In 1993, Michelle "Mickey" Koth (Yale University) completed the "Schumann Project."

At the February 1988 MOUG meeting in Minneapolis, Minnesota, reference services began to gain traction as a major topic of interest. One of the session topics was "Reference Use of OCLC" and during a discussion of "Future Goals and Objectives of MOUG," it was suggested that a "committee for reference services" be appointed. From its inception, MOUG had always been a mostly cataloger-dominated group. But as a result of this meeting, a MOUG Reference Task Force was formed, playing a vital role in advising OCLC on the reference products and services it was then in the process of developing. At this time, OCLC Market and Product Analyst Deborah Bendig began her long tenure as the reference services liaison between MOUG and OCLC. Don Hixon became chair, Linda Barnhart became secretary/newsletter editor, Candice Feldt (Tufts University) became treasurer, and Laura Snyder (Oberlin College) became continuing education coordinator. In December 1988, OCLC began to provide access to LC's subject authority records in addition to the name authority records. Also in 1988, Schuitema left OCLC and Ron Gardner became the fourth MOUG/OCLC Liaison.

During 1989, OCLC began to develop the "Musical Sound Recordings" subset of the bibliographic database that had been proposed in 1987, the *Search CD450 Music Library*, with considerable input from the MOUG Reference Task Force. OCLC moved into reference services in a big way in January 1990 with the introduction of its EPIC Service, aimed at expert librarian searchers, and then again in October 1991, with the debut of FirstSearch, the end-user counterpart. (In July 1999, the EPIC and FirstSearch services were merged under the latter name.) Browsable phrase searching of the OCLC authority files was implemented in May 1992.

When MOUG held its meetings in conjunction with MLA, the MOUG meeting usually preceded MLA. In March 1989, however, the MOUG meeting in Cleveland followed MLA. The experiment was never repeated. Out of that meeting came the suggestion that Jay Weitz, the newly appointed MOUG/OCLC liaison, revive the notion of a question-and-answer column in the *MOUG Newsletter*, started briefly by MOUG's first continuing education coordinator, Karl Van Ausdal. Weitz's first such column appeared in *MOUG Newsletter* no. 39 (May 1989). A collection of the columns from 1989 through 2002 was published under the title *Cataloger's Judgment: Music Cataloging Questions and Answers from the Music OCLC Users Group Newsletter* in 2004.[7]

In 1990, Jennifer Bowen (Eastman School of Music) became chair, Karen Little (University of Louisville) was elected secretary/newsletter editor, and H. Stephen Wright (Northern Illinois University) was elected continuing education coordinator. At the MOUG meeting in February 1990, the specter of MARC format integration rose from years of dark discussions and proposals at American Library Association meetings to the desert light of Tucson, Arizona. On 13 April 1990, MOUG reached an agreement to establish its official organizational archives at the University of Maryland, College Park. In 1991, Stanford and Yale became the first two RLG participants in the NACO-Music Project and Vassar's Ann Churukian was elected MOUG treasurer. At the February 1991 MOUG meeting in Indianapolis, both the advantages and the shortcomings of OCLC's EPIC Service for music materials were under discussion.

Laura Snyder (now of the Eastman School of Music) became chair; Sue Weiland (Wichita State University), secretary/newsletter editor; and Tim Cherubini (Duke University), continuing education coordinator in 1992. A highlight of the Baltimore meeting of MOUG in February 1992 was Papakhian's historical review of the NACO-Music Project. The next year, Christine Grandy (University of Oregon) was elected treasurer, and the MOUG Board appointed Ruthann McTyre (University of Iowa) as the first public services coordinator. MOUG met in San Francisco in February 1993, where Michael Colby (University of California, Davis) and Laura Gayle Green (Indiana University) relaxed the membership with a session about managing stress on the job.

In 1994, Ralph Papakhian became chair, Judy Weidow became secretary/newsletter editor, and Laura Gayle Green (University of Missouri–Kansas City) became continuing education coordinator. MOUG held a shortened March 1994 meeting in conjunction with MLA in Kansas City and then its second joint meeting with OLAC in Oak Park, Illinois, near Chicago, that October. Such cooperative ventures as the Associated Music Libraries Group's Retrospective Conversion Grants and the development of the Core Bibliographic Record were topics of the MOUG meeting in Atlanta in February 1995. In what remains the most celebrated feature ever to appear in the *MOUG Newsletter*, Papakhian's August 1995 "From the Chair" column in issue number sixty-one featured his essay on the psychological phenomenon known as "cataloger envy."

Karen Little assumed the position of chair, Lynn Gullickson (University of Northern Iowa) was elected secretary/newsletter editor, and Neil Hughes (University of Georgia) was elected continuing education coordinator in 1996. At the Seattle meeting that year, the MOUG Reference Products Interest Group was created. During 1996, Ralph Papakhian created the first MOUG website, based at Indiana University.

Jane Edmister Penner (University of Virginia) was elected treasurer in 1997. At the January 1997 MOUG meeting in New Orleans, Phillip De Sellem (LC) and Alice LaSota (University of Maryland) presented a Series Authority Workshop. In the May 1997 issue of the *MOUG Newsletter*, the PRISM Review Task Force, created in 1996 and consisting of Sue Weiland, Jean Harden, and Charles Herrold, issued its detailed final recommendations on the indexing, display, and other capabilities of OCLC's new PRISM platform in the context of music materials. (OCLC's WorldCat had begun to make the transition in 1991 from the First OCLC Online System to its new PRISM platform, and by 1994, most OCLC services had migrated.)

At its February 1998 meeting, MOUG celebrated its twentieth anniversary in Boston, the site of its first meeting in 1978. Special guest speakers included Sheila Intner (Simmons College) and Martha Yee (UCLA Film & Television Archive). H. Stephen Wright assumed the position of chair, Mickey Koth became secretary/newsletter editor, and Cheryl Taranto (University of Nevada, Las Vegas) was elected continuing education coordinator.

Los Angeles hosted the March 1999 MOUG meeting, where Debbie Herman-Morgan (University of Hartford) became treasurer. How cataloging can help users access web resources was a major topic of discussion. MOUG returned to Louisville in February 2000, when Jean Harden (University of North Texas) became chair and Margaret Kaus (University of North Florida) became continuing education coordinator. Brad Eden (University of Nevada, Las Vegas) spoke on "MARC Tagging for Internet Resources" and Jane Penner helped public service librarians make sense of music uniform titles.

MOUG-L, the MOUG electronic discussion list, was established in 2000 by Cheryl Taranto at the University of Nevada, Las Vegas. In July 2008, the list was moved to a new host at the University of Kentucky, where it is administered by Kerri Scannell Baunach.

In October 2000, MOUG met with OLAC in Seattle for their third joint conference. Martha Yee mused on "The Future of Libraries and Cataloging in a Networked Multimedia Publication Environment." Sherry Vellucci (St. John's College of Library and Information Science) contemplated how current trends in music, science, and technology would transform music libraries in the twenty-first century.

February 2001 saw MOUG meet in New York and Ruth Ann Inman (Kennedy-King College) become treasurer. David Procházka presented "A Beginner's Guide to OCLC Passport Macros." At the February 2002 meeting in Las Vegas, OCLC's Marty Withrow gave attendees a preview of the migration of WorldCat to its future Oracle platform. Ruthann McTyre ascended to chair of MOUG, Stephen Luttmann (University of Northern Colorado) became secretary/newsletter editor, and Martin Jenkins (Wright State University) took on the job of continuing education coordinator. At the MOUG business meeting, Ralph Papakhian became the first NACO funnel coordinator to be honored by the Program for Cooperative Cataloging (PCC) for his brainchild of the funnel concept and his longtime leadership of the NACO-Music Project.

In 2002, MOUG established its Distinguished Service Award to recognize "someone who has made significant professional contributions to music users of OCLC." The first recipient that year was Kathryn E. Burnett (Smith College), cited "as a role model . . . in advancing the case for high quality music cataloging in a cooperative environment." Judy A. Weidow became the second honoree in 2003, in particular for her work as compiler of five editions of *The Best of MOUG*. OCLC's Jay Weitz was the third recipient in 2004. Ralph Papakhian and Sue Ellen Stancu were jointly recognized in 2005 for their decades of work as catalogers, educators, mentors, and MOUG leaders. In 2006, Jean Harden (University of North Texas) became the sixth honoree for her long service to MOUG and the music cataloging community. Charles M. "Chuck" Herrold Jr. (Carnegie Library of Pittsburgh) was recognized in 2007, especially for his monumental contributions to the NACO-Music Project. Mickey Koth was honored in 2009 for her contributions to the NACO-Music Project, her editorship of both the *Music Cataloging Bulletin* and the *MOUG Newsletter*, and her creation of print and electronic resources for cataloging, among other things.

Marking MOUG's twenty-fifth anniversary, Judy Weidow and Steve Wright delivered warm reminiscences of their careers and involvement with the organization at the February 2003 meeting in Austin, Texas. Five librarians (Donna Arnold and Jean Harden from the University of North Texas, Kay Lowell and Steve Luttmann of the University of Northern Colorado, and Margaret Kaus of the University of Tennessee) spoke of the symbiosis between public and technical services in "The Truth about CAT(alogers) and DOG(ged Reference Librarians)."

Taking advantage of the fact that it was meeting in the Washington, D.C., suburb of Arlington, Virginia, in February 2004, MOUG had Joe Bartl and Henry Grossi of LC speak about "Relationships among the Various LC Catalogs and OCLC WorldCat." Ruthann McTyre led a MOUG "town hall meeting" to discuss the organization's future, the structure and scheduling of its meetings, its relationship to OCLC, and other topics. Mark Scharff (Washington University) took over as chair and Candice Feldt (now of Harvard University) became continuing education coordinator.

MOUG went international for the first time, meeting in Vancouver, British Columbia, Canada, in February 2005, where OCLC's Deb Bendig talked about the Functional Requirements of Bibliographic Records (FRBR) and what they meant for both public and technical services. The MARC bibliographic format was examined from the reference and the cataloging perspectives by Steve Luttmann and Sue Stancu, respectively. Holling Smith-Borne (DePauw University) took on the post of MOUG treasurer.

During 2005, MOUG began the multi-year process of changing from a 501(c)(6) nonprofit to a 501(c)(3) nonprofit, contributions to which are tax-deductible. Numerous MOUG members, including Karen Little, Jean Harden, Ann McCollough Caldwell (now of Brown University), Beth Flood (Kent State University), Deborah Morris (Roosevelt University), Holling Smith-Borne (Vanderbilt University), and Neil Hughes were involved in this effort.

How appropriate that when MOUG met in the music capital, Memphis, in February 2006, the focus was on sound recordings, including cataloging workshops by Margaret Kaus (Kansas State University), Howard Jaffe (Library of Congress), and Robert Freeborn (Pennsylvania State University). Neil Hughes became chair, Kerri Scannell Baunach (University of Kentucky) became secretary/newsletter editor, and Bruce Evans (Baylor University) became continuing education coordinator. In 2006, Deb Bendig left OCLC and so ended her long tenure as reference services liaison to MOUG, a position taken over by Mela Kircher. At its August 2006 summer meeting in Columbus, the MOUG executive board met with OCLC President Jay Jordan to discuss mutual concerns and the relationship between OCLC and its oldest user group. Also in 2006, Rebecca Littman (University of Wisconsin–Milwaukee) handed over the reins of MOUG web keeper to Nancy Sack (University of Hawaii at Manoa).

Open WorldCat and WorldCat.org were the topics of the opening plenary session, presented by Kathy Glennan (University of Maryland) and Chip Nilges (OCLC), at the February 2007 MOUG meeting in Pittsburgh. Martin Jenkins and OCLC's Tim Savage spoke about "OCLC and Outsourced Cataloging Services." Acquisitions of music materials were discussed by Anna Sylvester (OCLC), Bob Acker (DePaul University), and Richard LeSueur (Ann Arbor District Library). Deborah Morris took over as MOUG treasurer.

In April 2007, a Task Force to Revise MOUG's Mission and Objectives was created, consisting of Chair Joseph Hafner (McGill University), James L. Soe Nyun (University of California, San Diego), and Sue Stancu, with ex officio participation from Neil Hughes and Tracey Rudnick. The task force's final report, issued in July 2008, recommended some substantive updates to MOUG's goals, including stronger ties to MLA's Educational Outreach Program, the explicit inclusion of continuing education in the mission statement, and a closer advisory relationship with OCLC.

OCLC's Glenn Patton returned to MOUG at its February 2008 meeting in Newport, Rhode Island, to speak along with Paul Cauthen (University of Cincinnati) about "Vendor Bibliographic Record Quality in OCLC." Catherine Gerhart (University of Washington) led a session on OCLC's WorldCat Local. Tracey Rudnick (University of Connecticut) became MOUG chair and Alan Ringwood (University of Texas at Austin) became the secretary/newsletter editor.

For the fourth time, MOUG and OLAC met for a joint conference in Cleveland in September 2008. Lynne Howarth (University of Toronto) delivered the keynote address,

"Rocking the Metaverse: A/V Cataloging in a Web X.0 Environment." Heidi Hoerman (University of South Carolina) and Glenn Patton spoke about *RDA: Resource Description & Access*, Janis Young (Library of Congress) explained the ongoing genre/form heading projects, and Janet Swan Hill (University of Colorado at Boulder) closed the conference, looking toward the future of cataloging.

In February 2009, OCLC's Michael Sarmiento briefly became the new reference/public-services liaison between MOUG and OCLC, as MOUG met in Chicago. David Bade (University of Chicago) and Tom Caw (University of Wisconsin–Madison) discussed the recent and controversial LC Working Group's vision of the information future. Caitlin Hunter (Library of Congress) spoke about cataloging sound recordings of ethnic music. Wendy Sistrunk (University of Missouri–Kansas City) and Steve Luttmann presented the session "Authority Records for Public Services: Perspectives from Cataloging and Reference." Diane Napert (Yale University) took on the job of MOUG treasurer. Later in 2009, OCLC's Vince Wortman took over as reference/public-services liaison between MOUG and OCLC. In November 2009, MOUG conducted its first election of officers via electronic ballot.

OCLC's Matt Goldner introduced MOUG to "Web-scale Management Services" at the March 2010 meeting in San Diego. Maureen Russell of the UCLA Ethnomusicology Archive gave her presentation on "Archival Cataloging 101." Steve Luttmann became MOUG chair, Damian Iseminger (New England Conservatory) took the post of secretary/newsletter editor, and Catherine Gick Busselen (Brown University) became continuing education coordinator.

Just weeks before the 2010 MOUG meeting, Ralph Papakhian died on 14 January at the age of 61, following a long struggle with colorectal cancer. His Indiana colleague Sue Stancu delivered a tribute at the meeting. Soon thereafter, MOUG established the Ralph Papakhian Travel Grant in his honor. It is intended to support the attendance at the annual MOUG meeting of a student, paraprofessional, or professional in the first five years of her or his career. Thanks to a generous outpouring of donations in Papakhian's memory in 2010, MOUG was able to assist three recipients to attend the 2011 MOUG meeting in Philadelphia: Sally Bauer (New York Public Library), Sandra Schipior (Juilliard School of Music), and Tim Smolko (University of Georgia).

At its July 2010 summer meeting in Columbus, the MOUG executive board met again with OCLC President Jay Jordan, finding agreement in the desire to improve access to both new and hidden resources and to increase the usefulness of current and future OCLC products and services. In fall 2010, Tracey Snyder (Cornell University) took over as MOUG web keeper.

From the implementation of the MARC music format and the conversion to AACR2 through the rise of the World Wide Web and its resources to the advent of RDA and web-scale systems, the Music OCLC Users Group has worked alongside OCLC with the common goal of helping to further access to the world's information. MOUG has kept access to music, in all of its many forms, in the vanguard.

NOTES

[1] Library of Congress, MARC Development Office, *Music, a MARC Format: Specifications for Magnetic Tapes Containing Catalog Records for Music Scores and Musical and Nonmusical Sound Recordings* (Washington, D.C.: Library of Congress, 1976).

[2] Both documents were originally published on 27 September 1976 as parts of OCLC Technical Bulletin no. 13.

[3] Kay Guiles, "Guidelines for Subfielding Music Uniform Titles," *Music Cataloging Bulletin* 8, no. 5 (May 1977): 5–6.

[4] Joint Steering Committee for the Revision of AACR, *Anglo-American Cataloguing Rules*, 2nd ed., ed. Michael Gorman and Paul L. Winkler (Chicago: American Library Association, 1978).

[5] Ruth Patterson Funabiki and Karl Van Ausdal, *The Music OCLC Users Group Tagging Workbook and Reference Manual* (Newton, Mass.: NELINET, 1980).

[6] Music OCLC Users Group, *Best of MOUG* (Rochester, N.Y.: MOUG, 1987).

[7] Jay Weitz, *Cataloger's Judgment: Music Cataloging Questions and Answers from the Music OCLC Users Group Newsletter*, ed. Matthew Sheehy (Westport, Conn.: Libraries Unlimited, 2004).

PART 2

Cataloging Theory in Transition

As was the case a generation ago, the music cataloging community is again in a period of transition. Findings stemming from the 1997 final report of the IFLA Study Group on Functional Requirements for Bibliographic Records launched the cataloging community on a trajectory of both evolutionary and revolutionary change. As a result, the music cataloging community must again rise to the challenges unique to providing access to musical works and adapt cataloging procedures to keep up with technological innovations and changing theory.

At the heart of these changes is *Functional Requirements for Bibliographic Records* (FRBR), the intellectual model for providing access to bibliographic information in relationships based on a series of entities. For musical works, perhaps the most relevant are the Group 1 entities, including the concepts of *work, expression, manifestation*, and *item*. It is on FRBR principles that the new cataloging standard, *Resource Description & Access* (RDA)—slated to be implemented officially on 1 January 2013—is based. The music cataloging community is at the same time taking the opportunity to reevaluate subject and genre access to musical works. These efforts have been spearheaded by the MLA-BCC Genre/Form Task Force and the MLA-BCC Subject Access Subcommittee. At the heart of these efforts is the decision to separate musical genre terms from medium-of-performance terms in order to provide catalog users a more flexible way of accessing musical content.

All three authors of the articles in this part speak to the potential of these new theories in providing access to musical works, but they also address the challenges. Damian Iseminger discusses how the full potential of RDA cannot be realized until the community is able to move beyond the limitations of current metadata structures like MARC. Michelle Hahn proposes phased changes to AACR2 cataloging standards as a method of transitioning to future cataloging codes, which could include RDA. In her view, MARC could be adapted to accommodate these changes. Both Iseminger and Hahn speak to the potential of creating *work*-level records as a way of eliminating the redundancy of adding *work/expression*-level information to every bibliographic record representing a *manifestation*. Beth Iseminger discusses the evolutionary process utilized by members of the Genre Form Task Force in trying to separate genre and medium-of-performance terms, currently represented together in Library of Congress Subject Headings.

This current transition in music cataloging theory comes with enormous challenges. Patrons continue to expect materials to be provided in a timely manner, and as we make these transitions, we must examine the associated costs, especially in this fragile economic landscape. But these changes also come with enormous potential. As Ralph Papakhian and his colleagues did a generation ago, a new generation of catalogers is rising to these challenges and undoubtedly will (and must) come up with creative solutions to meet them.

WORKS AND EXPRESSIONS IN RDA
Problems and Solutions

Damian Iseminger

Abstract: The treatment of musical works and expressions in *Resource Description & Access* (RDA) is compromised by attempts to insure compatibility with today's cataloging environment and the metadata it currently produces. After reviewing the events that led to the birth of RDA, including problems with using *Anglo-American Cataloguing Rules*, second edition (AACR2) in the digital environment and the development of the conceptual models *Functional Requirements for Bibliographic Records* (FRBR) and *Functional Requirements for Authority Data* (FRAD), the problems with how RDA describes and provides access to music materials are enumerated. These include: problems with the "core element" concept in RDA; the expectation that data describing a work or expression will only be recorded in a form suitable for use as an element of an authorized access point, the equivalent of AACR2's uniform title; and the inability to uniquely identify musical expressions, using either stand-alone data elements or data that is part of an authorized access point. The root of these problems is RDA's attempt to be backwards-compatible with data produced using AACR2. If RDA is to be a standard for the future of resource description and access, it must loosen its ties to the past and embrace true innovation.

One of the signature achievements of A. Ralph Papakhian was the establishment in 1988 of the NACO-Music Project (NMP), for creating and contributing name and name/uniform-title authority records to the Library of Congress National Authority File. These records contain the headings that are needed for the retrieval of musical works and the persons associated with them. As a result of his efforts, creating name and name/uniform-title authority records has become some of the most important work performed by music catalogers, as evidenced by the over 190,000 name, name/title, corporate, and series headings that NMP contributors have produced.[1] Since the founding of the NMP twenty-three years ago, the wider cataloging community has increasingly devoted its attention to better understanding and describing the intellectual content contained within resources, culminating with the publication of *Resource Description & Access* (RDA) in summer 2010.[2] It is intended to be the successor to the current cataloging code, *Anglo-American Cataloging Rules*, second edition (AACR2).[3] The legacy of music access that Ralph Papakhian has bequeathed to his fellow music catalogers has put the community in an excellent position to understand and critique the instructions dealing with music access in RDA.

To do this, I will briefly describe how access to music content is treated in AACR2. I will then give an overview of the conceptual models underlying RDA, *Functional Requirements for Bibliographic Records* (FRBR) and *Functional Requirements for Authority Data* (FRAD), especially as it relates to the FRBR entities *work* and *expression* and their implications for cataloging.[4] Based on this, I will offer a critique of RDA's handling of works and expressions for music resources and provide possible solutions.

DESCRIPTION AND ACCESS IN AACR2

Cataloging, as envisioned by AACR2, is essentially a two-step process. The first part is describing all aspects of a resource. This includes the way the resource identifies itself, the physical aspects of the resource, the content of the resource, and those responsible for the content of the resource. The second part of the process is to combine these descriptions with headings representing the entities responsible for the intellectual content of the resource or the intellectual content itself, all constructed according to very specific rules. These headings, when used in a catalog, provide access to the intellectual content represented in the resources of a library collection. The construct resulting from the combination of a resource description and its headings is what is known as a bibliographic record.

The headings in bibliographic records provide a method for organizing the catalog in which they reside. It is expected that all records representing resources containing content created by a specific person or group can be found together under the heading for that person or group. Similarly, it is expected that resources containing the same work will also be collocated. The device that makes this possible is the uniform title.

As defined in the glossary of AACR2, a uniform title is:

1. The particular title by which a work is to be identified for cataloguing purposes.
2. The particular title used to distinguish the heading for a work from the heading for a different work.[5]

Rule 25.1A gives four purposes of a uniform title:

- for bringing together all catalogue entries for a work when various manifestations (e.g., editions, translations) of it have appeared under various titles
- for identifying a work when the title by which it is known differs from the title proper of the item being catalogued
- for differentiating between two or more works published under identical titles proper;
- for organizing the file[6]

The use of uniform titles is optional in AACR2. The decision to use a uniform title is based on numerous factors, including the nature of the work (e.g., how well known the work is, whether a translation is involved, and how many manifestations of the work are involved) and the purpose of the collection in whose catalog it will appear (e.g., a small browsing collection versus a large research collection).

Given the nature of music publishing, however, using uniform titles for musical works is generally considered to be necessary. Titles identifying a single musical work commonly appear in a variety of languages and forms within and across publications. There is often incorrect, incomplete, or misleading information. The fact that a work has been excerpted from a larger work or arranged for a medium of performance other than that originally intended by the composer may not be indicated anywhere on the item. It is not uncommon for a title on an item to consist solely of the name of a type of composition with no other identifying words. The cataloging process begins with the identification of the work.

Uniform titles are generally required for all types of composition—for example, forms (concerto, symphony, trio sonata), genres (capriccio, intermezzo, nocturne), commonly used terms (movement, piece), and chamber-music combinations (trio, quartet, quintet). Titles of this nature are considered to be generic and are given in the plural, unless the composer has written only one work of that type. Instrumentation, identifying numbers, quantitative numbers, and key are given in subordinate positions in the uniform title, or, in some cases, are omitted.

Titles that include more than the name of a musical form, genre, commonly used term, or chamber-music combination and other identifying elements (instrumentation, numbers, key, date of composition) are considered to be "distinctive." The title in the original language is preferred, but not necessarily in the original script.

When a musical work has been altered in a way that is considered important, words or phrases are also appended to uniform titles to bring these altered versions together in the catalog. These can indicate whether the work is an arrangement, is notated in a vocal or chorus score, is in translation, or is incomplete.

Because musical works are often known by multiple titles, it is not enough simply to construct the "correct" uniform title for a musical work. A music cataloger must also know the other possible titles under which a musical work might be sought. References, based on the rules for uniform title construction, are created from these alternate titles and in a catalog point to the uniform title under which all resources containing the work are filed. Authority records are used to record the uniform title of a work and its references and to document the decisions used in constructing them.

The model that AACR2 posits works well for a file that is linear in nature and which can only be accessed manually. In other words, the underlying principles of AACR2 are tailor-made for the construction of card catalogs. In the digital environment, though, the approach AACR2 takes to describing and providing access to resources is inadequate. AACR2 provides access to resources only if the initial element of a heading representing a person, corporate body, or title is known. In a linear file this makes sense, since the cost and labor required to provide access by other elements—such as language, medium of performance, or serial numbers—would be prohibitive. In the digital environment, there are no such constraints. Search queries can be formulated to search across all elements of bibliographic records in the database. To look at it another way, users have the power to organize a bibliographic database as they see fit. In order to do this in the most effective way possible, however, the standards that describe resources must acknowledge and take into account the possibilities of the digital realm. Because the AACR2 model is inadequate for resource description and access in the digital environment, extensive revision of the current cataloging code—based on a fresh approach to looking at knowledge organization and information retrieval—is needed to push cataloging into the digital age.

FRBR AND FRAD

FRBR

The *Functional Requirements for Bibliographic Records* (FRBR) and the *Functional Requirements for Authority Data* (FRAD) represent a new way of looking at cataloging. The International Federation of Library Associations and Institutions (IFLA), following the 1990 Stockholm Seminar on Bibliographic Records, formed the IFLA Study Group on Functional Requirements for Bibliographic Records. The purpose of the study group was to produce a framework for understanding what information the bibliographic record aims to provide and what it is expected to achieve in answering user needs. The study group completed work on the initial draft of FRBR in 1995, and after some revisions, a final report was submitted and approved by IFLA in 1997 and published in 1998.[7]

The report analyzed bibliographic records using the entity-analysis technique, which is widely used in the creation of conceptual models for relational databases. Objects ("entities") of interest to users of bibliographic data[8] were isolated and identified, then attributes were assigned to each entity, and relationships between entities were mapped, based on user needs in creating searches, interpreting search results, and navigating the bibliographic universe. More specifically, FRBR identified four functional requirements, or user tasks, that are performed by users when searching and using library data. The data provided should enable users to (1) find all materials relevant to specific search criteria; (2) identify whether an entity is of interest; (3) select material appropriate to the user's needs; and, finally, (4) obtain access to the materials described.

To support the user tasks, FRBR defined three broad groups of entities. Group 1 includes those entities that are the products of intellectual or artistic activity. These are the *work*, a distinct intellectual or artistic creation; the *expression*, the intellectual or artistic realization of a work; the *manifestation*, the physical embodiment of an expression of a work; and the *item*, an exemplar of a manifestation. The Group 1 entities will be discussed in further detail below. Group 2 includes those entities responsible of the creation, realization, production, or ownership of a work, expression, manifestation, and item, namely *person*, *corporate body*, and *family*.[9] Group 3 are those entities which can be the subject of a work: *concept*, *object*, *event*, and *place*. Entities in Group 1 and 2 may also be a subject of a work.

For music catalogers, perhaps the most intriguing part of the model is the set of Group 1 entities. Music catalogers, more so than other catalogers, have grasped the separability of content from carrier and have used mechanisms—such as uniform titles—to indicate to users that a work of music can exist across a multiplicity of materials. FRBR expands this duality conceptually by defining work and expression as intellectual or artistic content, and manifestation and item as the physical carrier of content. Since I am considering the treatment of works and expressions for music materials in RDA, works and expressions in FRBR as they relate to music materials are discussed in detail below.

FRBR defines *work* as "a distinct intellectual or artistic creation" (FRBR 3.2.1), defined in the abstract—that is, no single physical object can be said to be the work. The work, therefore, can only be recognized in the similarities between its various expressions. In music, for example, we recognize that the "Eroica" Symphony by Beethoven exists as a work because of performances that have been given or because it has been notated in written form and its ideational content in those expressions is the same or extremely similar.

Because of the abstract nature of the work entity, determining the point at which modifications in content create a new work can be difficult to determine and is often different between cultural groups or communities of practice. For music, FRBR takes the position of the music cataloging community when it comes to work boundaries for music. It considers revisions, versions with added accompaniment, transcriptions, and arrangements to be different expressions of the same work, not new works. Variations on a preexisting theme or free transcriptions of a work would constitute new works. In a more practical vein, the work entity also serves to gather all expressions of itself together.

An *expression* is "the intellectual or artistic realization of a *work* in the form of alpha-numeric, musical, or choreographic notation, sound, image, object, movement, etc., or any combination of such forms" (FRBR 3.2.2). Additionally, a new expression of a work is created each time it is realized. For example, a 1975 performance of the "Eroica" by the London Philharmonic Orchestra, conducted by Bernard Haitink, and the same work performed in 1991 by the London Philharmonic Orchestra, conducted by Klaus Tennstedt, are different expressions. Similarly, a score of the Bach violoncello suites edited by Janos Starker and a score of the same work edited by Pierre Fournier are different expressions. As with the work, the expression entity can also gather all manifestations that contain the same expression. In music, an excellent example of this would be the same performance of a work available on a compact disc and as an MP3 file or a particular edition of a work issued by C.F. Peters and later reissued by Kalmus.

For music, the attributes of the work include its titles, form (e.g., sonata, concerto, etc.), date of composition, medium of performance, numeric designations (serial, opus, and thematic index numbers), key, and any other characteristics needed to distinguish between two or more works. The attributes of an expression include (using the example of a score) a title associated with the expression, the form (notation, etc.), date, language, type of score (full score, close score, vocal score, etc.), and medium of performance, if it differs from the original medium. Note that persons, corporate bodies, or families associated with the creation of a work or realization of an expression are not listed as attributes. Rather, responsibility is indicated through the use of relationships between the Group 1 and Group 2 entities.

FRAD

In 2009, an expansion of the FRBR model was released by the IFLA Working Group on Functional Requirements and Numbering of Authority Records and was published as

Functional Requirements for Authority Data (FRAD).[10] Like FRBR before it, FRAD used the entity-analysis technique, this time to examine authority records. Entities that were of interest to users of authority data were identified, and relationships were mapped between the entities, with attributes identified for each entity.

In FRAD, the bibliographic entities of the FRBR model are each known by *names* and/or *identifiers*. These entities in turn are used as the basis for constructing *controlled access points*, which are governed by *rules* (such as AACR2 or RDA) and applied by *agencies* that create or modify controlled access points.

Name is defined as "a character or a group of words and/or characters by which an entity is known in the real world" (FRAD 3.4). Attributes of name include the type of name (e.g., a title, personal name, corporate body, etc.), name string (the sequence of characters identifying a name), the scope of usage (e.g., personal name used for certain types or classes of resources), dates of usage, language, script, and transliteration scheme. The identification of the name entity represents a subtle shift in the FRBR model. In the original report, titles of the Group 1 entities, names of the Group 2 entities, and terms of the Group 3 entities were considered attributes of the entity. In FRAD, this naming attribute is now considered an entity unto itself.

Identifier is "a number, code, word, phrase, logo, device, etc., that is associated with an entity" (FRAD 3.4) and serves to differentiate one entity from another entity within the same domain—that is, to distinguish a work from another work, an expression from another expression, and so forth. These identifiers could be standard identifiers, like ISBNs, issued by agencies; thematic-index numbers, assigned by a publisher or musicologist; and classification numbers. These identifiers, however, do not include numbers assigned to authority records, which can represent any type of entity. Rather, the identifier has to be domain-specific. The only attribute of an identifier is the type of identifier—that is, a work identifier, a manifestation identifier, etc.

Controlled access point is a "name, term, code, etc., under which a bibliographic record or authority record or reference will be found" (FRAD 3.4). It can be an authorized access point or a variant access point. Attributes of a controlled access point include the type of access point (personal name, corporate body, title, etc.), the status (fully established or provisional), usage (preferred or variant), undifferentiated, language and script of the access point, transliteration scheme of the access point, base access point (i.e., initial title element), and additions to the base access point (medium of performance, numeric designation, key, etc.).

There are many implications for cataloging in the FRBR and FRAD model, but let us consider those that are concerned with the description of and access to intellectual content, namely works and expressions. The emphasis placed on these entities within the FRBR/FRAD model implies that they should perhaps be the primary concern of catalogers. Music catalogers are in a unique position of understanding this shift, because content—and not so much format—tends to lie at the heart of music cataloging. Many, if not most, music catalogers catalog resources across formats. While formats can present challenges requiring special knowledge, generally it is providing access to content—whether in a score, sound recording, moving image, or other format—that is most important to a music cataloger.

FRBR/FRAD also suggests that works and expressions could exist as discrete, searchable objects within a library database. Currently, almost all bibliographic information is contained within a single record. This tends not to be a problem for resources where the only embodiment of its content is in a single manifestation. Problems arise, however, when a single work or expression is embodied in multiple manifestations across a database, as is often the case with music. In order to provide access, attributes of the work or expression must be repeated in every manifestation. The chance also increases that crucial information identifying a work or expression will be omitted or input incorrectly if entered multiple times, hence the possibility of not finding all instances. If works and expressions each had separate records, there would be less need for inputting redundant data. Work records could also serve as the primary collocating mechanism for all the manifestations containing its expressions, instead of using the current method of a precoordinated text string to gain access to all manifestations.

FRAD also suggests that authority records could perhaps be more robust than had been thought. A work is really nothing more than the sum of its attributes. To bring these attributes together, a work just needs to have a label that serves to identify this particular group of attributes. FRAD suggests that an identifier or a controlled access point could serve this labeling property. Currently, authority records related to works are generally used to document the decisions that led to the creation of the controlled access points contained within them. Some data concerning the attributes of the work may be present in the authority record, but usually only as it relates to establishing the access points. Since a controlled access point could conceivably function as a gathering mechanism for all attributes of a work, as suggested above, it follows that an authority record could contain not just the labels by which a work is known, but also all the attributes of that work, as separate data elements. For example, the authority record in MARC21 for Bach's Brandenburg Concerto no. 3, in addition to containing the authorized access point (Bach, Johann Sebastian, 1685–1750. Brandenburgische Konzerte. Nr. 3) could also contain the medium (string orchestra) coded in MARC21 field 382, the thematic index number (BWV 1048) coded in MARC21 field 383, and the key (G major) coded in MARC21 field 384. Authority records, instead of being records that validate authorized headings and generate references, could become the repository for data commonly considered to be part of the bibliographic record. In short, authority records could become work or expression records.

RDA: RAISON D'ÊTRE

The development of FRBR, the perceived inconsistencies in AACR2, and the inadequacy of AACR2 in describing current resources were the driving forces that led the Joint Steering Committee for the Revision of AACR (JSC) to call for a conference to be held in Toronto in October 1997 to review the underlying principles of AACR2 and to determine if fundamental rule revisions were necessary.

Following the conference, the JSC created a list of action items. Among these was a call to provide a logical analysis of the principles and structures underlying AACR2, completed in 1999 by Tom Delsey of the National Library of Canada, and a revision of rule 0.24 in AACR2 to advance the discussion on the primacy of intellectual content over physical format.[11] The work on rule 0.24 led to the JSC creating the Format Variation Working Group (FVWG) in 2001 to examine the feasibility of creating bibliographic records for expressions, to suggest methods for collocating expressions, and to determine the boundaries between expressions.

The logical analysis of AACR2, combined with the revision of rule 0.24 and the work of the FVWG, led the JSC to start work in 2004 on a new edition of the rules, then known as "AACR3." The initial work focused on revising part one of the rules based on Delsey's analysis.[12] In their strategic plan for the new edition, the JSC wanted a set of rules to cover all types of materials, to apply to and be able to operate in a web-based environment, to be compatible with other standards for resource description and retrieval, to be easy to use and interpret, and to be applicable beyond the library community.

Based on the feedback received of the initial AACR3 draft, the JSC decided in 2005 to go in a new direction. Instead of working toward a new edition of AACR, the JSC chose to develop a new standard for "resource description and access," designed for the digital environment. Additionally, the new standard would be written as a content standard—independent of guidelines for how the data would be presented and encoded—and would be more closely aligned with the FRBR and FRAD conceptual models. To reflect the new situation, the standard was given a new title: *Resource Description & Access* (RDA). After a recalibration of its structure in 2007 to make it even more aligned with FRBR and FRAD, RDA was released in draft form in late 2008, with revisions made in 2009. *Resource Description & Access*, after many fits and starts, was finally published in June 2010 by ALA Publishing.

RDA has four main objectives. The first objective, responsiveness to user needs, covers the user tasks of the FRBR and FRAD models, namely to find and identify resources and those associated with resources, to select and obtain resources, and to understand the relationships among the various entities and the forms chosen to represent these entities. The second objective is cost-effectiveness. Flexibility, the third objective, means that the data created using RDA should function independently of the systems used to encode and display the data. Finally, the data created using RDA should be able to be integrated into existing databases, especially those containing data created using AACR2. So, for our purposes, in order to determine how successfully RDA treats the concepts of works and expressions for music resources, we need only to compare the treatment with RDA's own objectives.

RDA: PROBLEMS WITH WORKS AND EXPRESSIONS

CORE ELEMENTS

The instructions in RDA that deal with the attributes (also known as "elements" in RDA) of a work and an expression are located in chapters 5–7. Chapter 5 is titled "General Guidelines on Recording the Attributes of Works and Expressions" and introduces the idea of "core elements" for works and expressions. The "core elements" concept is intended to address the RDA objective of cost-effectiveness. They are considered to be the minimum number of attributes needed to identify a work or an expression. For all works, a preferred title and identifier for the work are required, if readily ascertainable. For musical works with nondistinctive titles, the additional core elements are medium of performance, numeric designation, and key. For musical works with distinctive titles, medium, number, and key are core elements only if needed to differentiate between the same or similar preferred titles. For expressions of any kind, content type (e.g., notated music or performed music) and an expression identifier are required if readily ascertainable. Other expression attributes, such as language, date of expression, arrangement, vocal or chorus score, and sketches are considered core elements only if needed to differentiate between expressions.

The entire idea of "core elements" is problematic because of the implicit assumption that the recording of the attributes of works and expressions is necessary only when needed to distinguish between two or more works or expressions. I find this to be a strange way of identifying works and expressions. Any work or expression is necessarily the sum of its attributes. This problem is particularly acute when it comes to the RDA treatment of musical works. Why is there a distinction between those musical works that have nondistinctive titles and those that have distinctive titles? Aren't the attributes of medium of performance, numeric designation, and key important to most musical works, not just those that have "form" titles? Additionally, there are also other attributes—such as form/genre and date of composition—that users of music resources might also find helpful. In short, the "core elements" concept is simply too limiting when it comes to musical works and expressions.

Data that Identifies and Data that Describes

The specific rules for recording the attributes of works and expressions are found in chapter 6, "Identifying Works and Expressions," and chapter 7, "Describing Content." According to RDA, chapter 6 "provides general guidelines and instructions on choosing and recording preferred and variant titles for works, and on recording other identifying attributes of the work or expression . . . [and] provides guidelines on using the preferred title for a work with other identifying attributes of the work and/or expression to construct the authorized access point representing that work or expression, and using variant titles for the work to construct variant access points."[13] Chapter 7 "provides general guidelines and instructions on recording the attributes of works and expressions associated with the intellectual or artistic content of a resource."[14] With the exception of the guidelines for constructing access points in chapter 6, there appears to be little or no difference between the activities described in chapters 6 and 7. In fact, many of the activities described in chapter 6 are similar to activities described in chapter 7. The only real distinction seems to be between data that identifies and appears to be optimized for machine manipulation and data that describes, which is recorded in what appear to be natural language notes. For example, both chapters 6 and 7 contain instructions for recording the medium of performance. This is essentially the same task, so why is it necessary to establish two methods for doing the same thing?

The only logical reason is that RDA is making a distinction between data that would be recorded in an authority record and data that would be recorded in a bibliographic record, as they are understood today. RDA never explicitly states this, but its organization strongly implies it. This violates the third objective of the RDA project: flexibility, namely that the data recorded using RDA should function independently of the systems used to encode and display the data. It is clear that the data for works and expressions is intended to function in a system based on the current bibliographic/authority record model. While this may be the model in use at this time, it is by no means certain that this model will continue to be used in the future. The decision on what data should be used in an authority record or a bibliographic record and the formatting of that data should be left to those who are producing the data and should not be implied or proscribed by RDA.[15]

RECORDING DATA VS. CREATING AUTHORIZED ACCESS POINTS

There are two major activities described in chapter 6: one is to record the identifying attributes of works and expressions, and the other is to create an authorized access point to represent that work or expression. RDA defines an authorized access point as a "standardized access point representing an entity," which for a work or expression is the authorized access point representing the person, family, or corporate body, together with the title chosen as preferred title for the work, plus any other identifying attributes—in other words, the equivalent of a name/uniform-title heading.

The construction of an authorized access point, however, is not the only method for representing a work or expression. In a computer environment, a work or expression could just as easily be represented by an alpha-numeric identifier, as is implied by the FRAD report. For example, the Elgar Cello Concerto could be identified to a computer as work 3071978. There is no compelling reason why this work has to be represented to the computer as "Elgar, Edward, 1857–1934. Concertos, violoncello, orchestra, op. 85, E minor." Because of this, the data recorded to identify a work or an expression should be independent of the methods used to represent that work or expression in a library catalog.

Unfortunately, this does not appear to be the case in chapter 6 of RDA. There is an underlying assumption that most of the data recorded for works and expressions will have use only in an authorized access point. This problem is most readily apparent in the instructions for choosing and recording the titles of a musical work and the instructions for recording the medium of performance of a work.

Musical works, more so than other types of works, can be known by many titles. For example, Schubert's Piano Quintet in A major, D.667, is known by the titles " 'Trout' Quintet," "Forellen-Quintett," "Klavierquintett, A-Dur, Opus post. 114, D 667," and "Piano Quintet in A major, op. post. 114, D 667," just to name a few. Some of the titles are generic and some are distinctive, but they share one thing in common: they are titles by which this work by Schubert has become known through its various expressions and manifestations. If RDA is based in large part on the FRBR conceptual model, then it makes sense to record these various titles as one of the attributes of the work, regardless of whether the titles are generic or distinctive. But nowhere in RDA is there a suggestion that all titles of a musical work should be recorded. Instead, the musical titles that are recorded as work attributes in RDA are based on their suitability for use in an access point.

The method for recording a preferred title for music in RDA is mostly like the method of determining the initial title element for a uniform title in AACR2. Medium of performance, serial, opus, and thematic index numbers, designations of key, non-integral numbers, dates of composition, and adjectives and epitaphs not considered part of the original work title are all dropped from the title. Those titles that consist of only a generic or form title are further modified so that they are in the language of the cataloging agency and are made plural if the composer wrote more than one work of that particular type. Titles that contain more than just generic designations are considered distinctive and are recorded as is.

From a FRBR perspective, however, this presents a problem. The preferred title of a musical work is not the same as the actual title of a musical work. In RDA, the preferred title is an artificial construct. Its purpose is to serve as the initial title element in a precoordinated string that represents the musical work and is not at all intended to represent an actual title by which the work is known. This is perfectly acceptable if one intends to use authorized access points to provide access to works, but again, this is not the only way to provide access to works. If RDA is committed to a FRBR model, then it must also allow for the recording of all titles as work attributes. As it stands, there is no instruction in RDA that allows for this. Work titles may be recorded only as preferred or variant titles and must be constructed according to rules that will allow for their use in authorized or variant access points.

An examination of the instructions for recording medium of performance in chapter 6 further reinforces the idea that the way in which the attributes of works and expressions are recorded is based primarily on their utility as part of an authorized access point. RDA, much like AACR2, specifies a recording order for the voices and instruments. If the instrumentation for a work fits one of the "standard combinations of instruments," the medium is not recorded using the names of the individual instruments but rather using a group designation dependent on the preferred title. When individual instruments are listed, designations of key or range and alternative instrumentations are omitted from the statement. Designations for large instrumental ensembles are limited to "orchestra," "string orchestra," and "band." If a work includes solo voices together with a choir, the solo voices are not included in the medium statement.

Once again, these restrictions make sense in the context of constructing access points. The character strings would simply become too unwieldy if individual instruments were always listed in a work for string quartet or if designations of key or range were always included. The results, though, often do not accurately represent the medium of performance of a work. A work for alto saxophone and piano is misrepresented to users if the only way of recording the medium attribute for this work is as "saxophone, piano." Similarly, users lose information when the only permissible way of recording the medium for a group consisting of two violins, a viola, and a violoncello is either as "strings" when "Quartets" is the preferred title or as "string quartet" when it is not. A work for chamber orchestra is misrepresented when the only permissible term to use is "orchestra." To solve this problem, RDA must allow the recording of medium of performance to be independent of the methods used for including a medium-of-performance statement in an authorized access point. They are two separate activities: the first is intended to accurately represent the medium of performance of a work; the second is intended to create a statement that will be of use in a precoordinated string representing the work itself. RDA should not conflate them as it does now.

Based on the available evidence, it appears that the data generated from the instructions in chapter 6 are clearly intended for use in an authorized or variant access point. This violates the RDA objective of data that is independent of display and encoding standards. The data only makes sense in the context of an authorized access point—a display and organizational convention that is carried over from AACR2. The emphasis on recording work and expression attributes that are compatible with access points also undermines the FRBR user objectives of finding and identifying works and expressions. Titles recorded as preferred or variant titles may not be representative of titles found on manifestations of these works, hence limiting the ability of a user to find a work. The stringent rules for constructing medium statements may, for example, thwart users in attempting to identify works that contain an instrument whose name includes a designation of range or key. The one objective that RDA does fulfill is that the data is compatible with data produced according to AACR2, but in trying to make sure RDA data is AACR2-compatible, the authors of RDA are undermining the reasons why work on a completely new standard was considered necessary.

Identifying Expressions

Part of what makes cataloging materials related to music unique is the multiplicity of expressions that can be associated with one work. For example, here are just some of the expressions related to the work *The Marriage of Figaro* by Mozart:

- a performance recorded in 1990 in New York by James Levine and the Metropolitan Opera Chorus and Orchestra
- a performance recorded in 1990 in Munich by Colin Davis and the Bavarian Radio Symphony Orchestra and Chorus
- the critical edition of the score, with Italian words, edited by Ludwig Finscher, first published in 1973
- the vocal score, arranged by Erwin Stein, in Italian with an English translation by Edward J. Dent, first published in 1947

For users of music materials, the information relating to an expression of a work is just as important as the work itself. Unfortunately, RDA is lacking in its treatment of expression attributes that identify specific expressions of a musical work.

In chapter 6, RDA provides three expression attributes that cover all materials: "content type," which is how the content is meant to be perceived (for example, text, notated music, performed music, etc.); "date of expression" (expressed only in terms of a year or years); and "language of the expression."[16] RDA defines three further expression attributes for music that are considered to be "other distinguishing characteristics of the expression." These are "arrangements," "sketches," and "vocal or chorus scores."[17] Taken together, these attributes are not nearly enough to competently identify and differentiate between the various expressions of a musical work. Take, for example, the two performances of Figaro mentioned above. Both will have the same content type, date of expression, and language. The other three expression attributes defined for music are not applicable in this situation. Being able to record the names of principal performers as an identifying expression attribute would provide enough data to distinguish these two expressions.[18] Another situation that would be commonly encountered is a single work that has multiple arrangements. It would be helpful in differentiating between the two arrangements if an expression attribute existed in RDA for the medium of performance of the arrangement. Curiously, such an attribute does exist in the FRBR conceptual model. It is unclear why this does not appear as an element within RDA.

The underwhelming treatment of expressions of musical works in RDA is disappointing. It does not appear that the JSC clearly thought through what is required to identify a musical expression. It is as if elements that were identified as belonging to expressions within an AACR2 music uniform title were transferred to the text of RDA without any consideration of why they were present in an AACR2 uniform title to begin with. The purpose of appending "arr." or "Vocal score" to a uniform title was to provide a useful mechanism for organizing the file and for collocating certain classes of music materials into categories that made sense to users. These additions were never intended to differentiate between individual expressions. If the intent of chapter 6 concerning expressions of works is to provide enough attributes to distinguish between expressions, then more attributes must be added for expression identification to be of any value.

CREATING AUTHORIZED ACCESS POINTS

As mentioned above, I object to the implication in RDA that attributes that identify a work or expression have to be recorded in such a way that they will find use as an element within an authorized access point. That does not mean that I object to the use of authorized access points to represent works or expressions; they can still perform their traditional duties of collocation, differentiation, and file organization. Authorized access points could also be used as a way to systematically label work or expression records. Because authorized access points are tools for achieving these ends, it follows that the rules used to construct them may be as detailed and as specific as is necessary. So the question is, how well does RDA provide guidance in constructing authorized access points for works and expressions?

Access Points for Musical Works
For musical works, the rules for constructing authorized and variant access points are sufficiently specific. The instructions governing the construction of each element of the access point (preferred or variant title, medium of performance, numeric designations, and key) are well defined. The instructions are also clear on the order of elements within the access point. The access point for the creator of the work is followed by the preferred or variant title element. If the title element is distinctive, additions are needed only if the string is the same or similar to another string. If the title element is nondistinctive, it is followed by medium, then numeric designation, and finally key. As with distinctive titles, additions are made to the string if it is identical or similar to another string. In short, RDA is successful in creating usable access points for musical works. It also maintains continuity with AACR2 by using a similar manner in constructing the access point.

Access Points for Musical Expressions
On the other hand, the rules for constructing access points for musical expressions leave a lot to be desired. Expression access points in RDA serve a different purpose than their work counterparts. The major difference is that an expression access point is mostly intended to identify specific expressions. Its purpose is not as a collocating mechanism, although there are situations where it could be used as such.[19] Each expression access-point string, therefore, must be unique so as to identify each expression associated with a work.

For nonmusical expressions, RDA states that content type, the date of the expression, the language of the expression, and other distinguishing characteristics may be added to the access point representing the work in order to differentiate one expression access point from another. For music, the situation is more complex. If the work in question is an arrangement, contains an added accompaniment, is a sketch, is a vocal or chorus score, or has a text in a translation, the expression access point is constructed according to one set of rules. If the musical expression does not fall into any of these categories, the access point is then constructed according to the rules for nonmusical expressions.

Setting aside for a moment this division of musical expressions between (1) arrangements, added accompaniments, sketches, vocal/chorus scores, translations, and (2) everything else, there simply are not enough attributes in the first class of musical expressions to differentiate one expression of a work from another. Take as an example the myriad arrangements of Pachelbel's Canon in D. The original medium is three violins and continuo. Arrangements of this work exist for solo organ, solo piano, string quartet, solo violin and piano, three solo trumpets and orchestra, and string orchestra, to name just a few. These arrangements exist in performances and in scores. There is simply no way that the potential authorized RDA access point

"Pachelbel, Johann, 1653–1706. Canon, violins (3), continuo, P. 37.1, D major; arranged" can differentiate between all the different expressions of the Canon in D. Yet the application of the instructions in RDA allow for no other construction. The same would be true for two different vocal scores of the same work or a work that has English translations by two or more people. Instead of differentiation, it appears that the expression access points are intended to collocate types of musical expressions. In other words, the expression access point behaves exactly as it does within AACR2. This would not be a problem if the intention of RDA was to collocate types of expressions, but this is exactly the opposite of what RDA defines as the purpose of an expression access point. This is curious, because if there is one group of resources for which distinguishing one expression from another is important, it is music. RDA is making an exception for musical expressions and it is unclear why this is the case.

This decision is even more bizarre when one considers a musical expression that falls into the second category, covered by the nonmusic rules. Using rules for nonmusical expressions, the resulting expression access point would contain enough information to differentiate it from other expressions of the same work. Using the first three *Marriage of Figaro* examples above, the resulting expression access points could be:

> Mozart, Wolfgang Amadeus, 1756–1791. Nozze di Figaro. Performed music. Italian. 1990 (Levine)
>
> Mozart, Wolfgang Amadeus, 1756–1791. Nozze di Figaro. Performed music. Italian. 1990 (Davis)
>
> Mozart, Wolfgang Amadeus, 1756–1791. Nozze di Figaro. Notated music. Italian. 1973 (Finscher)

But if expression access points are created for the final example above—which would fall under the music rules—the results could be:

> Mozart, Wolfgang Amadeus, 1756–1791. Nozze di Figaro. Vocal score. Italian
>
> Mozart, Wolfgang Amadeus, 1756–1791. Nozze di Figaro. Vocal score. English

Because of this division between the expressions that fall under the music rules and everything else, RDA creates a situation where some expressions of one musical work might be adequately identified while other expressions of the same work might not.

On top of these flaws, RDA also does not provide enough guidance in constructing the text string of the expression access point. In contrast to the rules for work access points, the rules for the expression offer no instructions for the order of the elements within the text string and no instructions for when a particular element must be included. The first three expression access points above could just as easily have the language before the content type, could omit the language, or could use different types of other distinguishing information instead of the surnames of the conductors or editors. This lack of guidance undermines the effectiveness of using expression access points to differentiate between expressions and for organizing coherent browse lists. If expression access points are going to be of any use in a catalog, the instructions that govern them in RDA must be developed more rigorously.

WORKS AND EXPRESSIONS IN RDA: POSSIBLE SOLUTIONS

The problems in RDA with identifying and describing musical works and expressions are not intractable. The following remedies would help make RDA a standard that is more closely aligned with the FRBR and FRAD conceptual models, while insuring that the data produced using RDA would be compatible with the data produced using AACR2. Additionally, these solutions would provide a way forward for those who wish to use data produced according to RDA in data structures that go beyond those used in libraries today.

1. Expand the list of core elements for musical works and expressions.
According to RDA, the elements considered core for musical works are the title, medium of performance, numeric designations, and key, with the last three only being core for works with nondistinctive titles. RDA should move beyond using the form of the title as its determination of whether an element is necessary and should base its decision on the type of work being described. For music, there are a whole host of attributes that users could consider necessary in identifying and selecting a work. Fortunately, some work has been done on identifying necessary work attributes for music. In 2008, a task force appointed by the Bibliographic Control Committee of the Music Library Association produced a report identifying work attributes that should be present in records describing musical works.[20] The recommendations of the task force, which considered the characteristics that all musical works share and those characteristics shared between certain types of musical works (such as purely instrumental works or works containing sung music), could be a useful starting point for expanding the core elements of musical works in RDA.

2. Eliminate the distinction between elements that identify and those that describe.
As shown above, the separation between elements that identify and elements that describe implies that some are intended for machine manipulation and use in an authority record (those in chapter 6) while others are intended to be human-readable and used in a bibliographic record (those in chapter 7). All attributes of a work or an expression serve to identify or describe. The manner in which they are used should be left to the users of RDA. At the very least, when RDA instructs a cataloger to record an attribute of a work or an expression, it should provide the option of recording the element either as appropriate for machine manipulation or as a note, or both, with the decision based on system needs. For example, instead of applying two separate instructions for recording the medium of performance, only one instruction would be needed. It would be up to the cataloger to determine how the medium of performance would be recorded.

Consolidating the rules for work and expression elements into one chapter while providing options for how the elements are to be recorded would also allow catalogers to determine the appropriate implementation scenario for their institution. To be sure, many will still prefer to use bibliographic and authority records as currently conceived, so machine data could be recorded in the authority record, while natural language notes could appear in the bibliographic record. Other institutions may choose to put work or expression data in their own respective records. To help with these decisions, RDA could have an appendix that provides examples for how and where work or expression data could be recorded, depending on the implementation scenario envisioned.

3. Separate the instructions for constructing access points from the instructions for recording work or expression elements.

As demonstrated above, the data produced according to the instructions for recording work or expression elements in chapter 6 is intended for use in an access point that is formatted in the same manner as a name/uniform-title heading in AACR2. But the recording of a work or an expression element in a format conducive for its use in a precoordinated string can misrepresent the work or expression attribute, as has been shown in the way in which an RDA statement of medium of performance must be altered to "fit" an access point.

Furthermore, chapter 6 makes the recording of medium, number, and key for musical works dependent on whether the preferred title element (analogous to the initial title element in AACR2) is distinctive or nondistinctive. There is no good reason for this differing treatment, since these elements are important attributes of every musical work. The reason becomes apparent only in the context of the element being used as an access point.

An access point for a work or an expression needs only to be constructed in such a way that its form is different from other work or expression access points. It is by no means necessary—or even desirable—to construct an access point that contains everything that can possibly be known about a work or an expression. All that is necessary is to provide just enough information so that no two strings are the same. That is why the rules in AACR2 for constructing music uniform titles make a distinction between those titles that are types of compositions and those that are distinctive. It is simply not necessary to provide the medium of performance in a string representing a distinctive title, because it is more than likely that a composer will not compose two different pieces with the same distinctive title, but in two different mediums.[21] RDA makes the same determination.

The above, coupled with the fact that access points are not the only way of providing access to works or expressions, suggests that the process of constructing access points should be considered its own activity in RDA, separate from recording the attributes associated with a work or an expression. One activity should not be dependent on the other. The instructions for recording medium of performance, number, and key as elements within an access point should be governed by rules that are appropriate for differentiating between precoordinated strings.

Similarly, the criteria for recording an attribute of a work or an expression should not be dependent on its use in an access point.

4. Revise the instructions for constructing expression access points for music.
RDA makes an unwarranted distinction between certain music resources (those that are arrangements, include added accompaniments, are sketches, are vocal or chorus scores, or contain sung text in translation) and all other music resources. This not only leads to the creation of some expression access points that are suitable only for collocating certain types of musical expressions—the opposite of what RDA intends for expression access points—but also causes situations where some expressions of a work are uniquely identified, while other expressions of the same work are not. Additionally, the instructions for constructing expression access points do not provide enough guidance about ordering elements and determining when elements should or should not be included.

A persuasive argument could be made for not creating expression access points that identify specific expressions of musical works. There are a multitude of attributes that go into making a musical expression unique: whether the music is notated or is performed, the names of the persons involved in the editing or performing, the date of publication or performance, the performed duration, whether it is an arrangement, the medium of the arrangement, the arranger, added accompaniments, the type of notated music, the sung language, and translation of the sung language—to name a few. It appears to be a daunting task even to attempt to come up with instructions that will cover all possible permutations. Would the resultant string even be intelligible to users? Where does one begin?

As a first step, the concept of a musical expression must be freshly examined and evaluated. Those attributes that contribute to a realization of a musical work must be identified and then evaluated for their suitability in fulfilling the FRBR user tasks. Once identified, the attributes would then be evaluated for their suitability in a precoordinated string. Factors going into this evaluation could include the expressibility of the attribute as a succinct phrase and its commonality as an attribute among certain types of expressions. (For example, the attribute of performer would be common to music expressed in a performance, but not common to notated music.) Once this phase is complete, a list of required elements within an expression access point could be drawn up with instructions provided for what elements to add to resolve a conflict. In tandem with this step, an order for the elements within the expression access point could be established.

CONCLUSIONS

The RDA treatment of works and expressions, especially as it concerns music materials, is compromised by attempts to insure compatibility with today's cataloging environment and the metadata it currently produces. If RDA is to be truly revolutionary, it must move its thinking from what was and is possible to what will be possible. It would be ludicrous to suggest that

RDA should predict the future, but what it should not do is put obstacles in the path of future developments. RDA has the potential to transform the cataloging landscape for the better, but it first must shake off the shackles of the past and look to the future, not with fear and trepidation, but with hope and vision.

NOTES

[1] NACO-Music Project, "NACO-Music Project Cumulative Statistics," http://www.musicoclcusers.org/NMP/nmpstats.htm.

[2] Joint Steering Committee for Development of RDA, *RDA: Resource Description & Access* (Chicago: American Library Association, 2010).

[3] Joint Steering Committee for the Revision of AACR, *Anglo-American Cataloguing Rules*, 2nd ed., 2002 rev. (Chicago: American Library Association, 2002).

[4] In this article, the names of FRBR entities will appear in italics when first introduced and defined; subsequent appearances will be in the normal typeface.

[5] AACR2, appendix D-9. A uniform title is also defined as a "conventional collective title used to collocate publications of an author, composer, or corporate body containing several works or extracts, etc. from several works (e.g. complete works, several works in a particular literary or musical form)." Because this article is concerned with the treatment of individual works and expressions of music in RDA, this particular function is considered outside its scope of inquiry.

[6] AACR2, 25-5.

[7] IFLA Study Group on the Functional Requirements for Bibliographic Records, *Functional Requirements for Bibliographic Records: Final Report* (Munich: K. G. Saur, 1998), http://www.ifla.org/en/publications/functional-requirements-for-bibliographic-records (as amended and corrected through February 2009). Hereinafter "FRBR."

[8] FRBR broadly defines users to include not only patrons of libraries and library staff, but also publishers, distributors, retailers, and nonlibrary information providers.

[9] This entity was added by the IFLA Report on Functional Requirements for Authority Data.

[10] IFLA Working Group on Functional Requirements and Numbering of Authority Records, *Functional Requirements for Authority Data: A Conceptual Mode*, ed. Glenn E. Patton (Munich: K. G. Saur, 2009).

[11] Rule 0.24, as amended in 2001, reads: "It is important to bring out all aspects of the item being described, including its content, its carrier, its type of publication, its bibliographic relationships, and whether it is published or unpublished. In any given area of the description, all relevant aspects should be described. As a rule of thumb, the cataloguer should follow the more specific rules applying to the item being catalogued, whenever they differ from the general rules."

[12] Tom Delsey, "The Logical Structure of the Anglo-American Cataloguing Rules—Part I," August 1998, http://www.rda-jsc.org/docs/aacr.pdf.

[13] RDA 6.0, "Identifying Works and Expressions: Purpose and Scope."

[14] RDA 7.0, "Describing Content: Purpose and Scope."

[15] The decision to structure the works and expressions portion of RDA based on data that would be used in an authority or bibliographic record was perhaps an attempt to fulfill the fourth objective of RDA:

to integrate the data created using RDA with databases containing data created using AACR. This seems to highlight the difficulty—or impossibility—of creating a standard that attempts to look both ahead and backwards simultaneously.

[16] These are covered in RDA 6.9, "Content Type"; 6.10, "Date of Expression"; and 6.11, "Language of Expression."

[17] RDA, 6.18, "Other Distinguishing Characteristic of the Expression of a Musical Work."

[18] RDA 7.23, "Performer, Narrator, and/or Presenter" allows for the recording of performers associated with the expression of a musical work. But as has been discussed above, RDA intends the data recorded according to chapter 6 to be entered in an authority record and the data recorded according to chapter 7 in a bibliographic record. Given this dichotomy, an identifying expression element for performer needs to be added to chapter 6. Of course, this situation would be rendered moot if the distinction between elements that identify and those that describe was dropped.

[19] A good example of this use in music is when the same performance of a work appears in multiple manifestations, such as when a performance previously released on an LP is reissued on a CD.

[20] The full report is available at http://bcc.musiclibraryassoc.org/BCC-Historical/BCC2008/BCC2008WGWRM1.pdf.

[21] In those rare cases where this situation is encountered, AACR2 allows for the addition of a medium statement to resolve the conflict.

THE MUSIC GENRE/FORM PROJECT
History, Accomplishments, and Future Directions

BETH ISEMINGER

Abstract: In 2007, the Library of Congress embarked on a project to create a multidisciplinary genre/form thesaurus. The Music Library Association agreed to partner with LC to build the music portion of the thesaurus. The MLA-BCC Genre Form Task Force and the MLA-BCC Subject Access Subcommittee have been working with LC on the music genre/form and medium-of-performance facets. Goals of this work have included making medium of performance more accessible, enabling post-coordinated searching of the genre/form and medium vocabularies, and contributing additional vocabulary, especially in the areas of world and popular music. In the course of the work, existing music subject-heading strings have been deconstructed into separate genre, form, and medium aspects. The new music vocabularies will be different from existing subject headings. It is recommended that the music community wait until the music project is finished to implement music genre/form and medium-of-performance vocabulary together as a group.

GENRES, FORMS, AND MEDIUMS OF PERFORMANCE: HISTORY

The Music Genre/Form Project is an initiative to establish a vocabulary of genre, form, and medium terms for use with musical works. The goals of the project are to compile genre and form terms for addition to the thesaurus *Library of Congress Genre/Form Terms for Library and Archival Materials* (LCGFT)[1] and to compile medium-of-performance terms that will most likely reside with the *Library of Congress Subject Headings* (LCSH).[2] The project aims to update, improve, and simplify the language and terminology used to describe the substance of musical works.

Music subject headings have included terms for musical genres, forms, and mediums of performance since the early history of LCSH.[3] Genre and form terms most often stand for what an item *is*, rather than what it is *about*. A piece of music *is* a sonata. This difference between "is-ness" and "about-ness" is the primary distinction between genre/form terms and topical terms. Musical works also have the facet of medium-of-performance, which is what the work *is for*. A piece of music *is* composed *for* violin and piano. Genre, form, and medium of performance are facets that are inherent to musical works, and for that reason, genre, form, and medium vocabulary provide an important way to access music materials.

As early as 1989, there was interest on the part of the music library community in creating a new controlled vocabulary based on LCSH but with more emphasis on ethnomusicological terminology and constructed according to thesaurus standards.[4] The Music Thesaurus Project was undertaken by members of the Music Library Association (MLA) in an effort to create this kind of controlled vocabulary. Members of the Music Thesaurus Project Form/Genre Terminology Working Group used the book *Music Subject Headings: Compiled from Library of*

Congress Subject Headings[5] as a source of terms and deconstructed the music subject headings into form, genre, musical instrument or ensemble, and language lists. The thesaurus that was to be made from these lists was intended to be a source of metadata for digitization endeavors, such as Variations, the Indiana University Digital Music Library. The Music Thesaurus Project never came to fruition, perhaps due to the huge scope of the project, to changes in its directorship, and to the fact that it was not accepted by the Library of Congress (LC) and could therefore have been seen as less useful in a cooperative cataloging environment. The Music Thesaurus Project as an entity ceased to exist in 2007.[6]

There are several similarities between the Music Genre/Form Project and the former Music Thesaurus Project. These include: deconstructing subject headings by separating medium of performance into a distinct facet; attempting to identify the broader medium terms as medium, genre, or both (for example, "Orchestral music"); asking whether some music-related terms should actually be in other facets (for example, religion, ethnicity, or language facets); and a desire to add terminology from other sources to increase ethnomusicological vocabulary. While the Music Thesaurus Project attempted to separate genre and form into distinct categories, the Music Genre/Form Project decided early on to avoid this thorny area and categorize genre and form terms as one facet. Two other differences in the projects are scope and support. The scope of the Music Thesaurus Project was the entire vocabulary for music access, including topical terms, whereas the scope of the Music Genre/Form Project is limited to the (admittedly large) set of music genre/form and medium terms. The Music Thesaurus Project was sponsored by MLA, while the Music Genre/Form Project is a collaborative effort of MLA and LC, which is an important distinction. The support from LC for work in the area of genre/form access means that the project has the weight of national policy behind it. The ability of LC staff, processes, and systems to take on such a large project and handle the amounts of data involved is a benefit as well.

THE LIBRARY OF CONGRESS GENRE/FORM PROJECTS

When LC began to be interested in genre terms, the door was opened for new genre/form projects to commence. As the genre projects began, they had a pragmatic focus that was closely intertwined with traditional cataloging practice. The genre projects were initially seen as a way of creating a set of genre/form authority records, based more or less directly on LCSH vocabulary. As the projects progressed, there was a shift in the paradigm of what these projects were meant to accomplish. It became clear that simple conversion of terms from topical coding to genre/form coding was just an introductory step and that genre/form terms could form the basis of a complex vocabulary that was more hierarchical and more like a thesaurus. The projects took on a larger scope as an established vocabulary with the creation in June 2010 of LCGFT, which formally separates LC genre/form terms from LCSH.[7]

LC began working on genre terms for moving images, television programs, and videos in 2007. Using the terms from the Moving Image Genre Form Guide (MIGFG), LC created genre/form authority records for these terms. The MIGFG terms represented a small, defined vocabulary and thus provided a good test case that could inform future, larger projects. The moving-image project was followed by a similar project to identify genre/form terms for radio programs, with the Radio Form/Genre Terms Guide (RADFG) as a base. In 2008, LC approved a timeline for five more genre projects in the following disciplines: cartography, law, music, religion, and literature.[8] These projects were scheduled to begin in late 2008 and finish in 2012. The cartography and law genre projects were completed during 2010, the religion project was started in early 2011, and the literature project has not officially begun. The history and accomplishments of the music genre/form project through early 2011 will be discussed here.

THE MUSIC GENRE/FORM PROJECT

The music portion of the LC's genre projects began in early 2009. Geraldine Ostrove of the LC Policy and Standards Division (PSD) presented MLA's Bibliographic Control Committee (MLA-BCC) with a proposal for collaboration, which was discussed during the annual MLA meeting in February 2009. By this point, LC and MLA had come to the realization that music genre/form terms and medium-of-performance terms were two distinct categories, and the terms that combined genre/form with medium needed to be examined and potentially deconstructed.[9]

MLA members saw that LC's plans for the project emphasized the genre/form terms but were vague on the future of the medium-of-performance list being developed. It was understood that music genre/form terms were part of the larger LC genre project, but it was unclear where the list of medium-of-performance terms would finally reside and how much importance such a list would be given. If the new genre/form vocabulary was to be a substitute for music subject heading strings in LCSH (with LCSH containing only topical terms), then in MLA's view, including medium of performance as an integral part of the project was imperative.[10] The assurance by LC that both sets of terms would be kept up to date alleviated some of these worries and opened the way for the music project to continue as part of the larger scheme of genre projects, though disposition of medium-of-performance terms remained a complicated issue.

The MLA-BCC Genre/Form Task Force was created in March 2009 and was composed of volunteers from various MLA-BCC subcommittees and of additional MLA members, all of whom were appointed by the MLA president. The membership of the task force included: Ralph Hartsock, Caitlin Hunter, Beth Iseminger (chair), Martin Jenkins, Brooke Lippy, Nancy Lorimer, Mark McKnight, Casey Mullin, Thomas Pease, Karen Peters, Sheila Torres-Blank, and Hermine Vermeij. The original charge for the task force included specific dates corresponding to an ambitious initial timeline—which was soon extended—while the revised charge removed the dates and focused on the work itself.[11]

Throughout the project, the task force has worked primarily with Geraldine Ostrove, music specialist in PSD. As the project progressed, a core genre/form project group was formed at LC, comprised of members from various units in LC including the Motion Picture,

Broadcasting and Recorded Sound Division, the Recorded Sound Section, the American Folklife Center, and members of the Music Division. The LC Music Genre/Form Project Group now consists of Caitlin Hunter, Bruce Johnson, Margaret Kruesi, Geraldine Ostrove (chair), Lisa Shiota, Maarja Vigorito, and Stephen Yusko.

In March 2009, MLA-BCC and LC agreed on a project proposal and timeline. As part of the process, MLA agreed to place emphasis on medium-of-performance terms, establish procedures for the progression of the project, and address syndetic structure and technological issues. LC had already begun creating lists of music genre/form and medium terms culled from LCSH, which they shared with MLA and also posted on the website "Genre/Form Headings at the Library of Congress."[12] The following steps for MLA to accomplish were agreed to by both groups via the timeline: (1) work through LC-compiled lists of genre/form and medium of performance terms, indicating which terms belong on which list as well as terms that should be deleted from the lists; (2) add any overlooked LCSH music genre/form and medium terms to the lists; (3) examine reference sources and add missing genre/form and medium terms to the lists, focusing especially on terms from the *New Grove Dictionary of Music and Musicians*, second edition,[13] and *The Garland Encyclopedia of World Music*;[14] (4) vet the lists of new (non-LCSH) terms and present the lists, with MLA recommendations, to LC; (5) collaborate on creating a syndetic structure for the terms in each list; (6) work on training modules and usage guidelines for music genre/form and medium terms; and (7) collaborate in creating MARC genre/form authority records for music terms.

The members of the MLA task force held discussions and posted the working lists of terms on a private group wiki, using PBWorks software. The task force also established a public wiki as a place to post information and to gather comments and suggestions for new terms to be included in the music genre project.[15] While the public wiki has not garnered as much interest as anticipated, it will remain available for the duration of the project. It is hoped that individuals interested in specific areas of music, particularly popular and world music, will visit the public wiki and suggest specific terminology in their areas of expertise.

PRINCIPLES

The MLA task force used the following working definitions for genre, form, and medium of performance. Genre is "a class, type, or category, sanctioned by convention,"[16] including terms for styles of music. Form is "the constructive or organizing element in music."[17] The task force considered medium of performance to include terms for instruments, groups of instruments, vocal types and ranges, and objects used as instruments. The task force also referenced the definition of medium in the cataloging standard *Functional Requirements for Authority Data*.[18]

The desire to make medium terms more accessible is one of the most important goals of the music genre/form project. Because music subject headings in LCSH were constructed as pre-coordinated strings, medium of performance was often positioned after initial form or genre terms, causing medium to not be directly indexed in such strings. For example, in the headings "Sonatas (Violin and piano)" and "Concertos (Violin)," the medium "violin" is not listed first, and the heading strings are therefore indexed under "Sonatas" or "Concertos" Library users seeking music for specific instrumentation or performing forces had to either rely on imprecise keyword searching or search many subject strings that included the desired medium(s) of performance.[19] With the undertaking of the Music Genre/Form Project, many members of MLA saw an opportunity to separate medium terms from genre/form terms, thereby enabling direct searching on medium-of-performance terminology. Searching for scores and recordings by medium of performance is one of the primary ways that music library users approach a search for musical works, so creating a way to access music materials directly, via medium of performance, is a key to meeting the needs of users. The task force very quickly recommended that medium terms be decoupled from genre and form terms and put in their own list, and the LC music genre specialists agreed.

Enabling post-coordinated searching of separate medium and genre/form terms became another fundamental guiding principle for the Music Genre/Form Project. As the MLA task force began to see the potential of separating medium and genre/form terms, the desirability of post-coordination across the music vocabulary became more evident as well. The task force recommended decoupling in both the genre/form and medium lists.[20] Genre/form terms combining genres or forms with medium were decoupled, and medium terms that combined more than one medium of performance were also split into separate terms. This meant that the connecting terms "and" and "with" were no longer part of the medium vocabulary.[21]

An early decision on the part of the task force was removing genre/form terms containing specific languages and putting them in a separate list. In the case of a term such as "Hymns," which stood alone but was also qualified by many languages, the stand-alone term was included in the genre/form list, while the qualified terms were removed to a separate list of terms qualified by language. The task force saw language as a facet that is separate from genre, form, and medium of performance. The language facet can be accessed through other features of records, and it was thought that including language in the genre/form area of the record was not necessary. Other projects had previously made similar decisions about other facets, so the precedent existed.[22] De-duplicating the music genre/form list by removing headings qualified by language was an effective way of reducing the lists to more manageable size, and it fit with the desire to deconstruct terms in the interest of post-coordination.

The drawback to removing facets like language, nationality, or geography from genre/form terms is the potential to lose information about the ethnicity or national origins of world music. Fortunately these facets are being addressed by a subcommittee for genre/form implementation that is part of the American Library Association.[23] Their findings should help inform work by the music task force in this area.

The issue of ensemble terms has been discussed by MLA and LC and has yet to be formally decided. Because one of the guiding principles is to make terms more explicit—by listing specific instrumentation, for example—the issue of ensembles with commonly accepted instrumentation is problematic. String quartets, piano trios, and brass quintets are examples of this type of ensemble. The task force would not want to do away with or change these terms, given their prevalence in common parlance. However, terms like this can stand for both the common instrumentation and for alternative instrumentation.[24] One possible approach for dealing with these terms is to always list the individual instruments in addition to the ensemble term. Another approach is to provide the individual instruments only when they differ from the commonly accepted instrumentation. This would require a scope note in the authority records for these ensembles listing their common instrumentation.[25]

THE WORK OF THE MLA-BCC GENRE/FORM TASK FORCE

The first step the task force tackled was vetting the LC-compiled lists of genre/form and medium-of-performance terms taken from LCSH. LC's original medium list included only the terms for the instruments or other mediums themselves (for example, "Violin" and "High voice"). Terms for music of the medium, such as "Violin music" or "Piccolo and piano music," were in LC's original genre/form list. The MLA task force decided before vetting the lists that all terms including medium of performance currently in the genre list would be moved to the medium list. The task force split the genre/form and medium lists among the members and, using spreadsheets accessible via the group wiki, designated each term with the following labels: "keep" (terms kept in the list, including terms having minor changes), "add" (terms already in LCSH but not included on LC's lists), "from genre" (terms moved from LC's genre list to the medium list), "delete" (terms that should be deleted from the thesaurus or changed to a different form), "new" (new terms necessitated by changes to existing terms), "ambiguous" (terms that could be either genre or form, or were otherwise unclear), and "qualified by language" (core term that has been qualified by language and should be removed to the language list). Table 1 shows some examples from the spreadsheet.

One of the first big decisions the task force made upon embarking on the project was eliminating the word "music" following medium-of-performance terms in heading strings. The task force identified the patterns "[Instrument] music" and "[Instrument] and [Instrument] music" in headings and determined that these patterns represented medium-of-performance terms. The addition of the term "music" seemed more like a genre term pattern, similar to genre terms like "Rock music" or "Dramatic music." When the task force envisioned implementation scenarios, the group realized that simple instrument names would be preferable to more syntactically complicated terms. The term "music" was decided to be redundant in the context of medium-of-performance statements. This means that the medium terms themselves function as more than just labels for performing forces included in a work. They also signify that the work is in fact a piece of music, written for the particular instrument or instruments. This decision was consistent with the aforementioned desire to separate medium heading strings into terms for individual instruments alone.

Term	LC Number	Designation
Accordion	sh 85000385	Keep
Accordion and electronic music	sh2001 0025	Delete; From genre
Accordion ensembles	sh 85000396	Ambiguous; Keep; From genre
Audience participation	new	New - or "Audience participation (Musical medium of performance)"
Balloons as musical instruments	sh99004184	Keep; change to medium form—Balloons (Musical medium of performance)
Bands (Music)	sh 85011499	Ambiguous; Change to "Band (Musical medium of performance)"?

Table 1. An excerpt from the medium list, as vetted by the MLA task force.

After reviewing the two LC lists, the next steps for the task force were to collect terms from other sources which were not present in LCSH. The task force began with some relatively short lists including the controlled vocabularies from the Indiana University Variations Metadata site, the list "Types of Composition for Use in Uniform Titles," and the lists of medium and genre/form terms recommended by the International Association of Music Libraries, Archives, and Documentation Centres (IAML).[26] The Variations and "Types of Composition" lists proved to be quite useful for identifying common genres, forms, and mediums of performance that were not included in LCSH. The IAML lists were more problematic, because they included terms for the same concept in various languages, without designating one preferred term. After working on these lists, the task force moved on to the *New Grove Dictionary of Music and Musicians*. The group took the cumulative print index and divided it among the members, then searched for the terms using *Grove Music Online* or the print volumes of *New Grove*. *New Grove* was an excellent source of terms, not just for Western art music, but for world music as well. At this point in the project, some members of the task force also used the books *Selected Musical Terms of Non-Western Cultures* by Walter Kaufmann and *Practical Guide to Percussion Terminology* by Russ Girsberger as sources of new terms.[27] These sources provided terms in two areas that were more lacking in established vocabulary.

The final reference source used for collecting new terms for the music genre/form and medium lists was *The Garland Encyclopedia of World Music*. Nine of the twelve members of the task force had access to *Garland*, either online or in print. These nine members each took one of the volumes dedicated to music of a particular geographic region. The task force ran into many problems while working through the *Garland* volumes. Unlike *New Grove*, the *Garland Encyclopedia* was not a truly comprehensive encyclopedia, but rather a set of articles by different authors who often did not agree on the use or definition of terms. Now that this phase of the project is complete, the inconsistency of terms in the *Garland Encyclopedia*, even within a single volume, means that the task force will need to carefully vet the lists of new terms extracted from this source. Another problem with terms from *Garland* is that, especially for medium terms, the encyclopedia turns out to be too detailed for the purposes of the project. The task force will need to carefully consider literary warrant when deciding the level of detail for genre/form and medium terms added from the *Garland Encyclopedia*.

DISCUSSION PAPERS FROM THE LIBRARY OF CONGRESS

In the course of evaluating the MLA task force's recommendations regarding the lists of LCSH genre/form and medium-of-performance terms, the LC project group created discussion papers illuminating some of the more complicated issues. The discussion papers dealt with headings for psalms, headings for sacred music, and form subdivisions used with musical works.

Subject headings for musical settings of psalms, as they are currently constructed, contain an unconventional use of form subdivisions. All musical settings of psalms begin with the heading "Psalms (Music)" followed by a form subdivision containing the number of the psalm, for example, "—23rd Psalm." The authority records for some of the psalms contain a cross-reference for the first line of the Latin text. LC presented several options for changing the construction of psalm headings, and the MLA task force recommended the option of retaining the heading "Psalms (Music)" and creating related work entries for the individual psalm texts. This method separates the genre/form term from the descriptive access point, it mimics the way other texts in musical works are treated, and seemed to the task force to be the most theoretically sound of the proposed solutions. The task force also recommended that the Latin cross-references be included in authority records for the individual psalm texts, as well as King James and alternate numbering cross references when appropriate.[28] This method of treatment for musical settings of psalms is being considered by LC for musical settings of other sacred texts.

After a lengthy discussion on both sides, the MLA task force and the LC project group agreed on a plan for addressing genre/form headings for sacred music. While vetting the LC lists, the MLA task force had discussed post-coordinating the broad terms "Sacred music" and "Secular music" with the genre/form terms with which they were combined.[29] This method might have been conceptually consistent with other decisions of the task force, since individual terms combining the sacred/secular concepts with genre/form terms would be deconstructed, but in the end it was decided that the simplest method of dealing with these terms and reflecting the concepts of "sacred" and "secular" was to retain a small list of pre-coordinated terms.[30] A point of consideration in this decision was the usefulness the pre-coordinated terms for musicians and library users.

The MLA task force discussed subdivisions used with musical works and made recommendations in response to the LC project group paper on the topic. Most of these recommendations involved deleting the terms as subdivisions per se and making them genre/form terms that can be post-coordinated with other genre/form terms and with medium-of-performance terms. This method may differ from recommendations to be made by the ALA group working on genre/form implementation. The ALA group, and perhaps LC, may recommend keeping the terms as subdivisions and also creating new genre/form terms derived from them.

While reviewing subdivisions used with music terms, the MLA task force was prompted to analyze genre/form headings and subdivisions relating to children's music. There has been discussion in the broader genre community of changing the current term "juvenile" to something more descriptive of age level and with a less disparaging connotation in common language. The

MLA task force thus recommended that "Children's music," currently a cross-reference to the heading "Music—Juvenile," be preferred as the main heading and that it be the broadest term for other terms relating to music and children. The task force identified three facets present in headings for children's music: performer, audience, and level of difficulty. The terms recommended to LC by the task force were meant to reflect these facets with a better degree of clarity.[31]

FUTURE DIRECTIONS

With the genre/form and medium lists relatively complete, the next steps toward compiling the new genre/form and medium vocabulary will be to (1) create a hierarchy of the proposed terms; (2) review the hierarchy and edit or add to the vocabulary as needed; (3) make recommendations regarding genre/form terms that should be included in LCGFT and medium terms that should be added to or revised in LCSH; and (4) examine the new terms not in LCSH, look for literary warrant, and make proposals of new terms for LCGFT (genre/form) and LCSH (medium).

The MLA task force has begun placing the terms in a hierarchical structure. The purpose of this hierarchy is to illuminate the relationships that exist between terms and to identify relationships (broader terms, narrower terms, etc.) that need to be created. The hierarchy will also enable identification of "orphan terms," or terms without a broader term other than "Music." The task force began with a list of 626 genre/form terms that were agreed upon by MLA and LC for inclusion in LCGFT. The terms were divided into eleven broad categories[32] that were each assigned to a member of the task force. Starting with the broadest term in their category, task force members filled out a spreadsheet listing the relationships between the terms, including broader terms, narrower terms, related terms, alternate terms, and scope notes, when applicable. Terms were listed in both an alphabetical and a hierarchical arrangement. The alphabetical spreadsheet listed all relationships and other information, while the hierarchical spreadsheet shows only the hierarchy from the preferred terms up to the broadest terms. The MLA task force investigated thesaurus construction software for use in this process, but monetary support to purchase such software was not forthcoming, and spreadsheets were decided to be the simplest option for sharing the information.

In the process of creating these spreadsheets, the task force discovered additional broader terms that were needed beyond the eleven initial categories. These included "Occasional music" and a concept the task force referred to as "Music by function." "Occasional music" was applied to music for festivals, holidays, and other specific special occasions (music for secular festivals and holidays, secular music associated with sacred holidays, wedding and funeral music, and coronation music). "Music by function" was a way of referring to music used for particular activities (street music, computer game music, and exercise music).

One issue that arose in establishing the syndetic structure for music genre/form terms was that of selecting broadest terms for the top of the hierarchy. "Music" is naturally the broadest term for the genre/form list and perhaps the medium list as well. As a top term, "Music" serves several functions. It is a collective term for use with works having no specific genre or form, for works in multiple genres or forms, and for the complete works of a composer. It is also the broadest term for Western art music. A compelling argument can be made for reconceptualizing "Music" as the broadest term for all genres of music, including world and popular music. Currently, terms for what is traditionally thought of as "classical music" or "Western art music" are listed as see-references to the top term "Music," while terms for "non-classical" music are listed as narrower terms.[33] This arrangement clearly gives preference to Western art music as the top of the hierarchy and should be changed. "Music" should be the top term for all types and genres, and narrower terms should be established for Western art music and related concepts. For example, in order to identify Western art music as well as non-Western art music in the hierarchy, the task force used the term "Art music" as the broadest term for that category.

A discrepancy arose between LC's and MLA's understanding of the project scope. While LC has been focusing solely on terminology from LCSH, MLA undertook the music genre project under the assumption that it provided an excellent opportunity to add vocabulary in areas where historically there have been lacunae, such as world music and popular music. At a joint meeting of the MLA task force and the LC project group during the MLA 2011 annual meeting, several possibilities were discussed for incorporating the new terminology collected by the task force. The first option would be to search the new terms in OCLC and to submit those with literary warrant through the Subject Cooperative Program (SACO) process via the newly formed SACO-Music Funnel. Another option would be to put the terms together in an organized list with reference and scope notes and to present the list of new terms to LC as a whole.[34] Whichever option is ultimately chosen, both groups will need to balance the need to complete the project with the need for more vocabulary.

Another topic that both the MLA and LC groups are working on is the disposition of medium-of-performance terms. During the annual MLA meeting in February 2011, the MLA task force and the MLA-BCC Subject Access Subcommittee agreed to transfer responsibility for the medium-of-performance aspect of the genre/form project to the subcommittee. This was a logical step, given that medium-of-performance terms are separate from genre/form terms and will likely continue to be part of LCSH, thus falling under the purview of the subcommittee.[35]

The Subject Access Subcommittee spearheaded the writing of a discussion paper on medium-of-performance coding in MARC records.[36] While genre and form terms will be coded in the MARC 655 field "Index Term - Genre/Form," it is not clear that this is the best place for coding medium terms. The discussion paper suggests three possible fields that could be used for medium vocabulary: field 048 (Number of voices or instruments code), field 382 (Medium of performance), or a new 6XX field. While use has been made of the 048 field in the past,[37] the use of coded information is not ideal, and the number of codes needed would far exceed the capacity of the field as it is currently defined. To be useful as a vocabulary, medium of performance needs to be presented in human-readable as well as machine-readable form. The 382 field was created for use with the *Resource Description & Access* (RDA) cataloging standard,[38] where it was meant to function as a source of additional information for identifying works and expressions. Presumably, the medium terms used within this field would be structured according to instructions in RDA. The RDA rules focus on *identification* of works and expressions, while the medium-of-performance vocabulary would focus on *description* of the specific medium(s) for which a work or expression is written.[39] It could prove problematic to have one field serving two functions. Finally, a new 6XX field for descriptive medium-of-performance vocabulary would mirror existing MARC conventions (38X for identification, 6XX for description), but there are few unused 6XX fields available. No matter which field is eventually chosen, there are many functions that the field will need to provide: identification of the medium of performance, identification of the number of performers required, and identification of the number of each performing force required.[40]

IMPLEMENTATION

The MLA task force recommended early in the Music Genre/Form Project that the library community as a whole refrain from using genre/form terms for music until the music project is complete. The music project differed somewhat from the other projects in that the project involved deconstruction and post-coordination of terms as an integral part of the process. Medium-of-performance terms are being put into a separate category from genre/form terms. Therefore, the music genre/form and medium-of-performance terms as a completed vocabulary will be very different from the existing music subject headings. Because music genre/form and medium terms make up most of the vocabulary used to describe music scores and sound recordings, and because this vocabulary must support cooperative cataloging, it was agreed that the music community should implement this vocabulary as a group. If existing headings reflecting genre, form, and medium were used now, a large amount of cleanup would result when the new vocabulary is implemented. It will be simpler for the music cataloging community to switch from the existing topically coded headings directly to the new genre/form and medium headings.

REFLECTIONS

It has become clear, in retrospect, the extent to which the work of the music genre project is an evolutionary process. It has taken time for many of the decisions to come to fruition—LCGFT being a good example. Principles that seemed definite at first became more flexible as the project progressed. The development of the project from genre authority conversion to full-fledged thesaurus illustrates how the thinking of those working on the genre projects has changed over time. Understanding the progression of the project is an important part of understanding the conclusions reached and of envisioning future directions.

NOTES

[1] LCGFT authority records are distributed through three mechanisms: the MARC Distribution Service (as part of its Subject-Authorities product), through LC Authorities (http://authorities.loc.gov), and through LC's Authorities and Vocabularies (http://id.loc.gov). "LCGFT terms are also available for viewing online through Classification Web, and are available in printed form as part of Library of Congress Subject Headings." See "Frequently Asked Questions about *Library of Congress Genre/Form*

Terms for Library and Archival Materials (LCGFT)," June 2011, http://www.loc.gov/catdir/cpso/genre_form_faq.pdf.

[2] Latest edition: Library of Congress, Policy and Standards Division, *Library of Congress Subject Headings*, 5 vols. (Washington, D.C.: Library of Congress, Cataloging Distribution Service, 2010).

[3] "In 1933 the Music Library Association issued a 'provisional list' based on the music card catalogs of the Library of Congress and in 1935, a list of subject headings for the literature of music." Helen E. Bush and David Judson Haykin, "Music Subject Headings," *Notes* 6, no. 1 (December 1948): 39–40.

[4] "The time has come to redesign and eventually replace LCSH." Mark McKnight, "Improving Access to Music: A Report of the MLA Music Thesaurus Project Working Group," *Notes* 45, no. 4 (1989): 715.

[5] Harriette Hemmasi, *Music Subject Headings: Compiled from Library of Congress Subject Headings*, 2nd ed. (Lake Crystal, Minn.: Soldier Creek Press, 1998).

[6] "Music Thesaurus Project. MTP is not being revived, so need to explore other options." Music Library Association Bibliographic Control Committee, "BCC2007/Minutes," accessed 30 January 2011, http://bcc.musiclibraryassoc.org/BCC-Historical/BCC2007/BCC2007minutes.html.

[7] Library of Congress Policy and Standards Division, "Library of Congress to Formally Separate LC Genre/Form Thesaurus from LCSH," accessed 30 January 2011, http://www.loc.gov/catdir/cpso/genreformthesaurus.html.

[8] Library of Congress Policy and Standards Division, "Timeline and Plan for the Next Five Library of Congress Genre/Form Projects," accessed 30 January 2011, http://www.loc.gov/catdir/cpso/genretimeline.html.

[9] "However, it is now apparent that merely creating genre/form authority records using headings as they exist today would not be the best way to serve the user. Reasons to change these headings include the complexity of the existing heading structure and the fact that the present structure conflates genre/form terms with medium of performance." Library of Congress Policy and Standards Division, "Genre/Form Headings for Musical Works," accessed 1 February 2011, http://www.loc.gov/catdir/cpso/genremusic.html.

[10] "The Feb. 11, 2009 proposal from PSD does not address the future of the medium of performance headings list, beyond the creation of the list itself. . . . Because medium of performance is an essential part of 'non-topical' access to musical works, BCC recommends expanding the scope of this groundbreaking project to provide for the disposition of medium of performance headings in bibliographic records which employ genre/form terms." Music Library Association Bibliographic Control Committee, "BCC Response to Library of Congress PSD Proposal: Genre/Form Implementation at the Library of Congress: Musical Works," accessed 30 January 2011, http://bcc.musiclibraryassoc.org/PositionPapers/genre-form_2009.html.

[11] "The MLA-BCC Genre/Form Task Force will review the genre/form and medium of performance lists posted by the LC Policy and Standards Division (PSD) on their genre/form website. The group will suggest additional terms from LCSH, from other established lists (e.g., the MLA Types of Composition list, the Ethnographic Thesaurus), and from reference sources. Suggestions for genre/form and medium of performance terms will also be solicited from the MLA membership at large. The Task Force will vet the terms suggested by its members and by the MLA membership and will forward these terms on to PSD for possible inclusion in the genre/form and medium of performance lists. The second phase of the project will include working with PSD to establish syndetic structures for each list and to col-

laborate on coding and other issues, including making MARBI proposals if necessary. The final phase of the project will involve establishing training procedures, both for creation of genre/form/medium authority records and for practical application of the new terminology." Music Library Association Bibliographic Control Committee, "Subject Access Subcommittee: Genre/Form Task Force" [revised charge, August 2009], accessed 1 February 2011, http://bcc.musiclibraryassoc.org/SAS/SAS-genre_form.html.

[12] "Genre/Form Headings at the Library of Congress," accessed 10 June 2011, http://www.loc.gov/catdir/cpso/genreformgeneral.html.

[13] *The New Grove Dictionary of Music and Musicians*, 2nd ed. (London: Macmillan, 2001).

[14] *The Garland Encyclopedia of World Music* (New York: Garland, 1998–2002).

[15] MLA-BCC Genre/Form Task Force, "Music Genre/Form/Medium Project," accessed 1 February 2011, http://musicgenrepublicforum.pbworks.com/w/page/21942009/FrontPage.

[16] Grove Music Online, "Genre," accessed 30 January 2011, http://www.oxfordmusiconline.com.

[17] Grove Music Online, "Form," accessed 30 January 2011, http://www.oxfordmusiconline.com.

[18] "Medium of performance: The instrumental, vocal, and/or other medium of performance for which a musical work was originally conceived [FRBR]. Includes individual instruments, instrumental ensembles, orchestras, etc. Includes individual voices, vocal ensembles, choirs, etc. Includes other objects to be used in the performance of the work (e.g., spoons, washboard)." IFLA Working Group on Functional Requirements and Numbering of Authority Records, *Functional Requirements for Authority Data: A Conceptual Mode*, ed. Glenn Patton (Munich: K. G. Saur, 2009), 43–44.

[19] For example, a user seeking music for piccolo and piano could use the subject heading "Piccolo and piano music," but this would not retrieve music for piccolo and piano that was also in a specific form, covered by such subject headings as "Sonatas (Piccolo and piano)" or "Concertos (Piccolo)—Solo with piano."

[20] For example, the suffix ", Arranged" was used in many genre/form headings (for example, "Ballets, Arranged"). The MLA task force recommended separating the form heading ("Ballets") and creating a new term to represent the concept of arranged music ("Arrangements (Music)" or "Arranged music"). Another example of a heading that benefitted from deconstruction was "Piano music (Jazz)," which was split into "Piano" and "Jazz." The genre term ("Jazz") would not have been directly indexed as part of the existing heading string.

[21] For example, the medium string "Violin and violoncello with chamber orchestra" was split into the separate medium terms "Violin," "Violoncello," and "Chamber orchestra."

[22] The moving-image project decided not to allow geographical subdivision of film genre headings because of possible confusion between the subject of the film, its place of production, and its genre (for example, an American-made film about food in France, versus a film made in France, versus the genre "French films"). In the *OLAC Newsletter* of 7 April 2009, the moving image catalogers announced a MARBI proposal to change the MARC field 257 to allow country of production to be coded for all films (not just archival films). This was seen as a way to alleviate part of the problem of geography.

[23] The ALA/ALCTS/CCS SAC Subcommittee on Genre/Form Implementation was formed in 2008. From the minutes of their meeting at ALA Midwinter 2011, "The subcommittee developed a working list of aspects or facets associated in some way with genre/form. . . . For each aspect, a report will be created that includes the following: existing MARC fields in both bibliographic and authority formats where data may be recorded; common current practices (one or more that may be used in a record by some libraries) for recording such data; possible new MARC fields/subfields/indicator values for

data/possible new practices. The subcommittee will then review these reports at ALA Annual 2011 and decide on recommendations for best practices." *ALA Connect*, "Midwinter 2011 Report of the Subcommittee on Genre/Form Implementation," accessed 3 June 2011, http://connect.ala.org/node/131897.

[24] A string quartet may be written for the common instrumentation of two violins, viola, and violoncello, or it might be written for other combinations of these string instruments (three violins and violoncello; violin, two violas, and violoncello; etc.)

[25] Terms for common ensembles like string quartets and piano trios could hypothetically be considered genre terms as well as medium terms. While the task force agrees they should be included in the medium list, it has not been officially decided whether they belong in the genre list as well.

[26] "Variations Metadata," last modified 6 June 2008, http://www.dlib.indiana.edu/projects/variations3/metadata/guide/docs/controlVocab.html; MLA Working Group on Types of Composition, "Types of Composition for Use in Uniform Titles," last modified 11 July 2011, http://www.library.yale.edu/cataloging/music/types.htm; International Association of Music Libraries, "Unimarc Field 146 – Medium of Performance," http://www.iaml.info/en/activities/cataloguing/unimarc/medium; International Association of Music Libraries, "Unimarc Field 128 – Musical Forms," http://www.iaml.info/activities/cataloguing/unimarc/forms.

[27] Walter Kaufmann, *Selected Musical Terms of Non-Western Cultures: A Notebook-Glossary* (Warren, Mich.: Harmonie Park Press, 1990); Russ Girsberger, *A Practical Guide to Percussion Terminology* (Ft. Lauderdale: Meredith Music, 1998).

[28] Musical settings of psalms may use numbering on the source (score or recording) that differs from the numbering in the authority record for the psalm. This is due to differences in the numbering of the psalms in Hebrew and Greek texts. The task force felt that alternate numberings should be included as cross-references during the process of updating or creating the authority records for the psalm texts.

[29] For example, instead of the heading "Sacred musicals," the genre headings "Sacred music" and "Musicals" could both be used (separately) to reflect a musical based on a sacred text or intended for religious contexts.

[30] The specific terms to be included in the LCGFT are "Sacred cantatas," "Sacred dialogues (Music)," "Sacred dramatic music," "Sacred music," "Sacred musicals," "Sacred songs," "Secular cantatas," and "Secular oratorios." The two groups also agreed that (1) previously inverted terms should be uninverted ("Sacred cantatas" instead of "Cantatas, Sacred"); (2) "Sacred music" can be post-coordinated with other terms not on the sacred/secular list ("Sacred music" AND "Symphonies"); and (3) several other terms may involve medium of performance and need to be addressed as medium terms ("Sacred choruses," "Sacred monologues with music," "Sacred pantomimes with music," "Sacred part songs," "Sacred solo cantatas," "Sacred vocal music," "Secular choruses," and "Secular solo cantatas.")

[31] Terms relating to children's music that the MLA task force recommended for inclusion in the LCGFT: "Children's music," "Children's songs," "Elementary works (Music)," "Instructive editions (Music)," "Music for child audience," "Preschool music," "School music," and "Simplified editions."

[32] The broad categories used for the hierarchy are art music, dance music, dramatic music, folk music, jazz, instrumental music, popular music, sacred music, songs, vocal music, and world music.

[33] See references to the top term "Music" include "Art music," "Classical music," "Serious music," "Western art music," and "Western music." Narrower terms for the top term "Music" include "Folk mu-

sic," "National music," "Popular music," "Sacred music," and "World music." This arrangement suggests that "Western art music" is equal to the top term "Music" while "World music" and other narrower terms are merely sub-genres of "Music."

[34] "The MLA task force could possibly search our list of terms for literary warrant in OCLC and submit them to PSD through some type of expedited SACO process. The MLA task force feels there would simply be too many terms to go through the SACO process as it stands now. Another option might be for the MLA task force to put the new terms into some kind of organized list, possibly with references and/or scope notes, and to present this list to LC as a whole, similar to the way in which the MLA Working Group on 20th Century Music Terminology went about their recommendations." Music Library Association Bibliographic Control Committee, "BCC2010/GFTF/1," accessed 30 January 2011, http://bcc.musiclibraryassoc.org/BCC-Historical/BCC2010/BCC2010GFTF1.html.

[35] "Specifically, the Subcommittee is responsible for all matters concerning the Library of Congress Subject Headings." Music Library Association Bibliographic Control Committee, "Subject Access Subcommittee," accessed 3 June 2011, http://bcc.musiclibraryassoc.org/SAS/SAS.html.

[36] "MARC Discussion Paper No. 2011-DP05," accessed 3 June 2011, http://www.loc.gov/marc/marbi/2011/2011-dp05.html. The paper was presented at the MARBI (Machine-Readable Bibliographic Information) meeting held during the American Library Association annual meeting in June 2011.

[37] Most MARC field 048 search mechanisms suffered from the problem of retrieving works that included the desired instrumentation without being able to limit the results to works containing only the desired terms. Those that overcame this obstacle were searches limited to chamber music and a small number of specified instruments. The accuracy of searching on the 048 field codes, therefore, did not produce the sought-after solution to subject access via medium of performance. "KentLink Musical Instrumentation Search," http://www.library.kent.edu/kentlink_instrument_search.php; "Chamber Music Media Finder," http://www.bsu.edu/libraries/viewpage.asp?src=./librarycatalogs/chambermusic.html.

[38] Joint Steering Committee for Development of RDA, *RDA: Resource Description & Access* (Chicago: American Library Association, 2010).

[39] In older lingo, it might be said that the 382 field is currently intended for uniform title access, while the medium-of-performance project needs such a field for "subject" access. Ideally, medium of performance could be listed just once in the record, but the RDA guidelines as they now stand do not facilitate this option.

[40] "Results of MARC Advisory Committee discussion: The majority of participants agreed that field 048 should not be considered as an option for recording medium of performance. The group also felt that additional examples were needed in order to determine whether field 382 or the 6XX block would be preferable for recording this information. New examples will be posted on the MLA Bibliographic Control Committee's listserv. Additionally, general consensus was that Option 1 would be preferable, where all information related to the medium of performance is placed in a single field and the order of new subfields would be relied upon to give meaning. Predictability would be ensured by always pairing subfields $a (Name of instrument) and $p (Number of performers) together and having them be repeatable, with subfield $n (Total number of performers) always being placed at the end of the field. Discussion on the MARC list and more complex examples should inform development of a possible proposal for Midwinter 2012." Library of Congress MARC Standards, "MARC Discussion Paper No. 2011-DP05," last modified 2 August 2011, http://www.loc.gov/marc/marbi/2011/2011-dp05.html.

DREAMS FROM MY LIBRARY
Michelle Hahn

Abstract: Over 130 years ago, Charles Cutter outlined the purpose of a system for the description of information, and soon the card catalog came into being. More than eighty years later, those ideas were put through a revision, MARC was developed, and the OPAC was born. With FRBR should come more advancement, especially in the form of public access methods, so why does it feel like the catalog itself is moving backwards? The author looks at what FRBR, FRAD, and the like should mean for access to information and why we still are not getting there.

As I began writing this essay, I felt in no way qualified to make the claims in the following pages. The thoughts are mostly wayward daydreams, based on my experiences in a short period of schooling and an even shorter period of full-time employment, mixed with personal reactions to conversations among others who have a deeper understanding of cataloging and the like. The ideas are in their infancy, to be developed over the course of my lifetime. I am not an expert in any of the topics discussed.

INTRODUCTION

When asked what I do for a living, I am apt to simply say, "I am a librarian." In certain company, I may even be more specific: "I am a music librarian." I rarely say, however, "I am a music catalog librarian." When I do say it, I am always asked what it means. I use the following explanation that I spent a lot of time developing: *I describe music in a way that allows you to find it in a library and to determine whether you even want to find it in the first place.*

In this way, I try to define the raw purpose of bibliographic description to someone who has no prior knowledge of the concept. I think that most people would agree with my simple definition. Since the beginning of libraries, founded on many types of personal, ecclesiastical, or otherwise distinct collections, a variety of methods have been employed to maintain an inventory. Bibliographies, union catalogs, accession lists, and electronic databases are all examples. For the creation of these inventories, principles for the ways in which they are created and standards of input and display have been developed to create uniformly established content for each item or title listed. Those principles and standards include the "Statement of Principles Adopted by the International Conference on Cataloging Principles,"[1] the "International Standard Bibliographic Description" (ISBD),[2] *Anglo-American Cataloging Rules*, second edition (AACR2),[3] the Machine Readable Cataloging (MARC) format,[4] and the *Functional Requirements of Bibliographic Records* (FRBR).[5]

RDA

The talk these days is centered on FRBR, "a framework that identifies and clearly defines the entities of interest to users of bibliographic records, the attributes of each entity, and the types of relationships that operate between entities,"[6] with "entities" being "key objects of interest to users of bibliographic data,"[7] such as *works, persons*, and *concepts*.[8] *Resource Description & Access* (RDA)[9] has been developed to closely follow the entities described in FRBR and attempts to make the rules of description more malleable to match those entities. RDA could potentially supersede AACR2, though in 2011, RDA had only recently ended its test phase and a widely accepted implementation decision had not yet been made. With the potential of a major overhaul in policies and practices resulting from implementation of RDA, the cataloging community is facing a long and laborious process of change administration. It seems that with the backlogs of "hidden collections" behind everyone's doors, the time that will be invested in this process will push the discovery of those collections further into the future. Chances are, however, that administrators have no interest in losing that time, especially in a down economy.

While I agree that AACR2 does not do well in serving a good amount of the intellectual content in this world, I do not believe that its basic concepts are wrong or inapplicable. I also do not think that AACR2 as it stands needs to be tossed in the circular file. Rather, I think continual evaluation, revision, reworking, and adoption of changes to the existing AACR2—or the same with an Anglo-American adoption of ISBD—would be more useful and provide a more seamless transition to whatever future we choose. This approach would also meet the needs of a changing information environment and bring us in line with the standards of other information industries.

FRBR

The "Group 1 entities" described in FRBR are *work, expression, manifestation,* and *item*. A *work* is defined as "a distinct intellectual or artistic creation."[10] This entity is abstract, as is the description of it. Basically, in terms of music, a *work* is the idea of the piece itself, and not any particular notation or physical embodiment of that idea. For bibliographically descriptive purposes, use of this entity can aid in collocating many differing forms of a work, including print, audio, video, and digital instances, and ultimately physical embodiments of those instances. This is similar to traditional name/title authority control. Essentially, a name/title authority record is the equivalent of a FRBR *work* record. At this point, I stray from a strict interpretation of FRBR, which also considers the *work* entity to include both collections of individual works and segments of whole works. That makes the concept of a *work* overly confusing, and I would choose to use more descriptive terms such as "collection" and "segment" to represent those concept separately. Also, I would deem "collections" and "segments" to be more related to FRBR *expressions* and *manifestations*, with the understanding that multiple *works* can be embodied in one *expression* or *manifestation*.

An *expression* is defined as "the intellectual or artistic realization of a *work* in the form of alpha-numeric, musical, or choreographic notation, sound, image, object, movement, etc., or any combination of such forms."[11] This entity borders on the abstract, but starts to lean toward a more concrete, practical concept. For music, this entity describes the common characteristics of printed music as well as recordings of a given *work*. Those characteristics include information found in several of the transcribed areas of a bibliographic record such as title proper, edition statements, and musical presentation.

A *manifestation* is defined as "the physical embodiment of an *expression* of a *work*."[12] Here, we are looking at distinct printings of a print edition, or different media on which a commercial recording is issued—for example, a long-playing record and a cassette tape. Like the characteristics included in *expressions*, we currently see such information in existing bibliographic records—in this case, in the physical description area.

Finally is *item*, which is defined as "a single exemplar of a *manifestation*."[13] Simply put, my copy of this eight-track recording, not your copy. We associate these *items* with barcodes in our catalogs today.

However, it does not particularly matter how we describe the materials we have—the current Online Public Access Catalogs (OPACs) in which that information is displayed, disseminated, and accessed do not do enough with the information we already provide in the MARC coding format. Because of this, even though RDA may have the potential to bring practical bibliographic description in line with standards like FRBR, it is not beneficial for any institution to invest the time to implement it until a database and corresponding OPAC are created to handle it properly.

MARC

Why do we still use MARC numeric tags for the content of a bibliographic record? Roy Tennant framed the concern that underlies this question in 2002: ". . . fields are not explicitly labeled but coded with a numbering scheme that cannot be read by someone unfamiliar with the complicated syntax," describing it as "needless obfuscation."[14] As MARC was created in the late 1960s when each byte of computer memory represented a substantial expense, it would have been prudent to use a three-digit code rather than natural language to label the content of description: "245" was cheaper than "Title and statement of responsibility." Now, as we can literally watch our potential Gmail storage capacity grow by several millionths of a megabyte per second, using "Title and statement of responsibility" would not represent a significant expense.

But is it really a problem to learn a set of numeric codes in order to create a bibliographic record? For musicians, it is not the first time that they have learned an obscure code that is not decipherable by most people. What does musical notation mean to anyone but musicians? Did we not have to learn it before we could apply it? Does it have any natural connection to our written or spoken language? The same goes for other disciplines, such as software development or medicine. If I were to write a software program, I would first need to learn the appropriate programming language, which—though using actual words—is not understandable outside the context of software programming. Even 911, the widely known phone number for emergency service in the United States, would not mean anything to a person that was not taught the use of that number.

The problem is not with MARC itself. It is with two major flaws in the use of MARC coding: unused but potentially useful content designations and needless duplication between coded and descriptive data. There is a large amount of content designation for which the potential for use has never been exploited. This first flaw manifests itself in the 5XX fields, used for a variety of notes, where there are nearly fifty unused three-digit tags, yet a single tag—field 500—is used for a majority of descriptive notes. For the second flaw, a large amount of time is spent inputting duplicate information when only one instance of it actually displays to the user. For example, the 007 and 300 fields describe nearly identical physical attributes of material in coded and textual form.

The intent of MARC coding is to give a computer single-byte characters that it is programmed to display in a certain way depending on where they are located in the coding scheme. "If . . . then . . ." statements are a basic construct in programming. Rather than having to spell out "Compact disc" in a general 500 note in order for the phrase "Compact disc" to display to the user, the computer should be able to follow the programming instruction "if 007 $b equals 'd' and 007 $d equals 'f,' then display 'Compact disc,' " or something similar. It should follow that the coded information in a MARC record is the easiest for a computer to process and display.

MARC coding is a separate entity from the cataloging rules themselves, but there is no reason that the rules cannot reflect in some way the software and systems that will hold and organize the information. Those rules and codes could be integrated into one cohesive instrument to provide guidance and instruction in the coding and creation of a catalog record. For example, the physical description area of AACR2 could be eliminated, along with the use of the 300 field, and the integrated documentation could explicitly prescribe how to create an appropriate 007 field with corresponding codes for the physical description.

MY "FRBRIZED-LIKE" OPAC

FRBR simply describes a more efficient way to organize the "entities" of our descriptive information for greater collocation. What I see as the distinction between our current library catalogs and a "FRBRized-like" catalog is the separation of these entities visually and electronically, which would allow them to be linked in ways that are more complex, yet more efficient. I will attempt to paint the picture of how both the OPAC and catalog would look when utilizing my ideas.

As mentioned above, I see a *work* record as the equivalent of an existing name/title authority record. I imagine being able to click on a plus sign next to the name/title authority record to open a set of *expression* records. Then doing the same with those records and opening a set of *manifestation* records and subsequently *item* records. To give an example, I will use Dave Matthews (leader of the eponymous band).

Ideally, I could type "Dave Matthews" into my OPAC search interface, and the catalog would match the search string against the name in the name-heading index and take me to the index. I could click on the "Dave Matthews" for whom I was searching, and the catalog would show me a list of his songs. I could then click on the song I wanted, and it would bring up the name/title authority record, or *work* record for that song. The *work* record might have a hyperlink that instructs me to "Click here for 'expressions' of this work." Once I had done that, I could do the same for *manifestations* and *items*.

For example, Matthews wrote a song called "Gravedigger." The corresponding name/title authority record would be "Matthews, Dave. Gravedigger." By clicking on the appropriate link for expansion, I would see a list of *expressions*, such as:

- Sheet music
- Recordings
- Videos
- Related content

"Related content" would lead to books, articles, and other materials in which this piece is used as a subject heading. It may also lead to similar content that is related to Matthews himself, such as a biography, or his music in general. It could eventually help guide users toward a path of greater exploration into rock music.

If I chose "Recordings," I would then see a list of *manifestations*. As I mentioned in my discussion of FRBR entities, *manifestations* may include collections of individual *works* that include the individual work in which I am interested, such as an entire record album. This list would include:

- Gravedigger (single release)
- Some Devil (studio album)
- The Gorge 2002 (live album)
- Live Trax vol. 10: Pavilion Atlantico (live album)
- Live at Mile High (live album)

From that point, I could click on "Live at Mile High" and see the *items*—that is, single physical copies—associated with it, with the requisite information about where I could find them.[15]

MY FRBRIZED-LIKE CATALOG INTERFACE

Above, I briefly outlined my ideas for a catalog interface that would loosely follow the entities described in FRBR. I believe we could easily continue the use of MARC content designations as we know them, parsing the familiar three-digit tags, indicators, and subfields into the appropriate corresponding FRBR entity records until perhaps many of the fixed and descriptive data codes could be reassigned and easily converted through a system of mapping based on their location within the record structure.

A cataloger would interact with the database in a way similar to the OPAC I described earlier to create the records behind the scenes. *Work* records would be created in the same manner as a name/title authority record. The cataloger would then be given the option to create a linked *expression* record, inputting only the necessary information for that entity. The same process would continue through the creation of *manifestation* and *item* records.

Once a higher-level record is created (that is, the *work* or *expression* records), the amount of information to be input becomes less with each *manifestation* or *item*, as the more common information is already linked to those records. This in turn leads to a decreased amount of time spent in creating many of the records, leaving more time to provide access to a greater number of materials and thus eliminating hidden collections, increasing circulation, improving the quality of research, and so on.

IMPLEMENTING CHANGE

I wish I either were a software programmer or had the means to pay a programmer to do exactly what I asked. I am limited, though, to doing what I can from my position as an individual cataloger with no power to coerce an integrated library system vendor into making the changes to make my dreams come to life. I am at the mercy of whatever system my institution chooses and whatever upgrade or inadequate product will be bought and installed next.

Music description is ill-served by nonlibrary, commercial catalogs, such as publisher websites. The completeness of the information for music materials in external lists is far inferior to the content in library catalogs. Because of this—and because of the cooperative work of the music library community to create effective tools and interfaces specific to our needs—I think music libraries and catalogs will be among the last to hold on to cataloging as it looks today. I may even go so far as to suggest that the music library community pursue the creation of its own standards, much in the same vein as the Rare Books and Manuscripts Section of the Association of College and Research Libraries with the Descriptive Cataloging of Rare Materials series.[16] We are doing better than other subject areas, however, though with no thanks to our ILS vendors. The collective vigor of music librarians has allowed us to set ourselves apart from other library subdisciplines, and has positioned us for great success to this point.

It is the tireless efforts of music librarians like Ralph Papakhian that have gotten us to this point, and the continuing efforts of those to come that will keep us moving mightily into the future.

NOTES

[1] International Conference on Cataloguing Principles (Paris, 1961), *Report* (London: International Federation of Library Associations, 1963). Also published in *Library Resources and Technical Services* 6 (1962): 162–67, and at http://www.d-nb.de/standardisierung/pdf/paris_principles_1961.pdf.

[2] Working Group on the International Standard Bibliographic Description, *International Standard Bibliographic Description: For Single and Multi-Volume Monographic Publications* (London: IFLA Committee on Cataloguing, 1971).

[3] Joint Steering Committee for the Revision of AACR, *Anglo-American Cataloguing Rules*, 2nd ed., 2002 rev. (Chicago: American Library Association, 2002).

[4] Henriette D. Avram, John F. Knapp, and Lucia J. Rather, *The MARC II Format: A Communications Format for Bibliographic Data* (Washington, D.C.: Information Systems Office, Library of Congress, 1968).

[5] IFLA Study Group on the Functional Requirements for Bibliographic Records, *Functional Requirements for Bibliographic Records: Final Report* (Munich: K. G. Saur, 1998), http://www.ifla.org/en/publications/functional-requirements-for-bibliographic-records (as amended and corrected through February 2009). Hereinafter "FRBR."

[6] FRBR, 3.

[7] Ibid.

[8] In order to distinguish FRBR entities from generic terms, they will appear in italics.

[9] Joint Steering Committee for Development of RDA, *RDA: Resource Description & Access* (Chicago: American Library Association, 2010).

[10] FRBR, 16.

[11] Ibid., 18.

[12] Ibid., 20.

[13] Ibid., 23.

[14] Roy Tennant, "Digital Libraries: MARC Must Die," *Library Journal*, 15 October 2002, 26–27.

[15] All information related to the example of "Gravedigger" by Dave Matthews can be found on the Dave Matthews Band website, accessed 31 January 2011, http://www.davematthewsband.com.

[16] *Descriptive Cataloging of Rare Materials (Books)* (Washington, D.C.: Cataloging Distribution Service, 2007); *Descriptive Cataloging of Rare Materials (Serials)* (Washington, D.C.: Cataloging Distribution Service, 2008).

PART 3

Current and Emerging Standards in Practice

Cataloging practice is an outgrowth of cataloging theory. Sometimes it is a natural outgrowth, but more often than not, practice must be adapted to reflect realities either unknown or not considered at the time of the theory's inception. Music cataloging under AACR2 required such adaptation, and it most certainly will as RDA is adopted (or "adapted") over the next year and a half. At the same time, technological limitations will inform this adaptation as much as—if not more than—the theory itself.

Suzanne Mudge's article on cataloging ethnographic field recordings represents a case in point of how catalogers had to adapt to provide effective and accurate access to collections of non-Western art music and folk music under AACR2 music cataloging rules, which have a decidedly Western focus. In institutions like the Archives of Traditional Music (Indiana University) and the Archive of World Music (Harvard), this often meant supplementing AACR2 with standards such as *Describing Archives: A Content Standard* (DACS) and others. Over time, the unique challenges of providing access to these collections and the resulting adaptation of cataloging practice led to implementation of accessioning/cataloging systems that work well for them.

Peter Lisius exposes the challenges in attempting to provide controlled access points for musical works in digital music applications such as iTunes and Windows Media Player, and how these same challenges manifest themselves on digital music players such as the iPod Nano and Sony Walkman. Replicating AACR2-style (or soon, RDA-style) access points on digital music applications is problematic for catalogers who, when inputting records into Online Public Access Catalogs (OPACs), have striven for consistency in their work. Current technological limitations make replicating these same access points on both digital music applications and players difficult, if not impossible.

Jenn Riley provides a first-hand account of her experiences with Indiana University's Variations/ FRBR (or V/FRBR) project, in which principles of the *Functional Requirements for Bibliographic Records* (FRBR) conceptual model were applied to a discovery system intended to provide access to musical works. As Riley describes in her article, work done since FRBR's inception in 1998 (including that on the V/FRBR project) reveals what does and does not work with the model in practice. As the V/FRBR project illustrates, much work is still needed to build an effective system in which FRBR entities are presented in a way that will provide the best access to musical works.

That all said, it can be seen that, over time, cataloging practice can effectively adapt to emerging theories, as is evident in the achievements of catalogers for the Archives of Traditional

Music and Archive of World Music. Current work in the V/FRBR project reveals a concerted effort to convert FRBR theory into practice in providing access to musical works. Work such as this must continue if RDA, which in large part is based on FRBR, will succeed. Also, digital music applications and players will continue to evolve and increasingly be offered as a listening option for users of music collections, so providing consistent access to musical works on these applications and players should be as important to music catalogers as providing access to those same works through OPACs.

As mentioned in the introduction to part 2 (pp. 41–42), the current generation of catalogers is rising to meet these challenges. The volume concludes with a remembrance of Ralph Papakhian, the teacher, mentor, colleague, and friend who encouraged and inspired so many music catalogers to do their work at the highest level possible. It is with his spirit that we march into the future of music cataloging.

CATALOGING ETHNOGRAPHIC AUDIOVISUAL FIELD COLLECTIONS

SUZANNE MUDGE

Abstract: Although catalogers at audiovisual archives have used the MARC format to catalog ethnographic field collections on OCLC since the early 1980s, there is no definitive descriptive standard for cataloging these types of unpublished collections. This article provides an overview of the cataloging process for ethnographic audiovisual field collections, based on current practices at Indiana University's Archives of Traditional Music and Harvard's Loeb Music Library Archive of World Music. After reviewing cataloging-related principles and practices developed for accessioning archival collections, the article highlights relevant cataloging rules from AACR2 and DACS for each area of the collection-level description, illustrated with examples in the MARC format. The article provides strategies for addressing cataloging issues not covered by either standard, citing additional resources and the hybrid approaches adopted by both archives. The article also reviews subject-access guidelines for ethnographic collections and cites resources and programs available to help catalogers provide improved access to these holdings.

INTRODUCTION

The Archives of Traditional Music at Indiana University established its OCLC cataloging profile in 1983 and became one of the first institutions in the country to create MARC records for ethnographic audio collections in a union catalog. Mary Russell Bucknum, then the archives librarian, published two articles focusing on some of the issues she faced when cataloging field collections of music and American Indian languages.[1]

Today, most archives in the United States catalog their unpublished audio and moving-image collections using the MARC21 (hereinafter "MARC") format and OCLC Connexion.[2] Although cataloging rules have expanded to include some guidelines for unpublished audio and visual collections, catalogers still face multiple challenges in describing these complex collections, and there is as yet no definitive standard for cataloging nonpaper ethnographic field collections.[3]

This article will provide an updated summary of cataloging guidelines followed at the Archives of Traditional Music (ATM) and at Harvard's Loeb Music Library Archive of World Music (AWM).

The history of an audio and moving-image archive, its institutional context, scope, and size, and the types of available cataloging resources are among principal factors in determining cataloging practices. Some of these considerations are common to both archives. For example, the ATM and AWM both house commercial recordings as well as ethnographic field collections, and our field collections vary widely in their complexity of organization, formats, and intellectual content. However, the history, average collection size, and technical resources of the two archives run a less parallel course.[4]

Cataloging choices vary, but an outline of current practices (including a summary of the accessioning process and relevant cataloging rules and resources) may help the reader gain a sense of the overall process and the options for cataloging audio and moving-image ethnographic collections. Just as the various practices highlight the flexibility of the MARC format, they also affirm the need for a descriptive cataloging standard.

ACCESSIONING FIELD COLLECTIONS

The process of accessioning archival ethnographic collections is integrally linked with cataloging. Several archiving reference sources and local procedures reflect this relationship.

STANDARDS AND RESOURCES

Describing Archives: A Content Standard (DACS),[5] the descriptive standard for paper-based collections, provides a definitive explanation of archiving practices and the nature of archival description, and includes a statement of principles.[6] Audio and moving-image archivists and librarians are advised to become familiar with the archival principles outlined in DACS, even if they chose to adhere more closely to the format-based *Anglo-American Cataloguing Rules* (AACR2).[7]

Despite a long history of rich and varied resources for general archives management, including recent Society of American Archivists publications,[8] few sources discuss sound or moving-image archives. An exception is Alan Ward's *Manual of Sound Archive Administration*,[9] which the ATM has used to establish overall management and procedural guidelines. In "Access to Multi-Format Ethnographic Field Documentation," Catherine Hiebert Kerst provides a useful description of the American Folklife Center's framework for accessioning audio and visual ethnographic collections.[10] Similarly, in his chapter on archival collections in *Describing Music Materials*, Richard Smiraglia succinctly summarizes the first two steps of formal archival accessioning—arrangement and creation of a finding aid—and explains their relationship to cataloging.[11]

LOCAL ACCESSIONING PRACTICES

Ideally, an archive's accessioning process begins before materials arrive. When the ATM is approached regarding a potential donation, we make an effort to establish a relationship with the donor (who generally is the collector). Using the Archives' "Guide for Deposit of Field Collections" form, we begin a preliminary discussion of the content and scope of the collection, physical condition, rights and restrictions, and accompanying documentation. As a result, the donor better understands the Archives' process and will continue to work with the ATM archivist to complete relevant ATM accessioning forms when formal accessioning begins.

The ATM has developed a "Collection Summary" form over the course of many years (see appendix 1). When possible, this form is filled out by the collector. Through it we collect information on the collection's provenance and physical description and a summary of intellectual content—the minimal amount of information the Archives needs to accession a collection.[12] Completed summary forms are a first-hand account of the collector's research, and they provide the cataloger with much of the information needed to complete a collection-level MARC record. To adhere to the principle of original order, the ATM also endeavors to obtain item-level indexes, or an inventory, directly from the collector or depositor. Obtaining summaries and indexes or inventories is not always possible.[13] If necessary, the ATM archivist will complete the summary form after reviewing the contents and accompanying documentation for the collection. In addition, all archives require a contract for deposit between the donor and institution that specifies level of access to the collection and ownership of property rights.

Finally, within the formal accessioning process, nothing is more essential to cataloger and patron than acquiring the collector's contextual documentation for a collection.[14] What Bucknum noted over twenty-five years ago still holds true today: "[T]he quality of the database in general, is directly related to the documentation they [collectors] supply with their recordings. . . . [T]heir recordings are only as valuable to the scholarly world as the documentation they submit with them."[15] Fortunately, scholarly disciplines most closely affiliated with sound and visual archives increasingly emphasize the importance of fieldwork documentation in their courses and publications.[16]

DESCRIPTION

LEVELS OF DESCRIPTION

The levels of description for archival collections have been described as a pyramid.[17] The collection-level catalog record[18] serves as a surrogate and entry point for a more detailed finding-aid description. The finding aid, in turn, contains an inventory or item-level list of contents in the collection. Through these two levels of description an archive reconciles archival collection-level description, based on provenance and contextual unity, with the users' needs for item-level description and access.[19]

STANDARDS AND RESOURCES

The general introduction to AACR2 states, "These rules . . . are not specifically intended for specialist and archival libraries, but such libraries are recommended to use the rules as the basis of their cataloguing and to augment their provisions as necessary."[20] From the first years of cataloging its holdings, the ATM staff has followed AACR2's prescription. It has used AACR2 and MARC music (for sound recordings) and visual formats as a foundation,[21] augmented with guidelines from *Rules for Archival Cataloging of Sound Recordings* [22] and, more recently, *Archival Moving Image Materials: A Cataloging Manual* (AMIM),[23] based on AACR2, chapters 6 and 7, respectively. The ATM has, to a lesser degree, also adapted rules from *Archives, Personal Papers, and Manuscripts* (APPM)[24] and examples from *Cataloging Unpublished Nonprint Materials*.[25]

In contrast, AWM catalogers use AACR2 as the basis for describing their commercial holdings but have more recently adapted DACS as their principal standard for collection-level records. Principle 5 of DACS observes, "The rules apply to all archival materials regardless of form or medium . . . [however,] different media of course require different rules to describe their particular characteristics."[26]

Several authors have tried to fill in gaps in archival description for non–paper-based collections. In "Cataloging Sound Recordings Using Archival Methods," David Thomas cataloged a broadcast sound recording collection following the APPM standard and applying the Archival and Manuscripts Control (AMC) MARC format.[27] Similarly, Smiraglia has taken the lead by adding a chapter on archival music collections to *Describing Music Materials*.[28]

Although the creation of descriptive finding aids is beyond the scope of this article, it is important to note that audiovisual archives, including the AWM, have successfully adapted another standard—Encoded Archival Description (EAD), using Extensible Markup Language (XML) encoding—to create electronic finding aids for some of their ethnographic audio and moving-image collections.[29]

TECHNICAL READING AND TYPE OF RECORD

Unlike individual commercial recordings, an unpublished field collection[30] cannot be cataloged until it has been accessioned. That process, as we have seen, includes the presence or creation of some form of item-level description or finding aid. Cataloging also presupposes a summary of the extent and physical arrangement of a collection.

The technical reading for an ethnographic field collection includes a review of the various forms and documents that accompany the accessioned collection. The cataloger's first goal is to evaluate the physical arrangement and scope of a collection to determine if there is a predominant format and whether the collection should be subdivided into series. For example, the ATM may choose to subdivide the audio and visual components of a collection and create a collection-level record for each format-based series.[31] Classification of component formats may vary. The ATM tends to classify paper-based accompanying documentation as "accompanying matter," while AWM frequently includes this type of material as part of a "mixed materials" record.

CHIEF SOURCES OF INFORMATION

Archival cataloging standards have been quite flexible in defining the chief sources of information for collections. If there is no finding aid, APPM 1.0B1 instructs us to consider provenance and accession records, the materials themselves, and reference sources as the chief sources of information. For most elements, DACS 2.3.1 more broadly prescribes using any "reliable source," internal or external.

Because the specific chief sources of information for sound and visual recordings, as defined in AACR2 6.0B1 and 7.0B1, seldom provide adequate or consistent collection-level information, the cataloger will need to base the description on information found in the collection's finding aid or accompanying documentation.

TITLE

Ethnographic archival collections rarely come with a formal title. Consequently, one of the most problematic cataloging issues is how to construct collection titles that are both consistent and contain useful information for the patron. Furthermore, AACR2 and DACS offer somewhat conflicting guidance, with few relevant examples for ethnographic field collections.

AACR2 1.1B7 simply instructs the cataloger to "devise a brief descriptive title" for an item lacking a chief source. AMIM 1F1.6 elaborates, "Supply a descriptive phrase as the first part of the title proper. Include important elements such as personalities, events, dates, places, subjects, etc., as they apply. . . . Follow the descriptive phrase with the appropriate form term." The Dance Heritage Coalition weighs in specifically for ethnographic collections with 1F2.2b: "Base the collective title on appropriate factors such as dance group or culture, event, or dance genre."[32]

In order to provide both consistency and useful keyword searching, ATM catalogers create titles based on the geographic location of the field collection, the culture group recorded, and date of recording. As Bucknum noted, "This pattern . . . is loosely based on George Murdoch's *Outline of World Cultures* and has been used at the ATM since 1955" (see fig. 1).[33]

ATM patrons' modes of collection discovery continue to support this practice.[34] The resources cited above also include examples that closely resemble the ATM pattern (see figs. 2 and 3).[35]

In contrast, according to DACS 2.3.3, the names of those responsible for the creation or assembly of a collection are described in the name segment of a constructed title (MARC field 245 subfield $a). The title may include a term describing the nature of the archival unit, and optionally, a topical segment (see fig. 4). The first title in figure 4 is based on AACR2 guidelines and is enclosed in square brackets. The other two examples are based on DACS guidelines, which instruct us not to use brackets.

---

245 10 $a [Columbia, Putumayo, Sibundoy Valley; Kamsa, Inga, 1976, 1978-1979].

245 10 $a [Panama, Kuna Indians, 1970-1993].

Figure 1. Examples of ATM constructed titles.

---

245 00 $a [Papua New Guinea--Iatmul people, 1938--field footage. $n Roll 11].

Figure 2. Example from AMIM 1F1.6.

---

245 00 $a [Dances of the Tiskiouine from the Guidmioua Tribe, Grand Atlas Morocco] $h [motion picture]...

Figure 3. Dance Heritage Coalition example in 1F2.2b, with elements similar to ATM title elements, in a different order.

```
245 04 $a [The Eduard Alekseyev fieldwork collection of the musical culture of Yakutia, $f 1969-1990].

245 04 $a The Stephen Blum Collection of music from Iranian Khorāsān at Harvard University, $f 1968-2006.

245 00 $a Rubén Blades Archives at Harvard University, $f [19--?]-2009.
```

Figure 4. Example of AWM constructed titles that include the collector's name.

The decision whether to place the title in square brackets depends on the standard one follows. DACS 2.3.3 instructs us not to enclose supplied titles in square brackets. On the other hand, for most unprocessed sound and visual collections, constructed titles will *not* come from the chief source of information, as described in AACR2, chapters 6 and 7, and are placed in brackets. The issue of brackets, while a relatively small point, illustrates a difference in focus between AACR2 and DACS. The latter prescribes a range of possible sources for composing a supplied title. AACR2 gives a narrow set of options for the chief source of information—the prescribed source for titles—hence the need for brackets (AACR2 6.0B2). AACR2 1.1B1 also instructs us to create a note providing the source of the bracketed title.

GENERAL MATERIAL DESIGNATION

The inclusion of the General Material Designation (GMD) depends on whether the collection has a predominant format or consists of mixed materials. As noted earlier, the AWM tends to catalog its collections as mixed materials, which precludes the use of the GMD. If present, the GMD is recorded in MARC field 245 subfield $h, immediately following the title and enclosed in square brackets (see fig. 5).

STATEMENT OF RESPONSIBILITY

In accordance with AACR2 6.1F1,[36] the ATM transcribes the collector's name in the statement of responsibility area (MARC field 245 subfield $c; see fig. 5). A Dance Heritage Coalition ethnographic example (see fig. 6) closely resembles the ATM pattern.

If one follows DACS 2.3.3, however, the names of those responsible for the creation or assembly of a collection are described in the name segment of a constructed title (MARC field 245 subfield $a). For this reason, the collector's name would not be repeated in a statement of responsibility (see fig. 4).

PUBLICATION INFORMATION AND DATE(S)

Original field collections are not published; therefore, the ATM and AWM generally do not include a publication field, per AACR2 6.4C2. AACR2 1.4F9, however, requires date of production (i.e., recording) for unpublished items, and 1.4F10 specifically instructs us to provide a date or inclusive dates for unpublished collections.

> 245 10 $a [Africa, Nigeria, Abia, Ohafia, Igbo, 1990-1991] $h [sound recording] / $c collected by John C. McCall.
>
> 245 10 $a [Peru, Huancavelica, Ayacucho, Puno, Lima, Chanka, Quechua, 1984-1985] $h [sound recording] / $c collected by Nan Leigh Volinsky.
>
> 245 10 $a [Surinam, Pikilío Region, Saramaka Maroons, 1967-1968] $h [sound recording] / $c collected by Richard and Sally Price.

Figure 5. Examples of ATM constructed titles with GMD and statement of responsibility.

> 245 00 $a Dance at Irolerís store $h [videorecording] / $c collected by the American Folklife Center for the National Park Service [...]

Figure 6. Dance Heritage Coalition example of a title and statement of responsibility.

There are two options for the placement of dates in the MARC format. If dates are included in the constructed title field (MARC field 245), subfields $f or $g are prescribed subfields (see fig. 4).[37] If the date is not included in field 245, it can stand alone in subfield $c of field 260 (Publication, Distribution, etc. [Imprint]).[38]

PHYSICAL DESCRIPTION AND ADDITIONAL FORM ASPECTS

AACR2 provides basic guidelines for the physical description, based on format. For more complete cataloging guidelines, those issued by the Association for Recorded Sound Collections (ARSC) and AMI field in both iTunes field in both iTunesM are particularly helpful. They provide physical dimensions and examples for audiovisual formats not covered by AACR2, such as wires and cylinders.[39] *Music Coding and Tagging* is also valuable for the details Jay Weitz provides to help clarify the physical description coding in MARC fields 006, 007, and 300.[40]

A more complicated matter is determining if and how to make use of MARC field 006 to bring out aspects of the specific forms included in a collection, since the field 008 data elements for mixed materials (code "p" in Type of Record [Leader/06]), are not repeatable. Several catalog records for AWM collections illustrate the complexity and possible solutions (see fig. 7).

AACR2 1.5E1 and MCD 1.5E1 instruct us to mention accompanying documentation in either the physical description area *or* a note. Because documentation is critical to a collection's usefulness, the ATM generally deviates from these instructions by noting the presence of documentation in the physical description (MARC field 300) and also creating a MARC field 500 note for additional details (see fig. 8).

NOTES

The notes area forms the bulk of the description for unpublished audio and visual archival collections. Notes are perhaps the most important area in a collection-level bibliographic record,

```
Record Type p
006    jppnn         n
006    g---          vn
245 00 Rubén Blades Archives at Harvard University, $f [19--?]-2009.
246 3  Rubén Blades collection
300    70 sound discs : $b digital ; $c 4 3/4 in.
300    37 sound discs : $b analog ; $c 12 in.
300    12 CD-ROMs : $b digital, MP3 files ; $c 4 3/4 in.
300    30 videodiscs : $b sd., col. ; 4 3/4 in.
300    15 videocassettes : $b sd. col. ; $c 1/2 in.
300    1 CD-ROM : $b sd., col. ; $c 4 3/4 in.
300    1 sound cassette : $b 3 3/4 ips ; $c 7 1/4 x 3 1/2 in.
300    12 books.
300    16 kits.
300    41 magazines.
```

Figure 7. An AWM mixed format collection in which MARC field 006 is used to bring out the audio and visual aspects, reflecting the majority of the collection's content. Multiple MARC 300 fields are needed to describe physical description details for the wide range of forms contained in the collection.

```
300 ## $a 76 sound cassettes : $b analog, stereo. + $e documentation (163 p.).
500 ## $a Documentation consists of content summaries for each sound cassette and partial transcriptions of the interviews and performances.
```

Figure 8. ATM example of a MARC field 300 describing accompanying material and a corresponding MARC field 500 note.

not only for the descriptive detail they provide, but also for their function in providing uncontrolled access points. The choice and extent of notes depends on a range of factors, including the level and type of accompanying documentation for a collection, local cataloging practices, cataloging resources, and a cataloger's ability to synthesize salient features in the content of a collection.

Cataloging practices at the ATM and AWM illustrate two different approaches for supplying notes to collection-level records: (1) follow the note order prescribed by AACR2, based on the sound and visual formats, and supplement with archival-based notes, or (2) follow the DACS archival model, emphasizing provenance, historical context, arrangement, and contractual agreements, and supplement with format-based notes.

Beginning with the AACR2-prescribed notes and note order, I will focus on the MARC 5XX notes most commonly used at the ATM and AWM. For smaller collections, the ATM generally begins the notes area with a brief general note (MARC field 500) describing the nature or

> 500 ## $a Principally vocal and instrumental dance music from Peru.
> 546 ## $a Sung in Quechua and Spanish.

> 500 ## $a Music, interviews, and oral traditions.
> 546 ## $a In Teke, Mangala (Losengo dialect), and Ki-Koongo (Kongo dialect).

Figure 9. Examples of general notes for form and medium of performance and notes for language.

> 245 04 $a [The Kay Kaufman Shelemay Syrian-Jewish Collection, $f 1984-1995].
> 500 ## $a Collection title devised by creator of collection.

Figure 10. An AWM example of supplied title, with note regarding the source of information.

> 500 0# $a Principle performers are residents of the Sibundoy Valley, Putumayo state, Colombia. They include Bautista Juajibioy, Mariano Chicunque, Estanislao Chicunque, María Juajibioy, Justo Jacanamijoy, Francisco Narváez, members of the Kamsá indigenous community, and Francisco Tandioy Jansasoy, a member of the Inga indigenous community.
>
> 518 ## $a Recorded by John McDowell in 1976 and 1978-1979 in the Sibundoy Valley, Putumayo, Colombia.

Figure 11. Example of an ATM participant or performer note and history of recording note.

artistic form and medium of performance, per AACR2 6.7B1. Similarly, the construction of a language note for the audio or visual content (MARC field 546) may be indistinguishable from a note for a commercial recording (see fig. 9).

ATM catalogers always create titles for field collections. In AWM AACR2-based records, collectors as well as catalogers have composed titles. In these instances, both archives followed AACR2 1.1B1, adding a note to indicate the source of the title (see fig. 10).

The discussion in AACR2 6.7B6 regarding statements-of-responsibility notes offers an instance where item- and collection-level cataloging blend well for smaller ethnographic collections. Although DACS emphasizes the collector, notes regarding performers and other prominent participants are appropriate and often extremely important to archives' patrons (see fig. 11). On the other hand, the number of participants in large collections may prohibit transcribing a comprehensive performer or participant note. In those instances, this level of detail should be offered in a collection finding aid or index.

AACR2 6.7B7 includes unprocessed sound recordings in its instructions for creating the history of a recording in a note (MARC field 518; see fig. 11). The ATM includes this note for smaller collections; when the information is not so extensive, its inclusion becomes impractical. For larger collections, the recording information will be available in an item-level index, among the collection's accompanying documentation.

Additional information related to physical description, not included in a MARC 300 field, is often helpful to patrons. Such notes may, for example, include information on general physical condition or playback quality of the recordings in the collection (see fig. 12).

Including a general note (MARC field 500) to describe accompanying material will depend on the agency's overall approach to additional formats, and whether the additional materials are included as part of a "mixed materials" description. Figure 8 provides an example of the ATM's general approach to describing documents that accompany the field collection. Figure 7 illustrates the approach at the AWM, where photographs, for example, are more likely to be included as part of the mixed formats description, in which case the extent will be given in a MARC 300 field, augmented by item-level detail in the collection finding aid.

Both archives include a summary note (MARC field 520) and, if smaller-sized collections include song or descriptive titles, the ATM may also create a contents note (MARC field 505) as well (see fig. 13).

---

500 ## $a Acetate disc copies of the original wire recordings, reproduce from inside outward; sound quality fair.

500 ## $a Webster wire spools; sound quality fair to excellent.

Figure 12. Example of a general note for additional physical description information.

---

245 00 $a Malawi, Blantyre, Cewa and Yao, 1988] $h [videorecording] / $c collected by Mitchel Strumpf ; documentation by K. Wongani Katundu.

520 ## Recordings consist of video footage of the First Festival of Malawian Neo-Traditional Music held at the French Cultural Center in Blantyre and also a variety of miscellaneous footage shot in Malawi. The Festival performances consist of vocal and instrumental Neo-Traditional music performed by a variety of Cewa and Yao ensembles and soloists...

505 2# : tape 1. The First Festival of Malawian Neo-Traditional Music Held at the French Cultural Center in Blantyre on the 8th of May 1988, pt. 1 -- tape 2. The First Festival of Malawian Neo-Traditional Music Held at the French Cultural Center in Blantyre on the 8th of May 1988, pt. 2 ; Interview and performance by The Little Brothers Band ; Imitation of a Beni dance ; Interview about and performance of pounding songs by Yao women ; Preamble for performance by the Theatre of Development at the Department of Fine and Performing Arts of the University of Malawi ; Children's games ; Fishermen songs ; Children's games ; Synopsis of research by Dr. Chris Kamlongera ; Performance by Mbengwa Makanjila ; Performance by Black Paseli and K. Wongani Katundu.

Figure 13. Summary and contents notes for an ATM collection containing two videocassettes.

At this point in the description, the ATM adds notes based on archival guidelines. Using the ATM's deposit agreement form, the cataloger transcribes the immediate source of acquisition (MARC field 541), and the terms governing use (MARC field 540; fig. 14). The AWM follows a similar practice.

Lastly, the ATM frequently includes, if available, titles of works the collector has published based on the fieldwork, in the related publications note (MARC field 581).

DACS does not prescribe note order; nevertheless, the order generally reflects the order of description for a standardized finding aid. The AWM usually begins with a biographical/historical note (MARC field 545; fig. 15).

The AWM generally follows the biographical/historical note with a summary note (MARC field 520). Contrary to AACR2 practice, the AWM places the summary near the beginning rather than the end of the notes section. This placement reflects the prominent role a detailed abstract or summary plays in archival description. DACS provides comprehensive examples for the biographical and summary notes, which carefully define the detailed and narrative nature of archival description.

In addition to source of acquisition (MARC field 541) and restrictions on access (MARC field 540) notes, as described above, the AWM also includes a provenance/custodial history note (MARC field 561; fig. 16). If physical access is restricted, a MARC 506 field should also be included.

---

541 ## $c Deposit, option 1; $a John Doe; $d 10/14/2005.

540 ## $a Archival use and reproduction for non-profit educational or research purposes; $b Archives of Traditional Music.
OR
540 ## $a Obtaining copies or making published reference to the content of the materials in this collection is subject to the depositor's and Archives' approval; $b John Doe, Archives of Traditional Music; $c Contract for deposit, Archives of Traditional Music.

Figure 14. Examples of acquisition and terms governing use notes.

---

545 ## $a Stephen Blum is an ethnomusicologist who has taught at Western Illinois University, the University of Illinois at Urbana-Champaign, York University in Toronto, and the City University of New York (CUNY) Graduate Center, where he initiated a concentration in ethnomusicology. Blum's work concentrates on the music of Iran. Following the Iranian Revolution of 1979, Dr. Blum was unable to return to Iran until 1995, when he donated copies of his earlier recordings to the Ministry of Culture and Islamic Guidance, and made additional recordings in Khorāsān as well as in the city of Qazvin, northwest of Tehran. He began to make more frequent visits in 2006. Blum is collaborating with Dr. Ameneh Youssefzadeh on a series of critical editions of narratives (dāstān) in Khorasani Turkish. In 2007, the Mahoor Institute of Culture and Art began to issue compact discs drawn from his recordings.

Figure 15. An AWM example of a biographical/historical note.

> 561 1# $a Originally collected by Altan Ender Güzey; sound recordings in part made by Güzey in Salisbury, Maryland; radio broadcasts from the Istanbul, Ankara and Turkish National Radio Archives.

Figure 16. Example of an AWM provenance/custodial history note.

> 245 04 $a The Stephen Blum Collection of music from Iranian Khorāsān at Harvard University, $f 1968-2006.
>
> 555 0# $a Electronic finding aid available. $u http://nrs.harvard.edu/urn-3:FHCL.Loeb.Faids:mus00025

Figure 17. Example of a finding aid note for the Stephen Blum Collection at the AWM.

A crucial step for processing archival collections is the creation of a finding aid. For large collections, in particular, the finding aid is the most effective way for patrons to discover content at the item level. A finding aid note (MARC field 555) is used to indicate the existence of a finding aid for a collection. If an electronic finding aid is available, the Uniform Resource Locator (URL) will be coded in subfield $u (see fig. 17). As DACS 4.6 explains, however, "[because] some MARC systems may not yet have implemented $u in the 555 field," the MARC field 856 can be used for the electronic link. In addition, the AWM, and several other audiovisual archives, have begun to incorporate item-level audio files into their electronic finding aids (see appendix 2).

Catalogers of ethnographic collections have a rich array of MARC note fields from which to choose. AACR 26.7B tells us the order of notes is not random, but where AACR2 note order most significantly diverges from DACS archival practice is in the placement of the summary note (MARC field 520). An archive or library with archival collections will have to determine what practice will best serve its patrons, based on such factors as patron discovery expectations and search patterns, technical limitations (for example, OPAC notes order display), and documentary resources (for example, whether a finding aid has been or will be made).

ACCESS POINTS

Main Entry

Both AACR2 21.25 and DACS 2.6 (previously APPM 21.6.) consider the creator or collector to be the main entry, in the case of field collections (see fig. 7). Where there is more than one collector, a cataloger will make the necessary added entry headings.

Added Entries

While DACS focuses on the creator of the collection or the individual or corporate entities, AACR2 provides a broader scope for added entries for music audio and visual recordings.

According to AACR2, we may also create personal name and corporate body added entries for performers, videographers, and other assistants. A Library of Congress Rule Interpretation, LCRI 21.29D, explicitly tells us to make an added entry for all named performers, except for those whose performance is limited to a small number of works in the collection. Because collection size and scope vary greatly, the number of performers or participants in the events captured in a series of audiovisual recordings also varies. Cataloging decisions will necessarily reflect both the unique characteristics of a collection and simple practical considerations.

SUBJECT ACCESS AND REFERENCE SOURCES

The scope of subject content in our collections—including genre, geographic location, culture, language, and medium of performance—is vast. Fortunately, many useful reference works are available to aid in providing accurate subject access for each of these components, and most are available online. To help determine ethnic group and geographic location, one can turn to *Outline of World Cultures* and the Human Relations Area Files online entries (eHRAF World Cultures).[41] *Oxford Music Online* and the *Garland Encyclopedia of World Music* are indispensible for exploring genre and cultural context.[42] *Ethnologue: Languages of the World* and the Voegelins' *Classification and Index of the World's Languages* are excellent sources for language information, although the former is easier to use.[43] *The New Grove Dictionary of Musical Instruments* and *A Survey of Musical Instruments* have extensive entries for musical instruments and cultural context.[44]

While many of the ethnographic collections at the ATM and AWM are musical recordings, our archives also include spoken-word materials (for example, interviews, language elicitation, and lectures). The emphasis here will be on guidelines and collections with music content.[45]

The principal *Subject Heading Manual* (SHM) instruction sheet for ethnographic music collections is "Music of Ethnic, National, and Religious Groups," H 1917.[46] Its instructions provide a clear and systematic approach for the creation of subject headings, and have greatly improved subject access to non-Western music materials. The sheet covers five heading categories and provides examples of appropriate subdivisions. The categories are: ethnic or national group; music of individual religious groups; genre, type or style of music; place and language; and musical instruments. The examples cover the gamut of subject matter for collections with music content (see fig. 18).

A few specific points merit mention. Under genre, type, or style of music (H 1917 2.c.(1)), an important note has been added regarding the use of the term "Folk music." The term is fairly well understood for music from the United States, but its meaning and use are not universal. Furthermore, some cultures do not differentiate among folk music, art music, and popular music. A note for the revised rule states "Folk music" should no longer be used for cultures where the distinctions among these categories or types are not made. In these cases the "general term 'Music' is used."[47]

LC's description of "Music" as a general term helps illustrate an unresolved example of Western art music bias in LCSH. If "Music" is a general term, the inclusion of "Classical music" and "Art music" as cross-references to the heading "Music" is inaccurate, because they are not

650 #0 $a Dan (African people) $z Côte d'Ivoire $v Music.
650 #0 $a Bagpipe music $z Cape Breton Island (N.S.)
650 #0 $a Dansi (Music)
650 #0 $a Children's songs, Tibetan.
650 #0 $s Musical instruments $z Australia.

Figure 18. A sample of the types of subject headings covered in SHM H 1917.

hierarchically synonymous with music. The terms are similar to the terms "Folk music" or "Popular music"—subsets in the general and broader world of music. Furthermore, many of our archives' non-Western music collections *do* include a culturally differentiated mix of popular, folk, and classical music. We need to be able to provide the same level of specificity to "classical music" from around the world as we do to other narrower types.

Although inconsistencies linger in LCSH, the establishment of the Subject Authority Cooperative Program (SACO) in 1992 has been a great boon to catalogers of non-Western music collections.[48] Those who work with these materials may contribute new headings to supplement older ones. With the ever-increasing availability of terms for ethnographic music collections, it is also important not to assume narrower genres terms are missing from LCSH. As Terry Simpkins has noted, "before immediately resigning oneself to a general heading such as 'Popular music—Algeria,' catalogers should check to see if an established narrower term . . . is more appropriate."[49]

The range of MARC coding options for subject headings has been helpful over the years, particularly before SACO was established. Historically, both the ATM and the AWM have used MARC field 650, with a blank first indicator and a second indicator of "4," for local headings based on LCSH, and the ATM has used MARC field 690 to include Human Relations Area File (HRAF) numeric codes.[50] Today, we no longer create local headings. When a term is needed for more than one item or collection, and it has not been established in LCSH, the ATM proposes a new heading through SACO. The two archives also anticipate using the MARC 655 field with an expanded list of genre/form headings after the work of the Music Library Association's Bibliographic Control Committee Genre/Form Task Force is completed.[51]

SUMMARY

The SACO program, the development of the SHM H 1917 instruction sheet, and the MLA genre/form project have effectively responded to the need for more comprehensive subject headings for audiovisual collections with ethnographic content to improve collection access. Individual archives have also taken the lead in providing access to item-level description and audio content for their collections by creating electronic finding aids using the EAD standard.

For many years, audiovisual archives have adapted content standards for descriptive cataloging, from AACR2 to APPM, and have developed hybrid approaches for cataloging ethnographic collections at the collection level. After MARC format integration and the advent of MARC21 in the late 1990s, options for content display and hybridized description increased.

More recently, with some audiovisual archives turning to DACS as their foundation, a wider variation in description is beginning to emerge, as illustrated by the ATM and AWM examples.

For audiovisual archives still anchored in AACR2, the anticipated transition to Resource Description and Access (RDA) offers an opportunity to reexamine cataloging practices. We need to steer back toward standardization and away from continual adaptation, and with the advent of RDA, now is an ideal time to support collaborative efforts that promote supplementing descriptive standards to include archival audiovisual holdings.[52]

APPENDIX 1

COLLECTION SUMMARY
(condensed for publication)

Indiana University, Archives of Traditional Music

Collector/depositor: _____

Address: _____

Phone: _____ Email: _____

Date collection received: _____ Received by: _____

Date contract signed: _____ Option: _____

Provenance (if not collector): _____

Other contributor(s) (indicate role): _____

Materials in Collection:
  # of reels: _____ size: _____ feet: _____ ips: _____ track configuration: _____
  # of cassettes: _____ 60-min.: _____ 90-min.: _____ other: _____
  # discs: _____ 7": _____ 10": _____ 12": _____ 16": _____ other: _____
  # of cylinders: _____ 4: _____ 6: _____ concert: _____ other: _____
  # of videotapes: _____ b&w: _____ color: _____ beta: _____ vhs: _____ format: _____ soundtrack: _____
  # of digital rec.: _____ format: _____ byte size: _____ file type: _____ sampling rate: _____
  Duration: _____ Original format (if all copies): _____ Copy generation: _____
  Which recordings are originals?: _____ Which recordings are copies?: _____

Date/Location of Recordings:
  Date(s): _____ Countries: _____
  Province/State(s): _____ City/Town(s): _____
  Culture group(s): _____

Content of recordings (check all that apply):

Musical performances	Interview	Drama
Linguistic information	Narratives, stories	Biographical information
Historical information	Ethnological information	Festival
Ritual	Instructional materials	Concert

Other (describe):

Languages of recordings, documents, titles:

Performers/Informants:

Genre(s):
Primary research topics:
Summary:

Written documentation? yes / no   Length and type:
Content of written documentation:
Additional Information (related publications, general background information, definitions of terminology, etc.):

APPENDIX 2

Example of an EAD finding aid with links to audio files and documentation

Archive of World Music, Eda Kuhn Loeb Music Library, Harvard College Library

Boulton, Laura, 1899-1980. Collection of Byzantine and Orthodox Musics: Guide.
(condensed excerpt for publication)

Descriptive Summary
  Repository: Archive of World Music, Eda Kuhn Loeb Music Library, Harvard College Library
  Creator: Boulton, Laura, 1899-1980
  Title: Collection of Byzantine and Orthodox Musics
  Location: Archive of World Music
  Call No.: AWM 15000-15067
  Quantity: Sound recordings (351 reels, 12 discs) and accompanying materials (4 linear feet, 9 file boxes)

Abstract: Recordings collected by ethnomusicologist Laura Boulton between 1951 and 1969 primarily in Greece, Yugoslavia, Ethiopia, and various other countries. It consists primarily of Byzantine and other Orthodox Eastern church music and services from the liturgical cycles; it also contains folk and classical music, some of a religious nature, and miscellaneous commercial recordings and books.

Acquisition Information:
The Laura Boulton Collection of Byzantine and Orthodox Musics was given to the Archive of World Music by the Laura Boulton Foundation in 1994.

Access Restrictions:
Unrestricted

Scope and Content
The Collection represents Laura Boulton's field work and research throughout the Eastern Orthodox world between 1953 and 1969. It comprises reel-to-reel tapes and their accompanying logbooks, hand and typewritten notes, commercially issued LP's, published books, and ancillary materials such as essays, journal offprints, pamphlets, correspondence, and miscellaneous written items…

Historical Note
The music collector Laura Boulton, or musical anthropologist, as she was known in the early days of her fieldwork, recorded some 30,000 musical examples in the course of her 81 years. During a career which took her from hidden corners of the globe to urban centers alike, from royal palaces to tribal huts, she embarked on expedition after expedition at a time when such journeys were considered exotic, dangerous, and beyond the reach of the average traveler….

Inventory [Excerpt, showing links to audio excerpts and documentation]
- **AWM 15003 (9 reels)** Byzantine hymns and liturgies recorded in a monastery on Patmos, 1960.
    - **Reel 1** [awm rl 15003 (1)] Matins for Sunday after the Elevation of the Holy Cross. Logbook (Part I, p. 1-10)
    - **Reel 2** [awm rl 15003 (2)] Continues Matins, begins Divine Liturgy. Logbook (Part I, p. 11-14)
    - **Reel 3** [awm rl 15003 (3)] Continues Divine Liturgy. Logbook (Part I, p. 15-18)
    - **Reel 4** [awm rl 15003 (4)] Continues and concludes Divine Liturgy. Logbook (Part I, p. 18-24)
    - **Reel 5** [awm rl 15003 (5)] Great Vespers. Logbook (Part I, p. 24-27)
    - **Reel 6** [awm rl 15003 (6)] Continues and concludes Great Vespers, speech by Abbot Jeremiah. Logbook (Part I, p. 27-29)
    - **Reel 7** [awm rl 15003 (7)] (= LB's 15) Vespers. Logbook (Part II, p. 1)
    - **Reel 8** [awm rl 15003 (8)] (= LB's 16) Great Doxology from Divine Liturgy, portions of Holy Week and Easter Services. Logbook (Part II, p. 2)

NOTES

[1] Mary Russell, "Ethnic Field Recordings on OCLC," *Music OCLC Users' Group Newsletter*, no. 25 (1985): 3–6; Mary Russell Bucknum, "Cataloging Field Recordings of American Indian Languages," *Cataloging & Classification Quarterly* 17, no. 1–2 (1993): 15–27.

[2] "MARC 21 Format for Bibliographic Data," last modified 21 September 2010, http://www.loc.gov/marc/bibliographic/ecbdhome.html; "OCLC Connexion," accessed 14 January 2011, http://www.oclc.org/connexion.

[3] For this article, I use the American Folklife Center's definition of an ethnographic field collection: "An ethnographic field collection is a multi-format, unpublished group of materials gathered and organized by an anthropologist, folklorist, ethnomusicologist, or other cultural researcher to document human life and traditions. . . . An ethnographic field collection may bring together materials from a wide range of formats, including sound recordings, drawings, photographs, field notes, and correspondence." Website of the American Folklife Center, last modified 29 October 2010, http://www.loc.gov/folklife/ethno.html.

[4] "The Archives of Traditional Music began in 1948. Archives holdings document the history of ethnographic sound recording, from wax cylinders made during museum expeditions in the 1890s to recent commercial releases on compact disc. The core of the collection consists of some 2,500 field collections . . . collected by anthropologists, linguists, ethnomusicologists, and folklorists throughout the world." Website of the Archives of Traditional Music, Indiana University, last modified 13 January 2011, http://www.indiana.edu/~libarchm. "The Archive of World Music, a collection of the Loeb Music Library, was established in 1976 by Professor John Ward and in 1992 . . . moved to the Loeb Music Library to become one of its special collections. It is devoted to the acquisition of archival field recordings of musics world-wide as well as to commercial sound recordings, videos, and DVDs of ethnomusicological interest." Website of the Archive of World Music Collection, Loeb Music Library, Harvard University, last modified 5 April 2010, http://hcl.harvard.edu/libraries/loebmusic/collections/archive.cfm.

[5] Society of American Archivists, *Describing Archives: A Content Standard* (Chicago: Society of American Archivists, 2007). Hereinafter "DACS."

[6] The "statement of principle forms the basis for the rules in this standard. . . . These principles examine the nature of archival materials and their context, and reflect how those aspects are made apparent in description." DACS, xi.

[7] Joint Steering Committee for the Revision of AACR, *Anglo-American Cataloguing Rules*, 2nd ed., 2002 rev. (Chicago: American Library Association, 2002).

[8] The Society of American Archivists' new edition of the Archival Fundamentals Series provides a foundation for archival theory and practice. For general information, see http://www2.archivists.org/glossary/preface. In particular, see Frederic Miller, *Arranging and Describing Archives and Manuscripts* (Chicago: Society of American Archivists, 1990).

[9] Alan Ward, *A Manual of Sound Archive Administration* (Aldershot, Eng.: Gower Publishing, 1990). This is an excellent, though somewhat dated, resource. Topics include a sound archive's mission, acquisition procedures, collection processing, and audio preservation.

[10] Catherine Hiebert Kerst, "Providing Access to Multi-Format Ethnographic Field Documentation: Archival Practice in the American Folklife Center," *Folklore Forum* 35, no. 1/2 (2004): 29–34, http://hdl.handle.net/2022/2449. Her explanation of the significance of finding aids and their creation during the accessioning process is particularly helpful.

[11] As Smiraglia aptly notes, "Adherence to the principles of provenance and original order . . . will dictate the way in which the materials will be preserved and described." Richard P. Smiraglia, "Describing Archival Music Collections," in *Describing Music Materials: A Manual for Descriptive Cataloging of Printed and Recorded Music, Music Videos, and Archival Music Collections for Use with AACR2 and APPM*, 3rd ed. (Lake Crystal, Minn.: Soldier Creek Press, 1997), 12.

[12] The collection summary form also includes areas for describing geographic location, culture group, names of participants, etc. (see appendix 1).

[13] For example, if the collector is deceased, the designated collection depositor may have enough contextual information to complete the Archives' forms.

[14] Alan Ward offers the following definition: "[T]he term documentation, when applied to sound recordings, is understood to comprise all available information which purports to identify or make more fully comprehensible the audio event(s) captured on one or more sound recordings." Ward, *Manual of Sound Archive Administration*, 244.

[15] Russell, "Ethnic Field Recordings," 6.

[16] For example, ethnomusicologists describe their discipline's symbiotic relationship with archives and the need for archival documentation in their current fieldwork handbook. Written twenty years after Bucknam's article, the first chapter mirrors Bucknum's experience: "Accompanying documentation is as important as the recording itself, since the nature and content of recordings are not always self-evident. A recording without documentation cannot be cataloged by an archivist or effectively utilized by any future researcher." Society for Ethnomusicology, *A Manual for Documentation, Fieldwork, and Preservation for Ethnomusicologists*, 2nd ed. (Bloomington, Ind.: Society for Ethnomusicology, 2001), 5.

[17] "UCLA Film & Television Archive Cataloging Procedure Manual—Voyager Cataloging procedure manual," last modified 18 November 2010, http://old.cinema.ucla.edu/CPM%20Voyager/CPMV34A.html.

[18] Indicated in the MARC record by code "c" in the Bibliographic Level (Leader/07).

[19] For an excellent discussion of this topic, see David H. Thomas, *Archival Information Processing for Sound Recordings: The Design of a Database for the Rodgers & Hammerstein Archives of Recorded Sound* (Canton, Mass.: Music Library Association, 1992). Thomas discusses the need for item-level detail for archival sound collections and provides a comprehensive description of the database used at the Rogers & Hammerstein Archives for this purpose.

[20] AACR2 0.1.

[21] Because the ATM began cataloging ethnographic collections in 1983 before MARC21 format integration was implemented, the choice of the now obsolete Archival and Manuscripts Control (AMC) format would have precluded use of the MARC sound recording or projected medium formats.

[22] Association for Recorded Sound Collections, *Associated Audio Archives, Rules for Archival Cataloging of Sound Recordings* (Albuquerque, N.M.: ARSC, 1995). This useful resource aids catalogers in providing physical descriptions of sound recording formats not covered in AACR2 and supplies additional physical details appropriate to the notes area. Its focus, however, is on cataloging commercial recordings in an archival context, rather than on cataloging unprocessed, unpublished items or collections.

[23] Wendy White-Hensen and the Library of Congress AMIM Revision Committee, *Archival Moving Image Materials: A Cataloging Manual*, 2nd ed. (Washington, D.C.: Library of Congress, Cataloging Distribution Service, 2000). Since, as the AMIM introduction states, "[it] emphasizes the tracing of the

history of works and their relationships to other works," the focus is on iterations of a commercial work, rather than unpublished collections. Nevertheless, appendix C includes an excellent outline of archival fields catalogers may consider using in collection-level records.

[24] Steven L. Hensen, *Archives, Personal Papers, and Manuscripts: A Cataloging Manual for Archival Repositories, Historical Societies, and Manuscript Libraries*, 2nd ed. (Chicago: Society of American Archivists, 1989).

[25] Verna Urbanski, *Cataloging Unpublished Nonprint Materials: A Manual of Suggestions, Comments, and Examples* (Lake Crystal, Minn.: Soldier Creek Press, 1992). Although Urbanski states the book "is not intended for material entering an archival or special collection" (p. v), it, too, has been a useful resource. Its focus is on item-level cataloging, and despite the disclaimer, some examples represent ethnographic content and spoken-word collections.

[26] DACS, xiii–xiv. DACS refers readers to cataloging manuals from AMIM and the International Association of Sound and Audiovisual Archives for format-specific cataloging information.

[27] David H. Thomas, "Cataloging Sound Recordings Using Archival Methods," *Cataloging and Classification Quarterly* 11, nos. 3–4 (1990): 193–212. Thomas prescribes that we blend aspects of both bibliographic and archival description methods to meet the needs of varied users. Though dated, his theoretical discussion of bibliographic and archival description and the use of MARC fields for archival sound collections are still applicable.

[28] Smiraglia, *Describing Music Materials*. Smiraglia's work, though dated in its use of APPM (versus DACS), is extremely useful for its focus on archival processes and principles. Smiraglia also demonstrates AACR2 and APPM integration with his use of a performer note (MARC field 511). His audio examples are for broadcast collections, including the example from Thomas's article. Despite various supplemental resources, there is no uniformly accepted standard for cataloging archival audio and visual collections. An ARSC cataloging subcommittee recently synthesized the dilemma: "While DACS addresses the unique characteristics of archival materials in general and reflects archival principles of arrangement and description that are accepted throughout the United States, it does not attempt to include rules needed to describe sound recordings and other non-textual materials. The Anglo-American Cataloging Rules . . . are grounded in a bibliographic rather than an archival approach to description." "DACS for Archival Sound Recordings," accessed 14 January 2011, http://arsc-aaa.invisionzone.com/forums/index.php?showtopic =480.

[29] See Sarah Adams, "EAD for International Music: Digital Access to Archival Collections," unpublished paper presented at the annual meeting for the International Association of Music Libraries, Tallinn, Estonia, 2003. (Available from the author.)

[30] For the purposes of this article, it will be assumed that a field collection is unpublished. The use of the phrase here is meant to emphasize that such collections are not commercial materials, although selected items from a field collection may eventually be published. I will use the terms "noncommercial," "unpublished," and "unprocessed" interchangeably, again with the understanding that an ethnographic field collection, as defined earlier, is a specific type of unpublished group of materials.

[31] This information will be coded as a specific format or as mixed material in the MARC fixed field Type of Record (Leader/06). Appropriate Type of Record coding in the context of this article would be "g" for projected medium, "i" for nonmusical sound recording, "j" for musical sound recording, and "p" for mixed material.

[32] "Dance Heritage Coalition, Cataloging Moving Image Materials," accessed 14 January 2011, http://www.danceheritage.org/cataloguing/title.html.

[33] Bucknam, "Cataloging Field Recordings," 18.

[34] Sound Directions Metadata Team, "Sound Directions Interim Phase: Data Elements Useful for Discovery, Navigation, and Interpretation," unpublished internal report prepared for the NEH, Bloomington, Indiana, 5 March 2007. The Metadata Team found the collector's name, ethnic group, language or dialect, and genre to be the most frequently used terms for patron discovery. These were followed closely by date, geographic area, and instrument name.

[35] Figure 3 taken from "Dance Heritage Coalition, Cataloging Moving Image Materials," http://www.danceheritage.org/cataloguing/title.html.

[36] AACR2 6.1F1 specifically states that we should include "collectors of field material . . . [among] those persons or bodies credited with a major role in creating the intellectual content of the sound recording." In his chapter on the description of sound recordings, Smiraglia similarly notes "[t]he rule requires, of course, the transcription of names of composers . . . and collectors of field recordings." Smiraglia, *Describing Music Materials*, 45.

[37] Subfield $f is used for inclusive dates, "the time period during which the entirety of the contents of the described materials were created"; subfield $g is used to indicate bulk dates, "the time period during which the bulk of the described materials were created." Website for the MARC 21 Format for Bibliographic Data, http://www.loc.gov/marc/bibliographic/bd245.html.

[38] As the description of MARC field 260 subfield $c states, "The date of creation may be recorded for unpublished items, and, if they are collectively controlled, only the $c is used." Website for the MARC 21 Format for Bibliographic Data, http://www.loc.gov/marc/bibliographic/bd260.html.

[39] See AACR2 6.0A1.

[40] Jay Weitz, *Music Coding and Tagging: MARC 21 Content Designation for Scores and Sound Recordings*, 2nd ed. (Belle Plaine, Minn.: Soldier Creek Press, 2001).

[41] George Peter Murdock, *Outline of World Cultures*, 6th rev. ed. (New Haven, Conn.: Human Relations Area Files, 1983) and online as "eHRAF World Cultures," accessed 14 January 2011, http://www.yale.edu/hraf/collections.htm.

[42] *Oxford Music Online*, accessed 18 January 2011, http://www.oxfordmusiconline.com; Bruno Nettl and Ruth M. Stone, *The Garland Encyclopedia of World Music* (New York: Garland, 1998–2002).

[43] M. Paul Lewis, ed., *Ethnologue: Languages of the World*, 16th ed. (Dallas, Tex.: SIL International, 2009), also available at http://www.ethnologue.com; C.F. Voegelin and F.M. Voegelin, *Classification and Index of the World's Languages* (New York: Elsevier, 1977).

[44] Stanley Sadie, ed., *The New Grove Dictionary of Musical Instruments* (New York: Grove's Dictionaries of Music, 1997); Sibyl Marcuse, *Musical Instruments: A Comprehensive Dictionary* (New York: Norton, 1975).

[45] For ethnographic collections with language materials, see Bucknam, "Cataloging Field Recordings."

[46] Library of Congress, *Subject Headings Manual* (Washington, D.C.: Cataloging Distributions Service, 2008–). Hereinafter "SHM."

[47] SHM, H 1917, 3.

[48] Website of the Subject Authority cooperative Program, accessed 18 January 2011, http://www.loc.gov/catdir/pcc/saco. In 2010, the SACO Music Funnel Project was created, and Michael Colby

is the current coordinator. For more information, see http://www.loc.gov/catdir/pcc/saco/Music_Funnel.html.

[49] Terry Simpkins, "Cataloging Popular Music Recordings," *Cataloging & Classification Quarterly* 31, no. 2 (2001): 29.

[50] For example, "FJ22" is the code for the Nuer of southern Sudan and western Ethiopia.

[51] The MLA-BCC Task Force's current review of genre/form and medium-of-performance lists from various groups and its collaboration with the Library of Congress will undoubtedly be of great benefit to catalogers of ethnographic collections. For more information, see http://musiclibraryassoc.org/about.aspx?id=307. Furthermore, in a 23 May 2011 email exchange, Beth Iseminger, chair of the MLA-BCC Task Force, said the group will be addressing the issue of Western music bias and anticipates adding narrower terms to the term "Music."

[52] "The goal of the DACS for Archival Sound Recordings subcommittee is to supplement DACS with guidelines for describing the content and physical and administrative features of sound recordings while adhering to accepted archival descriptive practice." For more information, see http://arsc-aaa.invisionzone.com/forums/index.php?showtopic=480.

SQUARE PEGS IN ROUND HOLES

Adapting Cataloging Metadata Standards for Use with Digital Media Files

Peter H. Lisius

Abstract: The author examines two current digital music applications—iTunes and Windows Media Player—and the feasibility of combining their access capabilities with both what is currently prescribed under *Anglo-American Cataloguing Rules*, second edition (AACR2), and what will be prescribed under *Resource Description & Access* (RDA). The author then evaluates how these files appear when transferred to digital media players, specifically the iPod Nano and Sony Walkman. Technological limitations make replicating standards-compliant access on both digital music applications and digital music players very difficult—and at times impossible.

INTRODUCTION AND BACKGROUND

In order to meet student listening needs, libraries are increasingly offering digital audio services, supplementing the more traditional means of checking out physical recordings for limited personal use. For several reasons, this evolution has the potential to create unique challenges for music catalogers providing controlled access points for works. First, music catalogers have always striven for consistency in creating access points for musical works. As will be seen in this article, technological limitations make replicating this access on both digital music applications and digital music players very difficult—and at times impossible. Second, the very technologies discussed in this article will either significantly evolve or become obsolete in coming years. Issues surrounding electronic access to musical works will continue in libraries, and music will continue to be cataloged, regardless of either changing technologies or cataloging codes. It is therefore both timely and relevant to see the extent to which, however limited, digital music applications and players can work in conjunction with cataloging rules and guidelines.

I will examine two digital music applications—iTunes and Windows Media Player[1]—and the feasibility of using their metadata capabilities to store and access cataloging created under the *Anglo-American Cataloging Rules*, second edition (AACR2),[2] and, to a much more limited extent, *Resource Description & Access* (RDA).[3] I will then consider how the metadata for audio files created with these applications is displayed and accessed when the files are transferred to digital media players, specifically the Apple iPod Nano (used with iTunes) and the Sony Walkman MP3 player (used with Windows Media Player).

METHODOLOGY

I first selected a group of sound recordings of standard works performed by well-known artists that would probably be held in a large number of music or performing arts collections of various types. To create a diverse sample, I selected eight recordings representing several genres, including opera, choral music, solo vocal music, orchestral music, musical theater, and jazz: Verdi's *La Traviata*, performed by various soloists with the Bayerisches Staatsoper orchestra and chorus, conducted by Carlos Kleiber;[4] Mozart's Requiem, performed by the Gächinger-Kantorei Stuttgart and the Bach-Collegium Stuttgart, conducted by Helmuth Rilling;[5] the choral album *Americana*, performed by the San Antonio Chamber Choir, conducted by Scott MacPherson;[6] *A Portrait*, featuring mezzo-soprano Cecilia Bartoli singing various opera excerpts and Italian art songs with orchestral accompaniment;[7] Shostakovich's Symphony no. 11, performed by the Concertgebouworkest of Amsterdam, conducted by Bernard Haitink;[8] Sibelius's Symphony no. 2 and *Finlandia* performed by the Cleveland Orchestra, conducted by Yoel Levi;[9] an original cast recording of *West Side Story* with *Symphonic Dances from West Side Story*, performed by the New York Philharmonic, conducted by Leonard Bernstein;[10] and *Giant Steps* by John Coltrane on tenor saxophone, with various assisting musicians.[11]

After recordings were selected, I extracted each recording to iTunes and Windows Media Player. iTunes was selected for its high popularity, and since the purpose of this study was to compare digital music platforms and players, Windows Media Player was selected for its relative ease of use and the fact that it comes preinstalled with most Windows operating systems. On the hard drive of my computer, I created separate folders for both iTunes and Windows Media Player so I could manipulate data on each platform separately without running the risk of creating conflicting data on the other platform. iTunes files were saved in the AAC format, and Windows Media Player files were saved in the WMA format. I then manipulated data in both iTunes and Windows Media Player in accordance with rules for heading construction and note presentation found in AACR2. Throughout this process, I took "before" and "after" screenshots to document my work. (These are presented as mockups in this article.) Once this was accomplished, I synced the iTunes files to an iPod Nano, and the Windows Media Player files to a Sony Walkman MP3 player. The Nano was selected because I needed a basic player that worked directly with iTunes. The Sony Walkman was selected to work with the other platform, Windows Media Player; and, like the iPod players, it is another popular brand that patrons might likely purchase. I then took digital photographs of the screens of both the Nano and Walkman to show how data was presented once it was transferred from the respective digital media platforms. (Apple Inc. denied a request to reproduce the photographs of the Nano, so mockups are used in figures 19–24 to illustrate the screen display.)

In June 2007, Christia Thomason and Leslie Kamtman of the University of North Carolina School of the Arts (UNCSA) used the iTunes software available at the time to construct access points for musical works based on AACR2 rules. They then repurposed iTunes fields to best accommodate the AACR2 access points. They documented their project in a PowerPoint presentation entitled "The iTunes Project, or, We're All Pod People Now."[12] I will provide a summary of their work and then present my own analysis with a separate discussion of each media platform—first iTunes, then Windows Media Player. In each of these sections, I will discuss how my data transferred to both the iPod Nano and Sony Walkman, respectively. Finally, I will compare and contrast strengths and weaknesses of both platforms and related digital media players, in terms of how controlled access points and performer data are represented.

ACCESS POINT CONSTRUCTION AND NOTE PRESENTATION

When attempting to replicate AACR2 access points in both iTunes and Windows Media Player, I found it necessary to utilize both rules for access points and also rules for constructing formulated notes for performers. This was principally due to way I purposed the fields. For example, the "album artist" field in both iTunes and Windows Media Player replicated controlled access points for a single principal performer. Since multiple performers cannot be assigned their own individual fields on either digital platform, constructing AACR2-style formulated notes representing all performers on the given recording was the most logical course of action. These formulated notes were constructed in the "artist" field in iTunes and the "contributing artist" field in Windows Media Player. Chapters 22 and 24 of AACR2 cover rules for constructing access points for personal and corporate names, respectively. In chapter 25, sections 25.25 through 25.35 cover the construction of music uniform titles. Section 6.7B6 covers the construction of notes relating to performers. Catalogers often rely on supplementary materials for guidance on constructing these notes, specifically Ralph Hartsock's *Notes for Music Catalogers*[13] and Richard Smiraglia's *Describing Music Materials*.[14]

I will go into more detail on how these specific AACR2 rules come into play as I analyze my results. When I constructed access points in both itunes and Windows Media Player, I did so based on AACR2 rules. My discussion of RDA in relation to the construction of access points will be mostly theoretical.

CHRISTIA THOMASON AND LESLIE KAMTMAN'S PROJECT

In February 2007, at the annual Music Library Association Meeting in Pittsburgh, Pennsylvania, Christia Thomason presented on a project originally authorized at UNCSA in November 2004. The intent was to "provide copyright education and a delivery system of digital sound and image files for student coursework."[15] In this project, sound files were placed on an iTunes media server so students, at their convenience, could complete listening assignments. iPods were also loaded with this same music for checkout from the reserves.

iTunes was used to extract the files from compact discs. Thomason mentioned three challenges: the poor quality of metadata imported into iTunes; the limitations of iTunes as a database; and the limitations of the iPod display.[16] As I will discuss later, some of these same problems manifested themselves in my project. In Thomason's study, metadata was supplied by Gracenote, a commercial service based on the community-sourced CDDB service. In 2011, Gracenote is still used to extract metadata for iTunes. (Windows Media Player uses *All Music Guide* as its source for imported data.) The Gracenote metadata continues to have limited usefulness within an AACR2 (and now RDA) environment because of its varying quality and the fact that much of it is created by users who would largely be unfamiliar with either AACR2 or RDA cataloging standards. Thomason provided examples of the metadata coming from Gracenote.

Thomason's slides then shifted to the limitations of iTunes, using a popular-music and a classical-music example. She noted that the set of "view options" provided by iTunes—including album, artist, genre, size, and time—worked very well for popular music. She also noted that unfortunately only three of the data fields from iTunes—name, artist, and album—displayed on the iPod player. She then observed how this became a problem for a typical classical piece as well, using the example of the Gloria from Palestrina's *Missa Aeterna Christie Munera*. The display on the iPod listed only "Gloria," so the student could not determine the composer of the work and the larger work from which it was derived. She also provided a Mozart example where the "artist" field in iTunes showed the track name and character names rather than the actual performers on the album. After describing these various inconsistencies, Thomason provided background on the iPod index display functionality existing in 2004 and how it came into play to perpetuate those same inconsistencies. Thomason observed that the metadata from Gracenote is nonstandard and of uneven quality and concluded that the "metadata, limitations of iTunes, the iPod display, and index function all combine to create an unacceptable browsing experience for the user."[17]

Thomason then provided a solution to turn the inconsistent metadata imported from Gracenote into something that would provide a more useful browsing and retrieval system for students. Because much of the indexing and displays were based on the "name" and "songs" fields, the solution at the UNCSA was to repurpose the "name" field in iTunes. For each track, this "new and improved name field" now contained the last name of the composer, uniform title for the piece, track or movement number, act/scene (if applicable), and track name from the item.[18] Mapping this data against the contents of a MARC bibliographic record, the source of the data was the field 100 main entry, the field 240 uniform title, and the field 505 contents note. The goal was to give the iPod user an experience similar to "browsing a sound recording."[19] Figure 1, a mockup of a slide from Thomason's presentation, shows the edits made for this purpose, using the Palestrina example described above.

Thomason then describes the changes made to other fields. The "album" field was repurposed for call number. The "genre" field, which had provided a generic genre (such as "classical"), was repurposed to contain the name of the faculty member using the piece for reserves. By browsing this field, students could see all of the recordings a particular professor had on reserve. If two professors were using the same piece, both names were included in the field.

ACCESS TO MUSICAL WORKS IN iTUNES

There are four different views through which a user can view data in iTunes: "list," "album list," "grid," and "cover flow." I did all my editing in the "list" view, and it is within this context discussion below takes place. There are currently thirty-nine fields that can be selected for view (see appendix 1). The default fields employed by iTunes in 2010 are identical to those Thomason worked with in 2004: "name," "time," "artist," "album," "genre," and "date added" (see fig. 2).

The only difference is that, in the most current version of iTunes, the "album" field is labeled "album by artist/year." In my project, I also selected the fields "album artist" and "grouping" for display. In iTunes, the field "album artist" is usually applied to artists performing on the entire album, while "artist" can be limited to selected tracks. "Grouping" can be used in conjunction with the default "title" field to group uniform titles of whole works, where the "title" field is then used for separate excerpts. I did not repurpose the entire "name" field as Thomason did to include composer, uniform title, track number, and selected track. Instead, I

The Palestrina example:

	Name	Artist	Album
1	Missa Aeterna Christe Munera: Kyrie	Schola Cantorum of Oxford & Oxford Camerata	Palestrina – Allegri: Choral Works
2	Gloria	Schola Cantorum of Oxford & Oxford Camerata	Palestrina – Allegri: Choral Works
3	Credo	Schola Cantorum of Oxford & Oxford Camerata	Palestrina – Allegri: Choral Works
4	Sanctus	Schola Cantorum of Oxford & Oxford Camerata	Palestrina – Allegri: Choral Works
5	Agnus Dei	Schola Cantorum of Oxford & Oxford Camerata	Palestrina – Allegri: Choral Works

Becomes:

Palestrina – Masses, book 5. Missa Aeterna Christi munera – 01 – Kyrie	Oxford Camerata ; Summerly	CD-4620
Palestrina – Masses, book 5. Missa Aeterna Christi munera – 02 – Gloria	Oxford Camerata ; Summerly	CD-4620
Palestrina – Masses, book 5. Missa Aeterna Christi munera – 03 – Credo	Oxford Camerata ; Summerly	CD-4620
Palestrina – Masses, book 5. Missa Aeterna Christi munera – 04 – Sanctus	Oxford Camerata ; Summerly	CD-4620
Palestrina – Masses, book 5. Missa Aeterna Christi munera – 05 – Agnus Dei	Oxford Camerata ; Summerly	CD-4620

Which displays as:

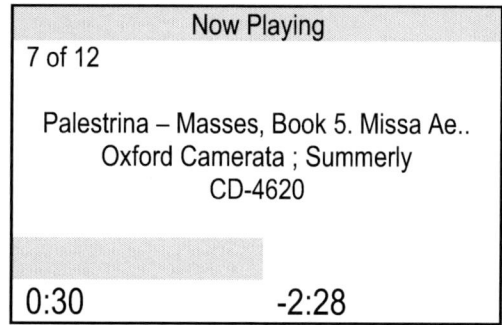

Figure 1. Palestrina example in iTunes (from Christia Thomason's 2007 presentation).

Name	Time	Artist	Album	Genre	Date Added
Giant Steps	4:47	John Coltrane	Giant Steps	Jazz	11/13/2010 2:06 PM
Cousin Mary	5:50	John Coltrane	Giant Steps	Jazz	11/13/2010 2:07 PM

Figure 2. Default fields used in iTunes.

tried to use fields provided by iTunes in a way that seemed logical to the construction of fields according to AACR2 rules.

Figure 2 shows how the metadata for the John Coltrane album *Giant Steps* appeared on the initial import from Gracenote into iTunes. I repurposed specific fields in the following ways.

First, I used the "album artist" field to provide the controlled access point for Coltrane himself (see fig. 3), following the form given in the national authority file (see fig. 4). I used the "album" and "name" field for album and track titles, respectively. The content of the "artist" field (see fig. 5) was constructed similarly to a MARC field 511 performer note in a bibliographic record (see fig. 6).

John Coltrane's *Giant Steps* represents a relatively simple repurposing of individual fields to replicate access found in a MARC bibliographic record. In iTunes, patrons can do relatively simple searches using the search box in the upper-right-hand corner to find specific tracks on which individuals perform. Five searching options are available: all (which allows the user to search all displayed fields by keyword), artist (allowing the user to search by both "artist" and "album artist"), album, composer, or song (which is the "name" field on the display). An implicit Boolean "and" is in effect when doing any of these searches.

In a MARC cataloging environment, controlled access points would also be given in MARC 700 fields for performers on each individual track (see fig. 7). I repurposed "album artist" for the main-entry access point for Coltrane, but the names of these other performers cannot be given controlled access individually in iTunes because they can only be recorded collectively in a single "artist" field.

A similar repurposing of fields was effected for the Concertgebouworkest recording of Shostakovich's Symphony no. 11, with the following differences (see fig. 8). The "composer" is given as a controlled access point. The "grouping" field is used to record the title in the form of a uniform title for the entire work constructed under AACR2 rules, while the "name" field is used for the individual movements (or "parts"). The successive placement of the "composer," "grouping," and "name" fields replicates the order in which a name-title main or added entry would be placed in a bibliographic record. The "album artist" listed here represents the controlled access point for the orchestra. I selected the orchestra, because under normal cataloging

Track #	Album Artist	Album by...	Composer	Grouping	Name
1 of 12	Coltrane, John, 1926-1967	Giant Steps			Giant Steps
2 of 12	Coltrane, John, 1926-1967	Giant Steps			Cousin Mary
3 of 12	Coltrane, John, 1926-1967	Giant Steps			Countdown
4 of 12	Coltrane, John, 1926-1967	Giant Steps			Spiral
5 of 12	Coltrane, John, 1926-1967	Giant Steps			Syeeda's Song Flute
6 of 12	Coltrane, John, 1926-1967	Giant Steps			Naima

Figure 3. Repurposed "album artist" field usage for *Giant Steps*.

```
100    1        Coltrane, John, ǂd 1926-1967. ǂ4 cmp ǂ4 prf
245    1    0   Giant steps ǂh [sound recording] / ǂc John Coltrane.
```

Figure 4. Authorized form of John Coltrane's name as found on a bibliographic record.

rules for sound recordings, the orchestra is generally assigned the main entry for a compilation of works by four or more composers; and, even though this album comprises a single work, it is for this reason that orchestra seemed like the best choice to be placed in the "album artist" field. Also, as was the case with the John Coltrane album, the "artist" field is used in the same manner as a 511 performer note field in a MARC bibliographic record (see fig. 8).

Name	Artist
Giant Steps	John Coltrane, tenor saxophone ; Tommy Flanagan, piano ; Paul Chambers, bass ; Art Taylor, drums
Cousin Mary	John Coltrane, tenor saxophone ; Tommy Flanagan, piano ; Paul Chambers, bass ; Art Taylor, drums
Countdown	John Coltrane, tenor saxophone ; Tommy Flanagan, piano ; Paul Chambers, bass ; Art Taylor, drums
Spiral	John Coltrane, tenor saxophone ; Tommy Flanagan, piano ; Paul Chambers, bass ; Art Taylor, drums
Syeeda's Song Flute	John Coltrane, tenor saxophone ; Tommy Flanagan, piano ; Paul Chambers, bass ; Art Taylor, drums
Naima	John Coltrane, tenor saxophone ; Wynton Kelly, piano ; Paul Chambers, bass ; Jimmy Cobb, drums
Mr. P.C.	John Coltrane, tenor saxophone ; Tommy Flanagan, piano ; Paul Chambers, bass ; Art Taylor, drums
Giant Steps [Alternate]	John Coltrane, tenor saxophone ; Cedar Walton, piano ; Paul Chambers, bass ; Lex Humphries, drums
Naima [Alternate]	John Coltrane, tenor saxophone ; Cedar Walton, piano ; Paul Chambers, bass ; Lex Humphries, drums
Cousin Mary [Alternate]	John Coltrane, tenor saxophone ; Tommy Flanagan, piano ; Paul Chambers, bass ; Art Taylor, drums
Countdown [Alternate]	John Coltrane, tenor saxophone ; Tommy Flanagan, piano ; Paul Chambers, bass ; Art Taylor, drums
Syeeda's Song Flute [Alternate]	John Coltrane, tenor saxophone ; Tommy Flanagan, piano ; Paul Chambers, bass ; Art Taylor, drums

Figure 5. Repurposed "artist" field for *Giant Steps*.

511 0   John Coltrane, tenor saxophone ; Tommy Flanagan, Cedar Walton, or Wynton Kelly, piano ; Paul Chambers, bass ; Jimmy Cobb, Lex Humphries, or Art Taylor, drums.

Figure 6. Performer note for *Giant Steps* in a MARC bibliographic record.

700 1   Flanagan, Tommy. ǂ4 prf
700 1   Walton, Cedar. ǂ4 prf
700 1   Kelly, Wynton. ǂ4 prf
700 1   Chambers, Paul, ǂd 1935-1969. ǂ4 prf
700 1   Cobb, Jimmy. ǂ4 prf
700 1   Humphries, Lex. ǂ4 prf
700 1   Taylor, Art. ǂ4 prf

Figure 7. Added entries as found on a bibliographic record for *Giant Steps*.

Composer	Grouping	Name	Album Artist	Artist
Shostakovich, Dmitriĭ Dmitrievich, 1906-1975	Symphonies, no. 11, op. 103, G minor	Palace Square	Concertgebouworkest	Royal Concertgebouw Orchestra ; Bernard Haitink, conductor
Shostakovich, Dmitriĭ Dmitrievich, 1906-1975	Symphonies, no. 11, op. 103, G minor	9 January	Concertgebouworkest	Royal Concertgebouw Orchestra ; Bernard Haitink, conductor
Shostakovich, Dmitriĭ Dmitrievich, 1906-1975	Symphonies, no. 11, op. 103, G minor	In memoriam	Concertgebouworkest	Royal Concertgebouw Orchestra ; Bernard Haitink, conductor
Shostakovich, Dmitriĭ Dmitrievich, 1906-1975	Symphonies, no. 11, op. 103, G minor	Tocsin	Concertgebouworkest	Royal Concertgebouw Orchestra ; Bernard Haitink, conductor

Figure 8. Repurposed "artist" field for Symphony no. 11 by Shostakovich.

As with the Coltrane album, additional controlled access points cannot be given for subsequent or additional performers. Since "Concertgebouorkest" was already used in the "album artist" field, Bernard Haitink's name is included in the "artist" field in direct order. Also, replication of metadata from a MARC bibliographic record in iTunes becomes problematic when dealing with art music. For example, I used the "composer," "grouping," and "name" fields to parse out data normally found in a name-title tracing on a bibliographic record. In the case of a single orchestra work on a recording, the composer would be given the main entry (see fig. 9).

When providing access to a complete work in a MARC bibliographic record constructed according to AACR2 rules, a name-title main or added entry would be given only for the complete work, not for individual tracks, which would be listed in a field 505 contents note (see fig. 10)—if at all. In order to provide access to individual tracks in a MARC bibliographic record in iTunes, however, it makes sense to treat each track as a distinct "work."

Similar issues arise when considering the recording of Verdi's *La Traviata*. As was the case with the Shostakovich work, the "composer," "grouping," and "name" fields are placed successively to represent how a name-title tracing would appear as either a main or added entry (see fig. 11). The "artist" field lists all the performers as they would appear in a MARC field 511 performer note (see fig. 12). Selecting the "album artist" for an opera is problematic, since performing groups and individuals on opera recordings are generally of equal prominence. For the purposes of my study and the opera *La Traviata*, I simply picked the first group listed on the sound recording itself to be placed in the "album artist" column, and listed it in the form found in the National Authority File (i.e., Bayerische Staatsoper München. Chor; see fig. 13).

For the original Broadway cast recording of *West Side Story* (see fig. 14), songs from the musical make up the first sixteen tracks. The *Symphonic Dances*, excerpts from the musical arranged by Bernstein for symphony orchestra, are provided as bonus tracks (tracks seventeen through twenty-five).

I used the "composer," "grouping," and "name" fields in the same way they were used for the *La Traviata* and Shostakovich Symphony no. 11 recordings. In an AACR2/MARC

100	1		Shostakovich, Dmitriĭ Dmitrievich, ǂd 1906-1975.
240	1	0	Symphonies, ǂn no. 11, op. 103, ǂr G minor
245	1	0	Symphony no. 11 ǂh [sound recording] / ǂc Dmitri Shostakovich.

Figure 9. Example of authorized composer main entry for Symphony no. 11 by Shostakovich.

| 505 | 0 | | Adagio : The palace square -- Allegro : 9 January -- Adagio : In memoriam -- Allegro non troppo : Tocsin. |

Figure 10. Contents note for Symphony no. 11 as found on a MARC bibliographic record.

Composer	Grouping	Name
Verdi, Giuseppe, 1813-1901	Traviata	Atto 1o. Preludio
Verdi, Giuseppe, 1813-1901	Traviata	Dell'invito trascorsa e gia l'ora
Verdi, Giuseppe, 1813-1901	Traviata	Libiamo ne lieti calici
Verdi, Giuseppe, 1813-1901	Traviata	Che e cio
Verdi, Giuseppe, 1813-1901	Traviata	Un dì felice, eterea
Verdi, Giuseppe, 1813-1901	Traviata	Ebben? Che diavol fate?
Verdi, Giuseppe, 1813-1901	Traviata	Si ridesta in ciel l'aurora
Verdi, Giuseppe, 1813-1901	Traviata	Ah, fors' è lui che l'anima
Verdi, Giuseppe, 1813-1901	Traviata	Sempre libera
Verdi, Giuseppe, 1813-1901	Traviata	De' miei bollenti spiriti

Figure 11. Repurposed "composer," "grouping," and "name" fields for *La Traviata*.

Artist
Ileana Cotrubas, soprano ; Plácido Domingo, tenor ; Sherril Milnes, baritone ; other soloists ; Bayerischer Staatsopernchor ; Ba
Ileana Cotrubas, soprano ; Plácido Domingo, tenor ; Sherril Milnes, baritone ; other soloists ; Bayerischer Staatsopernchor ; Ba
Ileana Cotrubas, soprano ; Plácido Domingo, tenor ; Sherril Milnes, baritone ; other soloists ; Bayerischer Staatsopernchor ; Ba
Ileana Cotrubas, soprano ; Plácido Domingo, tenor ; Sherril Milnes, baritone ; other soloists ; Bayerischer Staatsopernchor ; Ba
Ileana Cotrubas, soprano ; Plácido Domingo, tenor ; Sherril Milnes, baritone ; other soloists ; Bayerischer Staatsopernchor ; Ba

Figure 12. Repurposed "artist" field for *La Traviata*.

Album Artist
Bayerische Staatsoper München. Chor
Bayerische Staatsoper München. Chor
Bayerische Staatsoper München. Chor
Bayerische Staatsoper München. Chor

Figure 13. Repurposed "album artist" field for *La Traviata*.

Track #	Album by...	Composer	Grouping	Name
1 of 25	West Side story	Bernstein, Leonard, 1918-1990	West Side story	Prologue
2 of 25	West Side story	Bernstein, Leonard, 1918-1990	West Side story	Jet song
3 of 25	West Side story	Bernstein, Leonard, 1918-1990	West Side story	Something's coming
4 of 25	West Side story	Bernstein, Leonard, 1918-1990	West Side story	Dance at the gym
5 of 25	West Side story	Bernstein, Leonard, 1918-1990	West Side story	Maria
6 of 25	West Side story	Bernstein, Leonard, 1918-1990	West Side story	Tonight
7 of 25	West Side story	Bernstein, Leonard, 1918-1990	West Side story	America
8 of 25	West Side story	Bernstein, Leonard, 1918-1990	West Side story	Cool
9 of 25	West Side story	Bernstein, Leonard, 1918-1990	West Side story	One hand, one heart
10 of 25	West Side story	Bernstein, Leonard, 1918-1990	West Side story	Tonight (Quintet and chorus)
11 of 25	West Side story	Bernstein, Leonard, 1918-1990	West Side story	Rumble
12 of 25	West Side story	Bernstein, Leonard, 1918-1990	West Side story	I feel pretty
13 of 25	West Side story	Bernstein, Leonard, 1918-1990	West Side story	Somewhere (Ballet)
14 of 25	West Side story	Bernstein, Leonard, 1918-1990	West Side story	Gee, Officer Krupke
15 of 25	West Side story	Bernstein, Leonard, 1918-1990	West Side story	Boy like that
16 of 25	West Side story	Bernstein, Leonard, 1918-1990	West Side story	Finale
17 of 25	West Side story	Bernstein, Leonard, 1918-1990	Symphonic dances from West Side Story	Prologue
18 of 25	West Side story	Bernstein, Leonard, 1918-1990	Symphonic dances from West Side Story	Somewhere
19 of 25	West Side story	Bernstein, Leonard, 1918-1990	Symphonic dances from West Side Story	Scherzo
20 of 25	West Side story	Bernstein, Leonard, 1918-1990	Symphonic dances from West Side Story	Mambo
21 of 25	West Side story	Bernstein, Leonard, 1918-1990	Symphonic dances from West Side Story	Cha-cha
22 of 25	West Side story	Bernstein, Leonard, 1918-1990	Symphonic dances from West Side Story	Meeting scene
23 of 25	West Side story	Bernstein, Leonard, 1918-1990	Symphonic dances from West Side Story	Cool fugue
24 of 25	West Side story	Bernstein, Leonard, 1918-1990	Symphonic dances from West Side Story	Rumble
25 of 25	West Side story	Bernstein, Leonard, 1918-1990	Symphonic dances from West Side Story	Finale

Figure 14. Repurposed "album by artist/year," "composer," "grouping," and "name" fields for *West Side Story* and *Symphonic Dances*.

environment, when two works are contained on an item, the first work (in this case, the musical itself) is given the main entry and the second work (the *Symphonic Dances*) is given an added entry.

With the previous recordings, I had been able to select a single "album artist." This simply did not work with this recording. First, the orchestra used for the musical was unidentified, leaving only the vocalists, an unidentified orchestra, and a conductor, Max Goberman, who is not displayed prominently on the sound recording. *Symphonic Dances* is performed by the New York Philharmonic under the direction of Leonard Bernstein. To remain consistent in using a single term in the "album artist" field, I applied the generic term "Various artists," which of course would never be traced as a controlled access point in AACR2. The "artist" field, however, was again purposed to include all the artists performing in either the musical itself or the *Symphonic Dances* (see fig. 15).

The contents of *Americana* are typical of a recording of choral music: a mix of multiple works by various composers, traditional works with no composer attribution, and arrangements (see contents note in fig. 16). In an AACR2/MARC environment, these works are given as name-title added entries, and sometimes simply as title added entries. Works that were arranged from traditional hymns and songs, with no original composer attribution, are recorded in controlled 730 fields and uncontrolled 740 fields (see fig. 17).

In this bibliographic record, arrangers were not traced because of their large number (and relative obscurity). As with the ancillary contributors to the other sound recordings in my study, these arrangers could not be easily accommodated in iTunes. Therefore, all I did in the repurposing of the name field was add "arr." when appropriate and simply leave out composers for the traditional works with no attribution (see fig. 18).

Figure 18 also demonstrates that content of the "grouping" feature was a problem for individual works. When editing the "grouping" field for the previously discussed examples, I purposed it to include the title of the whole work, while the name field was used for the excerpt or part. My initial intent was to keep the individual works listed in the "grouping" field and to leave them out of the "name" field. This is not possible in version 10 of iTunes, because information must be input into the "name" field each time. The other option would have been to omit the title in the "grouping" field, but for other recordings of art music I had used the "grouping" feature, so in order to insure consistency I settled on the less-than-ideal option of placing the titles in both the "grouping" and "name" fields. The other fields, "album artist" and "artist," were treated the same way as in my other samples.

TRANSFERRING CONTENT TO THE iPOD NANO

After providing metadata in iTunes, I transferred the files to an iPod Nano. The current version of Nano[20] principally employs touch technology to navigate, browse, and select tracks. The central issue I encountered here was how the organizational features of iTunes sometimes did not transfer over to the Nano. Some of the features I made extensive use of on iTunes, including the "grouping" and "album artist," do not display on the Nano in the way I had initially intended them. Figure 19 shows the screen a user would see when first turning on the Nano. (Again,

Album Artist	Artist
Various artists	Carol Lawrence ; Larry Kert ; Chita Rivera ; Art Smith ; supporting soloists ; orchestra ; Max Goberman, conductor
Various artists	Carol Lawrence ; Larry Kert ; Chita Rivera ; Art Smith ; supporting soloists ; orchestra ; Max Goberman, conductor
Various artists	Carol Lawrence ; Larry Kert ; Chita Rivera ; Art Smith ; supporting soloists ; orchestra ; Max Goberman, conductor
Various artists	Carol Lawrence ; Larry Kert ; Chita Rivera ; Art Smith ; supporting soloists ; orchestra ; Max Goberman, conductor
Various artists	Carol Lawrence ; Larry Kert ; Chita Rivera ; Art Smith ; supporting soloists ; orchestra ; Max Goberman, conductor
Various artists	Carol Lawrence ; Larry Kert ; Chita Rivera ; Art Smith ; supporting soloists ; orchestra ; Max Goberman, conductor
Various artists	Carol Lawrence ; Larry Kert ; Chita Rivera ; Art Smith ; supporting soloists ; orchestra ; Max Goberman, conductor
Various artists	Carol Lawrence ; Larry Kert ; Chita Rivera ; Art Smith ; supporting soloists ; orchestra ; Max Goberman, conductor
Various artists	Carol Lawrence ; Larry Kert ; Chita Rivera ; Art Smith ; supporting soloists ; orchestra ; Max Goberman, conductor
Various artists	Carol Lawrence ; Larry Kert ; Chita Rivera ; Art Smith ; supporting soloists ; orchestra ; Max Goberman, conductor
Various artists	Carol Lawrence ; Larry Kert ; Chita Rivera ; Art Smith ; supporting soloists ; orchestra ; Max Goberman, conductor
Various artists	Carol Lawrence ; Larry Kert ; Chita Rivera ; Art Smith ; supporting soloists ; orchestra ; Max Goberman, conductor
Various artists	Carol Lawrence ; Larry Kert ; Chita Rivera ; Art Smith ; supporting soloists ; orchestra ; Max Goberman, conductor
Various artists	Carol Lawrence ; Larry Kert ; Chita Rivera ; Art Smith ; supporting soloists ; orchestra ; Max Goberman, conductor
Various artists	Carol Lawrence ; Larry Kert ; Chita Rivera ; Art Smith ; supporting soloists ; orchestra ; Max Goberman, conductor
Various artists	Carol Lawrence ; Larry Kert ; Chita Rivera ; Art Smith ; supporting soloists ; orchestra ; Max Goberman, conductor
Various artists	New York Philharmonic ; Leonard Bernstein, conductor
Various artists	New York Philharmonic ; Leonard Bernstein, conductor
Various artists	New York Philharmonic ; Leonard Bernstein, conductor
Various artists	New York Philharmonic ; Leonard Bernstein, conductor
Various artists	New York Philharmonic ; Leonard Bernstein, conductor
Various artists	New York Philharmonic ; Leonard Bernstein, conductor
Various artists	New York Philharmonic ; Leonard Bernstein, conductor
Various artists	New York Philharmonic ; Leonard Bernstein, conductor
Various artists	New York Philharmonic ; Leonard Bernstein, conductor

Figure 15. Repurposed "album artist" and "artist" fields for *West Side Story* and *Symphonic Dances*.

505   0   Shiloh ; I am the Rose of Sharon / William Billings -- Sixty-seventh psalm / Charles Ives -- Americana ; Alleluia / Randall Thompson -- I bought me a cat (David Short, Kay Sherill, soloists) ; Long time ago ; Ching-a-ring chaw / Aaron Copland -- The battle hymn of the Republic / arr. Peter Wilhousky -- Music from The sacred harp. Idumea : And am I born to die? ; Exhortation ; Lord, in the morning-- ; Wondrous love : What wondrous love is this! -- I dream of Jeannie / Stephen Foster ; arr. C Wills -- Camptown races / Stephen Foster ; arr. M. Hayes (Jennifer Whatley, Don Hill, soloists) -- Ride on, King Jesus / Spiritual ; arr. R. Shaw-A. Parker -- I couldn't hear nobody pray / Spiritual ; arr. H. Johnson (Mary Cowar, Angela Malek, Eric Schmidt) -- Soon-ah will be done / Spiritual ; arr. W. Dawson -- Encore : Hard times come again no more / Stephen Foster ; arr. Mark Keller.

Figure 16. Contents note for *Americana*.

because Apple Inc. denied my request to reproduce photographs of the Nano display, figures 19–24 are mockups.)

Using a finger to scroll over two screens will display two other organizational features I manipulated in iTunes: "songs" and "composers" (see fig. 20). The two organizational features on the iPod Nano that remained relatively unchanged from my initial intent for them on iTunes involved the "composers" and "artists" fields. For example, tapping the "composers" icon will display the list in figure 21. The first and third composers are from the *Americana* sound recording, and the names have been retained in the access-point construction style for which they were originally intended.

The "artists" feature remained relatively unchanged as well. Figure 22 shows the results of tapping the "artists" icon on the initial screen. The fields retain the information as I had intended. Unfortunately, the only way to display the "album artist" is to tap the "albums" icon on the last screen (see fig. 23). The "album artist" displays in gray beneath the album title.

The "grouping" feature is not implemented on the Nano. I had intended to use the feature to group larger "parts" of works so they would mimic the "whole" section of a "whole-part" uniform title. I could not find a feature on the Nano that maps it in this way. One can click on "songs" and see "artists" listed below them, but as becomes immediately obvious, the "grouping" feature where the larger work would be listed is non-existent on the Nano—it simply disappears (see fig. 24).

iTunes has limited capability for utilizing AACR2-style controlled access points, and these limits are also present in the iPod Nano. Also, the Nano did not always "scroll" the data to show it in its entirety.

ACCESS TO MUSICAL WORKS IN WINDOWS MEDIA PLAYER

As stated earlier, Windows Media Player imports metadata for recordings from *All Music Guide*. There are six default views currently available to users: "artist," "album," "songs," "genre,"

700	1	2	Billings, William, ǂd 1746-1800. ǂt Suffolk harmony. ǂp Shiloh.
700	1	2	Billings, William, ǂd 1746-1800. ǂt Singing master's assistant. ǂp I am the rose of Sharon.
700	1	2	Ives, Charles, ǂd 1874-1954. ǂt Psalm 67.
700	1	2	Thompson, Randall, ǂd 1899-1984. ǂt Americana.
700	1	2	Thompson, Randall, ǂd 1899-1984. ǂt Alleluia.
700	1	2	Copland, Aaron, ǂd 1900-1990. ǂt Old American songs, ǂn set 1. ǂp I bought me a cat; ǂo arr.
700	1	2	Copland, Aaron, ǂd 1900-1990. ǂt Old American songs, ǂn set 1. ǂp Long time ago; ǂo arr.
700	1	2	Copland, Aaron, ǂd 1900-1990. ǂt Old American songs, ǂn set 2. ǂp Ching-a-ring chaw; ǂo arr.
700	1	2	Foster, Stephen Collins, ǂd 1826-1864. ǂt Jeanie with the light brown hair; ǂo arr.
700	1	2	Foster, Stephen Collins, ǂd 1826-1864. ǂt Camptown races; ǂo arr.
700	1	2	Foster, Stephen Collins, ǂd 1826-1864. ǂt Hard times come again no more; ǂo arr.
730	0	2	Battle hymn of the republic (Song)
730	0	2	Sacred harp.
740	0	2	Idumea.
740	0	2	Exhortation.
740	0	2	Wondrous love.
740	0	2	Ride on, King Jesus.
740	0	2	I couldn't hear nobody pray.
740	0	2	Soon-ah will be done.

Figure 17. Controlled and uncontrolled access points on a MARC bibliographic record for the *Americana* recording.

"year," and "rating." "Recently added" is also an option to retrieve the most recently imported music. There are four other views available if desired: "contributing artist," "composer," "parental rating," "online stores," and "folders." Viewing a library by "songs" (see fig. 25) will display the most complete metadata for an album, and it is within this view I edited all my data. The fields available for use change with each view. The most comprehensive number of viewable fields are also found in the "songs" view (see appendix 1). Figure 25 illustrates an example of the default "songs" view.

Figure 26 shows the metadata for John Coltrane's *Giant Steps* as it was imported from All Music Guide.

Track #	Album by…	Composer	Grouping	Name
1 of 18	Americana	Billings, William, 1746-1800	Suffolk harmony	Shiloh
2 of 18	Americana	Billings, William, 1746-1800	Singing master's assistant	I am the rose of Sharon
3 of 18	Americana	Ives, Charles, 1874-1954	Psalm 67	Psalm 67
4 of 18	Americana	Thompson, Randall, 1899-1894	Americana	Americana
5 of 18	Americana	Thompson, Randall, 1899-1894	Alleluia	Alleluia
6 of 18	Americana	Copland, Aaron, 1900-1990	Old American songs, set 1	I bought me a cat; arr.
7 of 18	Americana	Copland, Aaron, 1900-1990	Old American songs, set 1	Long time ago; arr.
8 of 18	Americana	Copland, Aaron, 1900-1990	Old American songs, set 2	Ching-a-ring chaw; arr.
9 of 18	Americana		Battle hymn of the republic (Song)	Battle hymn of the Republic (Song)
10 of 18	Americana		Idumea	Idumea
11 of 18	Americana		Exhortation	Exhortation
12 of 18	Americana		Wondrous love	Wondrous love
13 of 18	Americana	Foster, Stephen Collins, 1826-1864	Jeanie with the light brown hair; arr.	Jeanie with the light brown hair; arr.
14 of 18	Americana	Foster, Stephen Collins, 1826-1864	Camptown races; arr.	Camptown races; arr.
15 of 18	Americana		Ride on, King Jesus	Ride on, King Jesus
16 of 18	Americana		I couldn't hear nobody pray	I couldn't hear nobody pray
17 of 18	Americana		Soon-ah will be done	Soon-ah will be done
18 of 18	Americana	Foster, Stephen Collins, 1826-1864	Hard times come again no more; arr.	Hard times come again no more; arr.

Figure 18. Repurposed "album by artist/year," "composer," "grouping," and "name" fields for *Americana*.

The metadata fields used in Windows Media Player are similar to those used in iTunes. In Windows Media Player, I repurposed several fields. (See appendix 2 for a chart mapping MARC data elements to fields used in Window Media Player.) I used the "album artist" field in the same way I used it in iTunes—to provide a controlled access point for the principal performer. The "title" field is analogous to the "name" field in iTunes, used for the titles of individual tracks. The "contributing artist" field is analogous to the "artist" field in iTunes, and I repurposed it in the same way by listing the performers as they would appear in a field 511 performer note. I also added the "conductor" field (which is not a separate option in iTunes), and removed the "rating," "genre," "release year," "size," and "parental rating" fields, so as not to

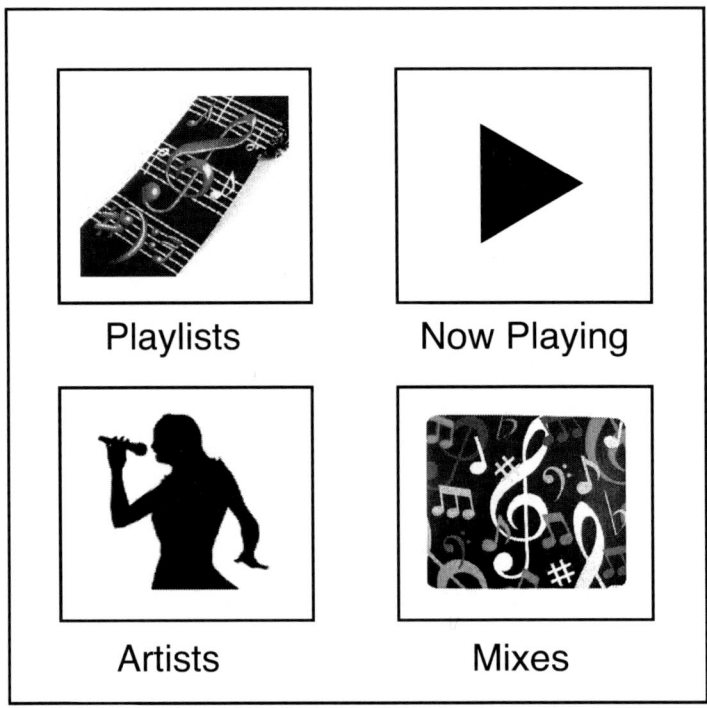

Figure 19. Opening screen on the iPod Nano (mockup).

confuse matters—the study focused on issues of name/work access. Figure 27 shows the edited metadata for *Giant Steps*. When trying to apply the " ; " punctuation convention used in the performer note in AACR2, Windows Media Player did not allow the semicolon to be preceded by a space. This is perhaps a minor detail, but iTunes did allow the preceding space.

I repurposed the "title" field in Windows Media Player to accommodate uniform titles as constructed per chapter 25 of AACR2. The "grouping" feature in iTunes does not exist in Windows Media Player, so I used the "title" field instead to record "whole-part" uniform title constructions for representative tracks and movements (see fig. 28). Figure 29 shows the use of the "conductor" field. Many of the issues manifesting themselves in iTunes were exactly the same in Windows Media Player. In the *West Side Story* example, the question of who to select as "album artist" was the same as in iTunes. Due to the lack of a single artist or performing group performing on each track, I employed the "various artists" option again (see fig. 30). For *La Traviata*, in the absence of a principal artist, I opted once again to place the chorus in the "album artist" column (see fig. 31).

Figure 20. Screen displaying "songs," "albums," "genres," and "composers" on the Nano (mockup).

In other cases, indexing was made easier in Windows Media Player by the lack of certain options. For example, I initially viewed the "grouping" feature in iTunes as a good way to employ the "wholes" of "whole-part" uniform title constructions, but this quickly fell apart when the data was transferred to the iPod Nano and the "grouping" field did not appear. Since this option does not exist in Windows Media Player, the dilemma of where to enter titles which would normally be the entire uniform title in an AACR2 does not exist—one simply enters both single and "whole-part" uniform titles in the "title" field (see fig. 32).

Windows Media Player and iTunes, however, are limited in some of the same ways. Arrangers cannot effectively be brought out on any either platform. And, of course, there is the problem of not being able to logically bring out controlled-access-point–style access to additional performers. As was the case with iTunes, in Windows Media Player I also attempted to provide access in fields that matched as closely as possible the analogous MARC fields. In doing so, however, providing controlled access points to all performers was simply not possible.

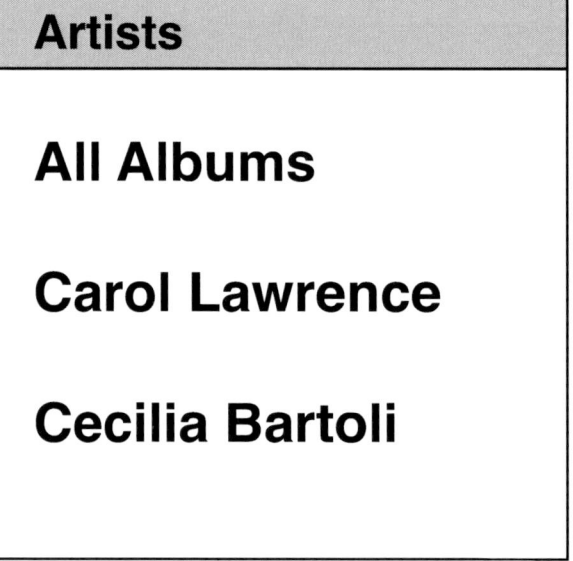

Figure 21. "Composers" display on the iPod Nano (mockup).

Figure 22. "Artists" display on the iPod Nano (mockup).

```
┌─────────────────────────┐
│ Artists                 │
├─────────────────────────┤
│                         │
│      All Songs          │
│      136 Songs          │
│                         │
│      Americana          │
│      San Antonio        │
│                         │
│      Giant Steps        │
│      Coltrane, John     │
│                         │
└─────────────────────────┘
```

Figure 23. "Albums" display on the iPod Nano (mockup).

```
┌─────────────────────────┐
│ Songs                   │
├─────────────────────────┤
│                         │
│   Dammi tu forza        │
│   Ileana Cotrubas       │
│                         │
│   Dance at the gym      │
│   Carol Lawrence        │
│                         │
│   De' miei bollenti     │
│   Ileana Cotrubas       │
│                         │
└─────────────────────────┘
```

Figure 24. "Songs" display on the iPod Nano (mockup).

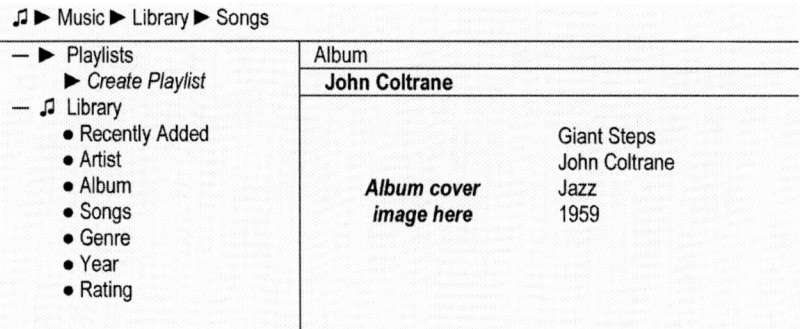

Figure 25. Default view "songs" highlighted in Windows Media Player.

Album			Title	Length	Rating	Contributing Artist	Composer	Size	Parental Rating
John Coltrane									
Album cover image here	Giant Steps John Coltrane Jazz 1959	1	Giant Steps	4:46	•••○○	John Coltrane	John Coltrane	3.3 MB	
		2	Cousin Mary	5:49	•••○○	John Coltrane	John Coltrane	4 MB	
		3	Countdown	2:25	•••○○	John Coltrane	John Coltrane	1.6 MB	
		4	Spiral	6:00	•••○○	John Coltrane	John Coltrane	4.1 MB	
		5	Syeeda's Song Flute	7:05	•••○○	John Coltrane	John Coltrane	4.9 MB	
		6	Naima	4:24	•••○○	John Coltrane	John Coltrane	3 MB	
		7	Mr. P.C.	7:02	•••○○	John Coltrane	John Coltrane	4.8 MB	
		8	Giant Steps [*][Alternate…	3:44	•••○○	John Coltrane	John Coltrane	2.5 MB	
		9	Naima [*][Alternate…	4:31	•••○○	John Coltrane	John Coltrane	3.1 MB	
		10	Cousin Mary [*][Alternate…	5:48	•••○○	John Coltrane	John Coltrane	4 MB	
		11	Countdown [*][Alternate…	4:35	•••○○	John Coltrane	John Coltrane	3.1 MB	
		12	Syeeda's Song Flute [*][Alternate…	7:03	•••○○	John Coltrane	John Coltrane	4.9 MB	

Figure 26. Example of metadata for *Giant Steps* after initial import. (The symbols in the "Rating" column appear as stars on the interface.)

Album			Title	Length	Contributing Artist	Composer
Coltrane, John, 1926-1967						
Album cover image here	Giant Steps Coltrane, John…	1	Giant Steps	4:46	John Coltrane, tenor saxophone; Tommy Flanagan, piano; Paul Chambers, bass…	Coltrane, John, 1926-1967
		2	Cousin Mary	5:49	John Coltrane, tenor saxophone; Tommy Flanagan, piano; Paul Chambers, bass…	Coltrane, John, 1926-1967
		3	Countdown	2:25	John Coltrane, tenor saxophone; Tommy Flanagan, piano; Paul Chambers, bass…	Coltrane, John, 1926-1967
		4	Spiral	6:00	John Coltrane, tenor saxophone; Tommy Flanagan, piano; Paul Chambers, bass…	Coltrane, John, 1926-1967
		5	Syeeda's Song Flute	7:05	John Coltrane, tenor saxophone; Tommy Flanagan, piano; Paul Chambers, bass…	Coltrane, John, 1926-1967
		6	Naima	4:24	John Coltrane, tenor saxophone; Wynton Kelly, piano; Paul Chambers, bass…	Coltrane, John, 1926-1967
		7	Mr. P.C.	7:02	John Coltrane, tenor saxophone; Tommy Flanagan, piano; Paul Chambers, bass…	Coltrane, John, 1926-1967
		8	Giant Steps [*][Alternate…	3:44	John Coltrane, tenor saxophone; Cedar Walton, piano; Paul Chambers, bass…	Coltrane, John, 1926-1967
		9	Naima [*][Alternate…	4:31	John Coltrane, tenor saxophone; Cedar Walton, piano; Paul Chambers, bass…	Coltrane, John, 1926-1967
		10	Cousin Mary [*][Alternate…	5:48	John Coltrane, tenor saxophone; Tommy Flanagan, piano; Paul Chambers, bass…	Coltrane, John, 1926-1967
		11	Countdown [*][Alternate…	4:35	John Coltrane, tenor saxophone; Tommy Flanagan, piano; Paul Chambers, bass…	Coltrane, John, 1926-1967
		12	Syeeda's Song Flute [*][Alternate…	7:03	John Coltrane, tenor saxophone; Tommy Flanagan, piano; Paul Chambers, bass…	Coltrane, John, 1926-1967

Figure 27. View of *Giant Steps* metadata after fields were repurposed.

Album		Title	Length	Contributing Artist	Composer
Concertgebouworkest					
Album cover image here	Shostakovich: S... Concertgebouw...	1 Symphonies, no. 11, op. 103, G minor. Palace square	15:53	Royal Concertgebouw Orchestra; Bernard Haitink, conductor	Shostakovich, Dmitriĭ Dmitrievich, 1906-1975
		2 Symphonies, no. 11, op. 103, G minor. 9 January	19:54	Royal Concertgebouw Orchestra; Bernard Haitink, conductor	Shostakovich, Dmitriĭ Dmitrievich, 1906-1975
		3 Symphonies, no. 11, op. 103, G minor. In memoriam	11:23	Royal Concertgebouw Orchestra; Bernard Haitink, conductor	Shostakovich, Dmitriĭ Dmitrievich, 1906-1975
		4 Symphonies, no. 11, op. 103, G minor. Tocsin	14:26	Royal Concertgebouw Orchestra; Bernard Haitink, conductor	Shostakovich, Dmitriĭ Dmitrievich, 1906-1975

Figure 28. Repurposed "album," "title," "contributing artist," and "composer" fields for Symphony no. 11 by Shostakovich.

Composer	Conductor
Shostakovich, Dmitriĭ Dmitrievich, 1906-1975	Haitink, Bernard, 1929-
Shostakovich, Dmitriĭ Dmitrievich, 1906-1975	Haitink, Bernard, 1929-
Shostakovich, Dmitriĭ Dmitrievich, 1906-1975	Haitink, Bernard, 1929-
Shostakovich, Dmitriĭ Dmitrievich, 1906-1975	Haitink, Bernard, 1929-

Figure 29. Repurposed "composer" and "conductor" fields for Symphony no. 11 by Shostakovich.

Album	
Various artists	
Album cover image here	West Side Story [Bonus... Various artists

Figure 30. "Album artist" display for *West Side Story*.

Album	
Bayerische Staatsoper München. Chor	
Album cover image here	Verdi: La Traviata Bayerische Staatsoper…

Figure 31. "Album artist" display for *La Traviata*.

	Title	Length	Contributing Artist	Composer
1	Suffolk harmony. Shiloh	2:01	San Antonio Chamber Choir; Scott MacPherson, conductor	Billings, William, 1746-1800
2	Singing master's assistant. I am the rose of Sharon	4:05	San Antonio Chamber Choir; Scott MacPherson, conductor	Billings, William, 1746-1800
3	Psalm 67	2:22	San Antonio Chamber Choir; Scott MacPherson, conductor	Ives, Charles, 1874-1954
4	Americana	17:03	San Antonio Chamber Choir; Scott MacPherson, conductor	Thompson, Randall, 1899-1984
5	Alleluia	5:15	San Antonio Chamber Choir; Scott MacPherson, conductor	Thompson, Randall, 1899-1984
6	Old American songs, set 1. I bought me a cat; arr.	2:15	San Antonio Chamber Choir; Scott MacPherson, conductor	Copland, Aaron, 1900-1990
7	Old American songs, set 1. Long time ago; arr.	3:21	San Antonio Chamber Choir; Scott MacPherson, conductor	Copland, Aaron, 1900-1990
8	Old American songs, set 2. Ching-a-ring chaw; arr.	1:55	San Antonio Chamber Choir; Scott MacPherson, conductor	Copland, Aaron, 1900-1990
9	Battle hymn of the republic (Song)	5:43	San Antonio Chamber Choir; Scott MacPherson, conductor	
10	Idumea	2:51	San Antonio Chamber Choir; Scott MacPherson, conductor	
11	Exhortation	1:39	San Antonio Chamber Choir; Scott MacPherson, conductor	
12	Wondrous love	2:27	San Antonio Chamber Choir; Scott MacPherson, conductor	
13	Jeanie with the light brown hair; arr.	3:13	San Antonio Chamber Choir; Scott MacPherson, conductor	Foster, Stephen Collins, 1826-1864
14	Camptown races; arr.	3:18	San Antonio Chamber Choir; Scott MacPherson, conductor	Foster, Stephen Collins, 1826-1864
15	Ride on, King Jesus	2:41	San Antonio Chamber Choir; Scott MacPherson, conductor	
16	I couldn't hear nobody pray	3:27	San Antonio Chamber Choir; Scott MacPherson, conductor	
17	Soon-ah will be done	3:37	San Antonio Chamber Choir; Scott MacPherson, conductor	
18	Hard times come again no more; arr.	1:53	San Antonio Chamber Choir; Scott MacPherson, conductor	Foster, Stephen Collins, 1826-1864

Figure 32. Repurposed "title," "contributing artist," and "composer" fields for *Americana*.

TRANSFERRING CONTENT TO THE SONY WALKMAN

In contrast to the iPod Nano, the Sony Walkman[21] does not employ touch technology—navigation is achieved by buttons located below the screen. Once one turns on the player, the home screen displays a series of icons. To play music, a user will select the two-eighth-note icon. Figure 33 illustrates the location of the buttons and the home screen. Tapping the two-eighth-note icon will display the list of options from which to select music (see fig. 34).

"All songs" displays all song titles, "album" displays all album titles (see fig. 35), and "artist" displays all names included in the "contributing artist" field of Windows Media Player (see fig. 36). The only way to access the "album artist" field as entered in Windows Media Player is to view the screens for individual "songs."

Figure 36 shows that the Sony Walkman does not handle diacritics well. The player cannot display the "ä" in the name of the second to last artist, "Gächinger Kantorei." This is true of diacritics in other languages as well.

CONCLUSION

The cataloging community is in the midst of a possible change in code from AACR2 to RDA. Regarding personal and corporate names and their tracings in bibliographic records, instead of being treated as "main entries" or "added entries," they will be described in terms of "preferred access points." "Uniform titles" will now be "preferred titles." My study was based on constructing access points per AACR2 rules and their respective rule interpretations. Had I constructed them per RDA guidelines, the way in which I repurposed fields in either iTunes or Windows Media Player would have changed very little. This is because the extent to which access-point construction has changed or will change in RDA would require one simply to either add or change the data in iTunes or Windows Media Player.

In both applications, simple keyword searches can be performed in boxes in the upper right-hand corner of the application. These searches can retrieve all the data prescribed in constructing authoritative names and uniform titles. By repurposing these fields to include this data, it is possible to closely replicate the experience of conducting similar searches in a library catalog. In this way, regardless of whether the user is searching the library catalog for a score or compact disc recording, or using iTunes or Windows Media Player on a library workstation, the bibliographic information would be presented in the same way, thus giving the user the most cohesive experience possible when using a library's resources.

As can be seen throughout this study, however, the digital music platforms and respective players fall very short of being able to replicate the same access provided by catalogs in an AACR2/MARC environment. Providing access to additional performers as controlled access points is problematic in both the iTunes and Windows Media Player environments. When compared with AACR2, the trend in RDA guidelines seems to be toward more rather than less access to a larger number of contributors. Because of this, the current capabilities of digital-music platforms and players will not do any better in replicating access points under RDA. In order to become most useful to libraries in the way my study prescribes, music librarians must find a way to work with the software developers of both digital music platforms and players.

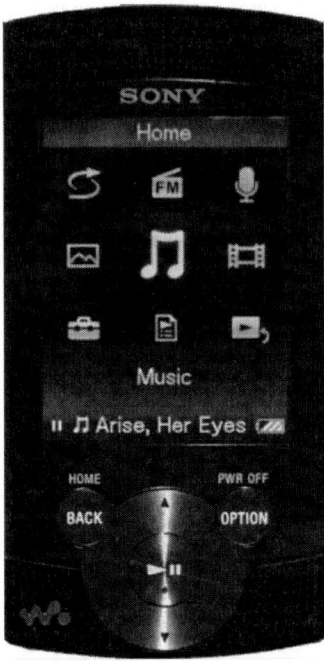

Figure 33. Location of buttons and home display screen for Sony Walkman.

Figure 34. "Music" display on Sony Walkman.

Figure 35. "Album" display on Sony Walkman.

Figure 36. "Artist" display on Sony Walkman, showing mishandled diacritics.

This may be a difficult feat considering these players are designed to provide access to popular music, the market for which is far greater than that of either Western art music or jazz. Only when this happens can the ideas discussed in this study be transformed from the theoretical to practical.

Finally, there is a question of the future of applications like iTunes and Windows Media Player, and devices like the iPod Nano and the Sony Digital Walkman. As with all technologies, they will either become obsolete or transformed at varying degrees within the next five years. That said, however, the issues surrounding electronic access to music will continue to be present in institutions, and music will continue to be cataloged under AACR2, RDA, or whatever new code appears in the future. Digital media already has a strong presence and appears to have a future of continual progress, so when the next group of media applications and devices becomes available, another study could be done to examine their usefulness in providing access to musical works.

APPENDIX 1

METADATA FIELDS IN ITUNES AND WINDOWS MEDIA PLAYER

iTunes (All views)	Windows Media Player (Songs view)
Album	Action
Album Artist	Album
Album Rating	Album Art
Artist	Album Artist
Beats Per Minute	Bit Rate
Bit Rate	Composer
Category	Conductor
Comments	Content Provider
Composer	Contributing Artist
Date Added	Copyright
Date Modified	Custom 1
Description	Custom 2
Disc Number	Data Provider
Episode ID	Date Added
Episode Number	Date Created
Equalizer	Date Last Played
Genre	Date Recorded
Grouping	File Name
Kind	File Path
Last Played	Genre
Last Skipped	Key
Plays	Keywords
Purchase Date	Language

Rating	Length
Release Date	Media Info
Sample Rate	Mood
Season	Parental Rating
Show	Period
Size	Play Count
Skips	Protected
Sort Album	Publisher
Sort Album Artist	Rating
Sort Artist	Release Year
Sort Composer	Size
Sort Name	Subgenre
Sort Show	Subtitle
Time	Title
Track Number	Track number
Year	Type
	Writer

APPENDIX 2

CHART MAPPING REPURPOSED MARC FIELDS

MARC Field Number/ Name/Function	iTunes Data Element(s)	Windows Media Player Data Element(s)
100—Main Entry (Personal Name)	Album Artist	Album Artist
110—Main Entry (Corporate Name)	Album Artist	Album Artist
100-240—Main Entry (Personal Name-Title)	Composer-Grouping-Name	Composer-Title
511—Participant/Performer	Artist	Contributing Artist
700—Added Entry (Personal Name)		Conductor
700—Added Entry (Personal Name-Title)	Composer-Grouping-Name	Composer-Title

NOTES

[1] iTunes version 10 (and subsequent updates through version 10.2.2) was used for files extracted onto that platform. Windows Media Player version 11 was used for files extracted onto that platform. All files were initially extracted in November 2010. Both players were run on Windows XP.

[2] Joint Steering Committee for the Revision of AACR, *Anglo-American Cataloguing Rules*, 2nd ed., 2002 rev. (Chicago: American Library Association, 2002).

[3] Joint Steering Committee for Development of RDA, *RDA: Resource Description & Access* (Chicago: American Library Association, 2010).

[4] Giuseppe Verdi, *La Traviata*, conducted by Carlos Kleiber, Deutsche Grammophon 415 132-2 (1986), CD.

[5] Wolfgang Amadeus Mozart, *Requiem d-moll, Kyrie d-moll*, conducted by Helmuth Rilling, Hänssler Classic 98.146 (1997), CD.

[6] San Antonio Chamber Choir, *Americana*, San Antonio Chamber Choir, conducted by Scott MacPherson (2009), CD.

[7] Cecilia Bartoli, *A Portrait*, London 448 300-2 (1995), CD.

[8] Dmitri Shostakovich, *Symphony no. 11*, Concertgebouw Orchestra, conducted by Bernard Haitink, Decca 425 072-2 (1993), CD.

[9] Jean Sibelius, *Symphony no. 2*, Cleveland Orchestra, conducted by Yoel Levi, Telarc CD-80095 (1984), CD.

[10] Bernstein, Leonard, *West Side Story (with Symphonic Dances)*, Columbia Broadway Masterworks SK 60724 (1998), CD.

[11] John Coltrane, *Giant Steps*, Atlantic 1311-2 (1988), CD.

[12] Christia Thomason and Leslie Kamtman, "The iTunes Project, or, We're All iPod People Now" (presentation, Music Library Association Annual Meeting, Pittsburgh, Pa., 2007).

[13] Ralph Hartsock, *Notes for Music Catalogers* (Lake Crystal, Minn.: Soldier Creek Press, 1994).

[14] Richard Smiraglia, *Describing Music Materials*, 3rd ed., rev. and enl. (Lake Crystal, Minn.: Soldier Creek Press, 1997).

[15] Thomason and Kamtman, slide 3.

[16] Ibid., slide 11.

[17] Ibid., slide 22.

[18] Ibid., slide 25.

[19] Ibid.

[20] The iPod Nano used is a sixth-generation player with 16 GB storage capacity. Player was purchased in January 2011

[21] The Sony Walkman used is a 16 GB, NWZ-S545 model. Player was purchased in January 2011.

THE FRBR MODELS

Thinking More Deeply about Library Metadata

JENN RILEY

Abstract: Examines the role of conceptual models as the basis for library metadata standards, focusing heavily on the FRBR suite of models as examples. The potential for conceptual models to provide rationale for decision-making is examined in some detail, along with the improved discovery potential these models provide. The Variations/FRBR initiative at Indiana University is discussed as an example of a next-generation music discovery system that realizes the benefits of the FRBR models, including its discovery, cataloging, and data-sharing features.

SIGNIFICANCE OF A "CONCEPTUAL MODEL" IN LIBRARY METADATA

The Functional Requirements for Bibliographic Records (FRBR) suite of conceptual models[1] has been the source of significant dialogue, debate, hand-wringing, and general interest within the cultural-heritage community since the initial publication of the FRBR report in 1998. FRBR analysis and discussion appears in a wide variety of forms, including a community LISTSERV,[2] an enthusiast-hosted blog of FRBR-related news,[3] no fewer than three books in English,[4] a *Cataloging & Classification Quarterly* special issue,[5] a volume of the ALA TechSource series *Library Technology Reports*,[6] a Library of Congress formal pamphlet,[7] an entry in the library technology online reference resource *TechEssence*,[8] an ALA/ALCTS preconference,[9] an OCLC–hosted workshop,[10] and, of course, the widespread and ongoing debate over *Resource Description & Access* (RDA), which is grounded in FRBR concepts.[11] The IFLA-maintained "FRBR Bibliography"[12] runs fifty-seven pages at the time of this writing. There is no shortage of attention being paid to FRBR in the library community, and this attention has had at least one profound effect: increasing the thoughtfulness of libraries' approach to resource description.

FRBR as a conceptual model forces an analytical and thoughtful approach to its implementation. While the original FRBR report does say it defines a conceptual model, it does not at any point explicitly define what it means by this term. In the report's introduction, however, some clues may be found. There we learn that FRBR as a conceptual model is not a set of rules to be followed; it is not a database structure or other formal data model listing fields or elements to fill in; it is not even fully prescriptive. "The model operates at the conceptual level; it does not carry the analysis to the level that would be required for a fully developed data model."[13] Instead, FRBR paints a picture of the core ideas the bibliographic community revolves around, offers a structured way of thinking about library resources, and provides a specific vocabulary that the community can use to discuss aspects of library resources in formal terms. "The aim of the study was to produce a framework that would provide a clear, precisely stated, and commonly shared understanding of what it is that the bibliographic record aims to provide information about, and what it is that we expect the record to achieve in terms of answering user needs."[14] Ralph Papakhian, the dedicatee of this volume, from time to time also commented on the role of shared understanding in the library community functioning as the basis for cataloging rules, for example in this MLA-L mailing list post from 1993:

> I'm not sure common sense has anything to do with rules either. [Another poster's] explanation of the rules and how to deal with them is fine. But cataloging rules have some kind of underlying principles which really are conventions rather than scientific truths. For a long time, scholarly convention was to enter lists of books (et al.) under author (surname then forename). This was a convention developed over time that allowed for bibliographic communication.[15]

FRBR's explicitly articulated user needs mark the reflective nature of the model, yet the concept of meeting user needs is not entirely new in cataloging principles. Indeed, William Denton tracks the role of explicitly stated user needs as the basis for cataloging codes throughout library history, including their articulation by Thomas Hyde in 1674, Panizzi in the mid-1800s, Cutter in the late-1800s, Ranganathan in the 1930s, Lubetzky in the 1950s, and the Paris Principles in the 1960s.[16] Denton also looks to these and other writers to track the use of "axioms" underlying library cataloging, but he (and the writers he cites) limits the use of these axioms to "a core set of simple, fundamental principles that form the basis for complete cataloging codes such as *Anglo-American Cataloguing Rules*."[17] These axioms and the user needs that cataloging rules are built upon are not yet full conceptual models, but are surely their predecessors.

The development of the FRBR suite of models marks a new era for cultural-heritage metadata, one in which conceptual models are clearly articulated and have the potential to be used explicitly by both metadata structure standards and metadata content standards. FRBR is not the only conceptual model that has emerged in this time and in this space; other alternatives with slightly different foci include CIDOC/CRM from the museum community,[18] the indecs framework for e-commerce applications,[19] and to a lesser extent the Dublin Core Metadata Initiative (DCMI) Abstract Model,[20] which is less concrete than FRBR or CIDOC/CRM yet shares their focus on explicit functional definitions. However, metadata structure standards (also known as metadata formats or element sets) such as MARC, MODS, and Dublin Core, and content standards such as AACR2 that are in common use in the library community typically predate the development of these conceptual models. Implementers of these standards, therefore, have difficulty using them in a way that clearly conforms to a relevant conceptual model since there is no explicit and planned connection between them. Indeed, "only recently has the idea of defining a conceptualization separately from its specification gained real traction in the library metadata community."[21] Work being performed under DCMI auspices reveals just how explicit a connection between an underlying model and its binding into a specific metadata encoding must be in order to achieve true interoperability. Nilsson summarizes this idea:

Note that it is possible to produce applications that process metadata without regard to [an] abstract model. Such ad-hoc processing of metadata records requires that the precise content of the records is well-known in advance, which is the case in many systems where extensibility, modularity and refinements are not design requirements. In contrast, the kind of interoperable processing based on the abstract model described above is necessary when an application needs to be prepared for metadata constructs that do not fall within the limits of such a precise, pre-conceived description. Thus, it should be clear that interoperable processing is a basic prerequisite for metadata interoperability.[22]

The emergence of conceptual models and a growing focus on true metadata interoperability mark a renewed reflectiveness in cultural-heritage metadata. The thoughtful approach to cataloging that FRBR's focus as a conceptual model promotes is one that Ralph Papakhian both practiced and preached. This can be seen clearly in Papakhian's comments on the use of the uniform title in AACR2-based cataloging. Despite persistent questions about the opaqueness and seemingly multiple functions of uniform titles, he frequently called for a simpler and more direct interpretation. For example (sometimes using his trademark all-lowercase style):

> it's not clear to me that uniform titles have to be comprehensible. that is not one of their purposes (25.1a: —the means for bringing together all catalogue entries for a work . . .—provides identification for a work when the title by which it is known differs from the title proper of the item being catalogued).[23]

> . . . let's remember that uniform titles have only one purpose: to order files. They should not be expected to provide subject access, useful information, nor anything close to truth. The system of uniform titles in cataloging is simply a filing device (used to be called "filing titles"). Uniform titles are not supposed to be pleasant, meaningful, or illuminating. Other elements of bibliographic records may be all these other things, and may meet all of these expectations. But don't look to uniform titles for the meaning of life or to account for the deficencies [sic] of any given online catalog.[24]

In his habit of always asking "why?,"[25] Papakhian maintained a healthy skepticism about FRBR. While the conceptual model methodology matches well with his approach to interpreting and applying the cataloging rules, this in and of itself does not necessarily mean that the specific model the FRBR reports outline is the most effective for music cataloging going forward. The rest of this chapter will examine the FRBR models in more detail, analyzing the ways in which they do (and don't) offer specific benefits to the description of library resources in general, and music resources in particular.

WHAT THE FRBR MODELS PROMISE TO PROVIDE

The raw potential of the FRBR models to provide powerful discovery experiences is well documented.[26] FRBR's work-centered nature is a natural fit for the discovery of Western art music, as this tradition values a "canon" of core works that are performed, reproduced, and discussed in many iterations. The notion of the "work" in music predates the issuance of the original FRBR report, most notably in the writings of Richard Smiraglia.[27] While the FRBR Group 1 entity *work*[28] is of obvious benefit, the exact application of the other FRBR entities, attributes, and relationships to musical materials requires more careful analysis. Many authors have concluded that, despite some challenges, the FRBR models overall have a great deal of promise for representing music metadata.[29]

The FRBR models, however, are not ends unto themselves. As conceptual models, they require further specification and detailed technical planning to implement, and many systems might be considered "FRBR compliant" but still be architected very differently from each other. In the library community, few data models are explicitly based on formal conceptual models, though approaches to tie the two more closely together have been proposed.[30]

To achieve the powerful benefits of the FRBR models, the metadata provided by libraries will need to be more highly structured than in the past. Full analyses of *works* present in a specific *manifestation*, for example, is not currently done for many types of materials, though it would be essential for a full FRBRized discovery-and-display experience for musical sound recordings. Certainly there are good arguments to be made for providing this extra level of analysis and discovery capability. Papakhian was consistently in favor of this approach, at least in an AACR2/MARC environment, saying: "I cannot imagine anyone complaining about 'too many added entries' or 'too much information' in a catalog record."[31] At a time when libraries are increasingly looking to scale back and streamline cataloging and metadata creation activities, moving towards true FRBR implementation represents a significant challenge. Papakhian summarized these types of questions many have about FRBR in a 2003 MLA-L post, again with his characteristic all-lowercase style:

> it is going to be very interesting to see if the library community will be willing to pay for the increased authority work required by a FRBRized AACR2 (to distinguish various expressions of works). my impression is that much of the library community is currently unwilling to pay for the authority work now implied by AACR2. it is hard to imagine what would need to happen in order for that community to change its attitude so that it would be willing to finance the greater complexities required by genuine FRBRization.[32]

The value of resource description in libraries, however, is not calculated solely on the cost of this activity; it is a function of cost relevant to the benefit and services it provides. More clearly articulating these benefits and services and demonstrating them in concrete ways will be necessary in order to adequately understand this side of the equation and make intelligent decisions about the future of library-based resource discovery systems.

In addition to the questions surrounding what it means to "implement" FRBR in a technical sense, the very scope of what is meant by "FRBR" is unclear in many contexts. There are significant differences among the models presented in FRBR, FRAD, and FRSAD. FRAD extends FRBR with new entities, new relationships between entities, and new attributes on FRBR Group 1 and Group 2 entities. FRSAD collapses the Group 3 entities into a unified set and adds features to distinguish the entities themselves from how they are referenced or named. A FRBR implementer at this time has no clear guidance on how to reconcile these differences in order to be "compliant" with the models. IFLA, however, appears to be beginning the process of collapsing the three reports into a unified model. In the IFLA FRBR Review Group's "Report of Activities, 2009–2010," they state that following the official 2010 committee approval of FRSAD, their "work can expand to consider the three models at once" and that their "attention [has] turned to the task of preparing a consolidated or harmonised statement of IFLA's conceptual models."[33]

Building discovery and resource description systems that truly realize the promise of the FRBR models is difficult at this time. Yet there is progress. As experimental systems implement FRBR, more is learned about what the model offers, in terms of both benefits and challenges. Further work in this area is needed, and indeed was explicitly called for by the Library of Congress Working Group on the Future of Bibliographic Control's 2008 report:

> [T]he impact of the FRBR model on cataloging practice and on the machine-readable bibliographic record has not been extensively explored. There is no standard way to exchange Work-based data, and no cataloging rules that yet support the creation of records using the FRBR model. . . . Until carefully tested as a model for bibliographic data formation for all formats, FRBR must be seen as a theoretical model whose practical implementation and its attendant costs are still unknown.[34]

The working group followed this discussion with a specific recommendation addressed to the Library of Congress, OCLC, the IFLA FRBR Working Group, and representative system vendors: "4.2.1. Develop Test Plan for FRBR."[35]

The Variations/FRBR: Variations as a Testbed for the FRBR Conceptual Model (known in short as "V/FRBR") project at Indiana University aims to answer this call from the Library of Congress Working Group on the Future of Bibliographic Control. Funded through a National Leadership Grant from the U.S. Institute of Museum and Library Services, the project runs from 1 October 2008 through 30 September 2011. It is "focused on testing FRBR in a real-world environment, and on providing data, code, and system design specifications that can be reused by others interested in FRBR."[36] Some of the systems and lessons learned from the V/FRBR project are the focus of the remainder of this article.

WHAT'S FULFILLED (SO FAR) FROM THE FRBR PROMISE

DISCOVERY

One of the primary specific outcomes of the V/FRBR project is "[a]n openly-accessible system for searching FRBRized music data for community testing and analysis."[37] This system, found at http://vfrbr.info/search, is seeded with data automatically converted into a FRBRized form from MARC bibliographic and authority records representing the approximately 80,000 audio recordings and 105,000 scores at the Indiana University William and Gayle Cook Music

Library. As of this writing, the discovery system is still in an experimental stage. It is, however, designed to make the most of the FRBRized data model that underlies it. A primary feature of the interface is the presentation of search results in separate groups for *works* and for *manifestations*. When a user search is based on *work* data, all *works* that match their query are displayed, then all *manifestations* of those *works*. This display is shown in figure 1.

If a specific *work* is selected from the *work* result list, both the *work* and *manifestation* lists are then adjusted. The *work* list, obviously, reduces to the single *work* selected. The *manifestation* list reduces to only the *manifestations* of the newly selected *work*, as seen in figure 2.

The display of both *works* and *manifestations*, with a clear distinction between them, allows users seeking specific *works* to easily locate information on those *works*. This is possible even when the user's initial search was not overly precise (for example, not a full or correct uniform title), allowing for a more flexible and powerful discovery experience. Late in the project's development cycle, the V/FRBR team has experimentally introduced scores to the search interface, which previously only included sound recordings. This will likely require a parallel addition of a mechanism to group *manifestations* according to their format (recording vs. score), perhaps through the use of an additional facet. A system that expands in scope even further to provide access to *works* about music in addition to the music itself would need to provide a mechanism to distinguish instances of a *work* from other *works* about that *work*. Such a mechanism would be significantly easier to implement on a *work* list than on a *manifestation* list, such as appears in current library catalogs.

The V/FRBR discovery system's results display features facets for navigating and refining a result set. The use of facets in library discovery interfaces has grown significantly in the past few years. Faceted interfaces benefit from FRBRized treatment, as facet values are clearer when explicitly connected to a FRBR Group 1 entity, though FRBRized data is not a prerequisite for implementing a faceted interface. The V/FRBR interface provides facets for "instrumentation" (the medium-of-performance attribute for the *work*), "composer" (here, any Group 2 entity related to the *work*), and "performer/conductor" (here, any Group 2 entity related to the *expression*). While these facets benefit from the underlying FRBRized data model, their use is still experimental and far from ideal.

The label "instrumentation" for the facet in this interface does not make it clear to the user that the instrumentation presented is that of the original *work*, which may not match the instrumentation of the *expression* that is contained in a selected *manifestation*. Moving forward, determining the most user-friendly way of presenting facets devoted to the medium of performance of a *work* as distinct from the medium of performance for an *expression* (e.g., what instrument a specific recording uses in the performance of a *work*) will be necessary. The V/FRBR project has not to date worked in depth towards a solution to this problem, chiefly because the underlying data store does not have reliable information on instrumentation in general. The mapping of data from MARC to FRBR *works* developed by V/FRBR parses strings out of subfield $m (Medium of performance for music) in uniform titles located in 240, 130 and 7XX

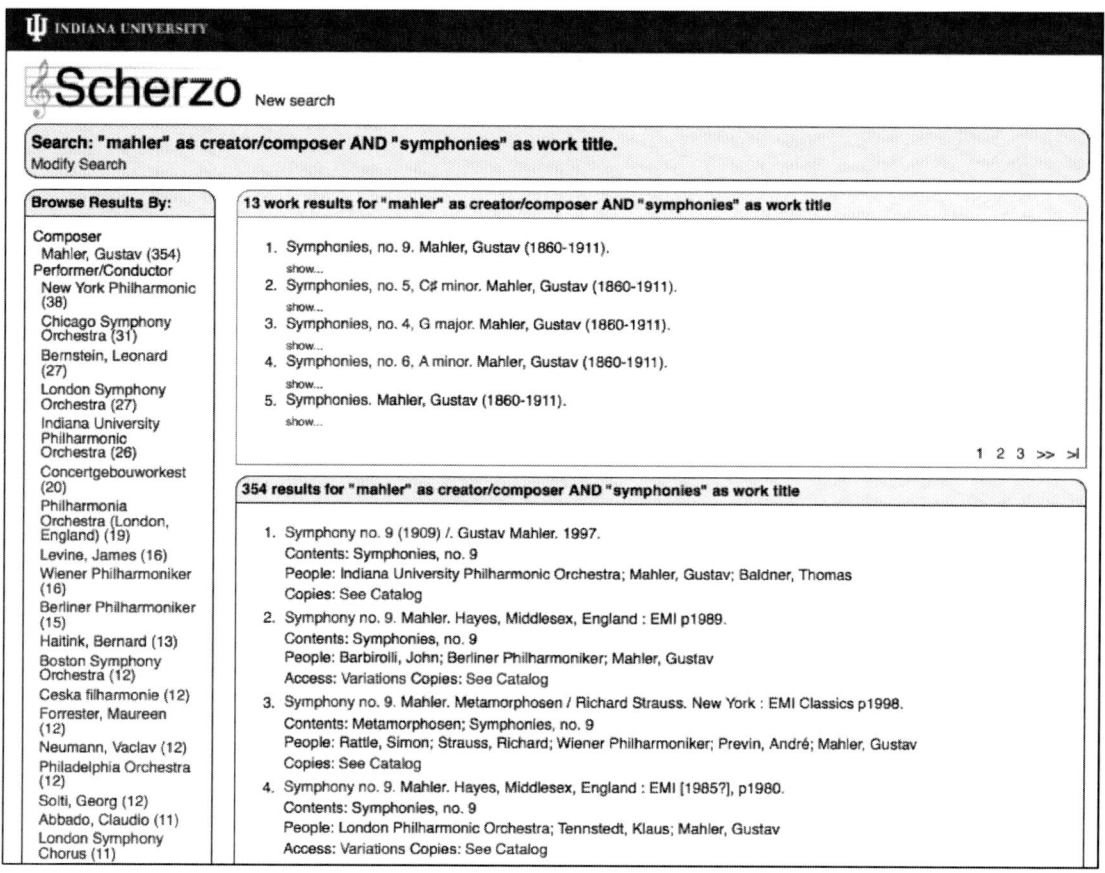

Figure 1. Results from a *work* search.

fields (when the uniform title does not indicate an arrangement) into the *work* "medium of performance" attribute.[38] This is frequently not effective, however. Not every *work* identified by the FRBRization process comes from a uniform title, not all uniform titles have subfield $m, and the strings that are present in subfield $m are not always reliably parsable. Therefore, while many *work* records in the V/FRBR system have a medium of performance, this is not as reliable a means of refining results as the inclusion of the facet in the interface might imply to the user. The mapping of instrumentation for *expressions* is even less reliable. If there is no indication the *expression* is an arrangement, the medium of performance is copied to the *expression* from the *work*. If the *expression* is found to be an arrangement, or no medium of performance is found for the *work*, an attempt is made to fill in this information from the MARC bibliographic field 048

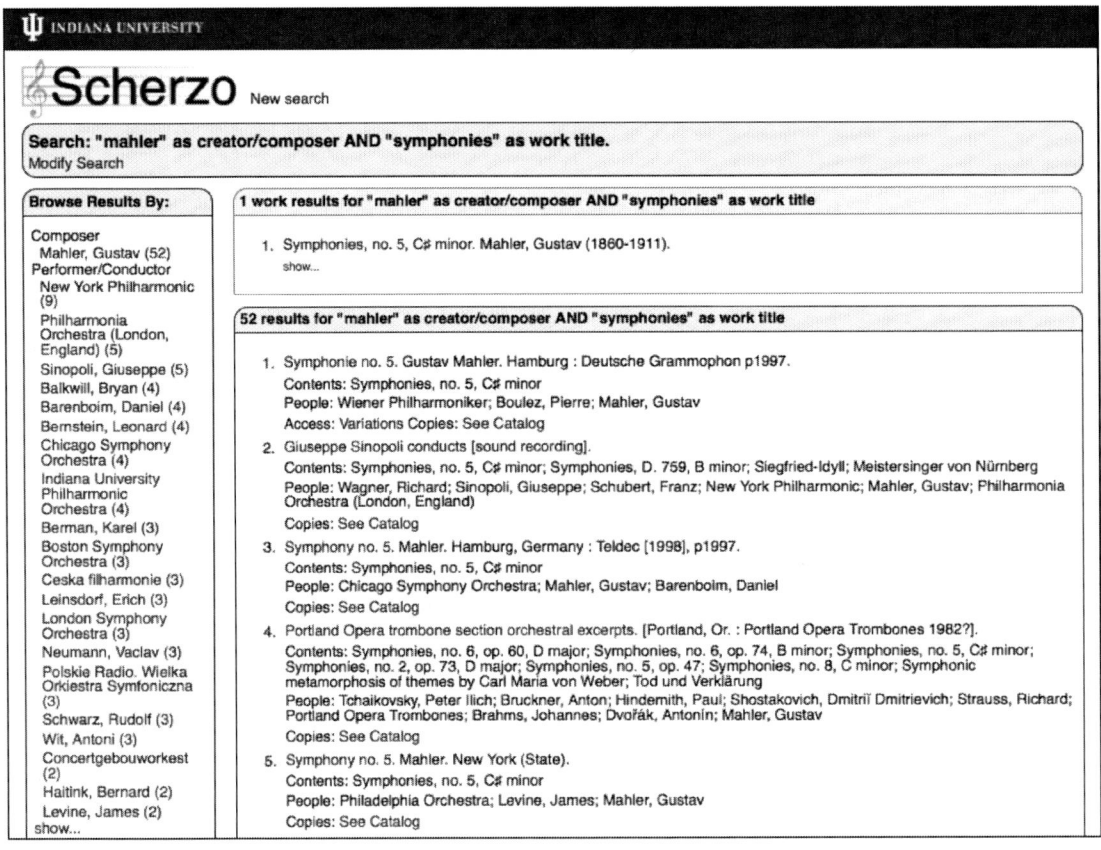

Figure 2. Results from a *work* search, refined to a single selected *work*.

(Number of Musical Instruments or Voices Codes). Since field 048 applies to the *manifestation* as a whole and not necessarily individual *expressions* on that *manifestation*, this method adds additional unreliability beyond what is already present from relying on uniform title subfield $m for instrumentation data.

The facets for composer and performer/conductor in the V/FRBR search interface are currently implemented in an oversimplified way. The FRBR models make relationships between Group 2 entities and the Group 1 entities, and label the type of relationship based on which Group 1 entity is being used. The models do not explicitly provide for the typing of those relationships to distinguish, for example, between a composer and a lyricist. In the first pass, the V/FRBR mapping algorithm worked within these strict constraints and presented all Group 2 entities connected to *works* as "composers" and all Group 2 entities connected to *expressions* as

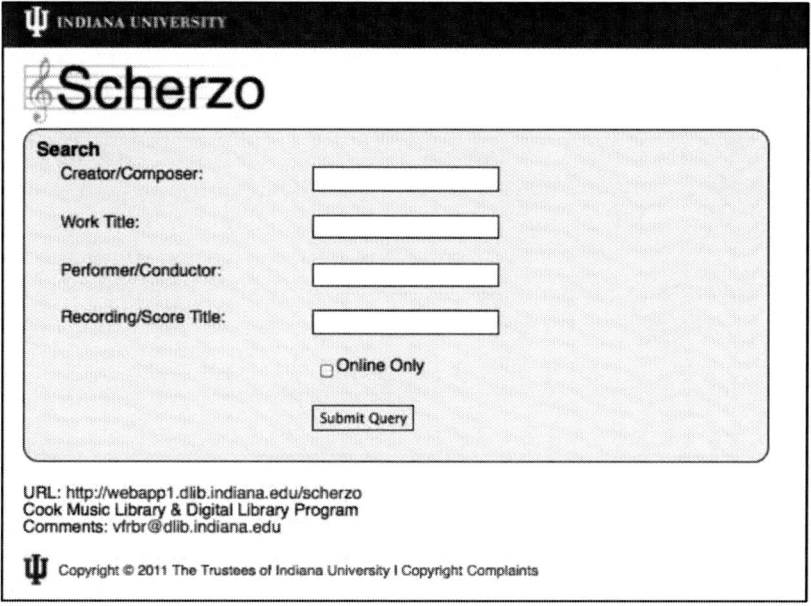

Figure 3. The initial V/FRBR search interface.

either "performers" or "conductors." The facet names in the search interface reflect these initial assumptions. Yet these are obviously incorrect assumptions in many cases. The V/FRBR project has more recently extended its internal data model beyond the core FRBR reports to allow for an indication of role on the relationship between a Group 2 and a Group 1 entity. Work is underway to use MARC relator codes (when they exist in references in bibliographic records) and potentially some other common-sense logic to guess when a Group 2 entity's role in connection to a *work* or *expression* should be other than the default assumed role. If these adjustments are found to produce reasonably reliable data, the discovery interface could then be adapted to show the more specific role to end-users, and potentially use these roles in the facet lists as well.

The initial search feature in the V/FRBR discovery system, in order to simplify the technical implementation, provided only search indexes explicitly connected to either *works* or *manifestations*, as seen in figure 3. The "Creator/Composer" and "Work Title" fields search *work* data (including Group 2 entities connected to *works*), and the "Performer/Conductor" and "Recording/Score Title" fields search *manifestation* data (including Group 2 entities connected to *manifestations*). If terms are entered into search fields for both *work* and *manifestation*, the result set shows only *manifestations* that both meet the entered *manifestation* criteria and contain *expressions* of one or more *works* that meet the *work* criteria.

Keyword search in a FRBRized environment is significantly more difficult than in one with a flatter data model. The search algorithm must make intelligent use of the connections between entities in order to benefit from the entity-relationship structure. Yet exactly what that intelligent use should be is not immediately clear. If search terms match a name and a title, must they be connected to the same entity, or at least entities in the same "tree"? What if they match two different *works* on the same *manifestation*? If a title word and a musical key match two different *works* on a *manifestation*? What should the results display look like if a search term matches a *manifestation* title and a title of a *work* that does not appear on that *manifestation*? These and many similar questions show that significant planning is necessary for the results of a keyword search to be intelligible in a FRBR context. The V/FRBR project has implemented a simple keyword search that makes use of a flattened, *manifestation*-based index. It does not at this time make use of the relationships between FRBR entities for matching queries to results. Regretfully, the project will likely not have the resources to explore in much depth questions about how to make an effective FRBR-based keyword search.

METADATA SHARING

In one respect, the FRBR models make it easier to effectively share metadata. As a conceptual model, FRBR promotes a shared understanding of what is being described that is essential for interoperability. Yet in many other ways, FRBR presents challenges to data sharing. Since FRBR "compliance" is still poorly understood, the shared understanding that FRBR promotes is not yet fully realized in practice. In addition, since the specific metadata structure standards in common use in the library community predate FRBR and implement this model by retrofitting at best, there are few if any common data formats that can be used to exchange FRBRized metadata in a production environment. The cataloging rules presented by RDA, as based on FRBR, should go partway toward alleviating this issue. Implementing the RDA rules in the MARC structure, however, will bring with it the limitations (in the FRBR sense) of MARC. It remains to be seen whether the implementation of RDA as Resource Description Framework (RDF) metadata properties—as distinct from use of RDA as cataloging rules—will prove influential in the library community.[39]

The most significant issue related to metadata sharing that FRBR presents is the inherent connection of every attribute to a specific FRBR entity. An attribute name itself does not indicate the full meaning of a data element; the meaning that comes with the associated entity contributes to the full understanding of the data. This design gives FRBR a great deal of power, but also makes it more difficult to share metadata with communities that do not subscribe to the worldview that FRBR presents. Hillmann, Coyle, Phipps, and Dunsire discuss one method to address this issue;[40] the solution presented, however, is (necessarily) grounded in an RDF representation of RDA/FRBR data. Alternative methods would be needed to effectively share metadata that is not structured according to the RDF model.

The V/FRBR project is attempting to provide the community with concrete data formats and encodings that are FRBR compliant in order to promote interoperability and the exchange of FRBR data between systems and institutions. The first product of this work was a FRBR-compliant XML format developed and released by the project team.[41] This XML format allows for one of three different representations of the data to be chosen: "frbr," a structure that shows strict conformance to the letter of the FRBR reports; "efrbr," which extends the FRBR model with features we believed were necessary for production data; and "vfrbr," which is a music-specific implementation that removes attributes that are not applicable to scores or sound recordings and adds additional attributes useful for music materials that the FRBR reports do not include.[42] A full data export from the V/FRBR system in the efrbr XML format is available, with the hope that actual data that supplements theoretical modeling can help promote the use of the FRBR model.[43] In addition, the V/FRBR project is working towards RDF representations of its data and will release both specifications and actual data in these formats before the end of the grant-funded project.

METADATA CREATION

In order to get a large corpus of data to experiment with (and to demonstrate to the community how legacy data might be leveraged in a FRBR context), the V/FRBR project team focused its early efforts on converting data from a traditional library catalog into FRBRized structures. An additional explicit goal of the project originally was to "[d]esign and implement a new, web-based cataloging system for FRBRized Variations data, hiding the complexity of the metadata model to the degree both possible and desirable, and promoting efficient data entry."[44] The project team, due to some unforeseen challenges, will not in the end be able to build a full cataloging interface, but the team has released a number of detailed design wireframes that other initiatives can use in the future as the basis for an actual implementation. Several screencasts illustrating these design wireframes with commentary explaining the planned cataloging process are also available.[45] These designs present a semiguided cataloging process, separating the creation of metadata from the various entities into a logical sequence, but at the same time attempting to streamline the process. Expanding and collapsing panes are used rather than multiple windows, for example, to assist with an efficient workflow.

The cataloging process envisioned by the V/FRBR project team does explicitly connect the metadata created to FRBR entities, unlike traditional MARC cataloging, where a record has fields that contain data related to several different entities, and many fields are not consistently applicable to the same FRBR entity. The approach taken by V/FRBR allows records for the various FRBR entities to be more effectively reused in the cataloging process. A *work* record once created does not need to be created again, though it could be enhanced when a new *manifestation* containing that *work* is cataloged. Current MARC cataloging practice does this to some extent, through MARC authority records. In the MARC environment, however, there is still some duplication of effort; for example, the composer associated with a *work* is entered as a full heading into each bibliographic record for that *work*, and other *work* data elements such as medium of performance, date of composition, and form/genre may all be entered in each bibliographic record as well. In the V/FRBR cataloging tool designs, the structure of the FRBR models is leveraged to eliminate this duplication. *Expressions* are also explicitly reused as their own records, whereas it is rare in the MARC environment for individual *expressions* to be represented by authority records.

Both in designing the V/FRBR cataloging interface and in writing FRBRization specifications, our project team discovered many cases where significant interpretation of the text in the FRBR reports would be necessary in order to actually create FRBRized data in a production environment. Specific guidelines and best practices are needed for individual disciplines to determine where, for example, something represents a new *expression* of a pre-existing *work* or a new *work*. In music, the application of the notion of the *work* to non-Western music is a prime example of this need for interpretation. Many authors have questioned the utility of the *work* construct for many formats of material, including Ralph Papakhian himself on MLA-L. In this forum Papakhian responded to a message expressing concerns about the "work-ness" of some types of music: "[The original poster's] observations about jazz improvisations, renderings, 'versions of versions of works,' etc. are at least one reason why the current FRBR will probably be impossible to apply to musical works in any consistent fashion."[46] The Variations project itself has in the past attempted to outline the issues related to non-Western music in work-based metadata models.[47] The V/FRBR project team is more optimistic than Papakhian about the ability to apply FRBR concepts to music outside of the Western-art-music tradition, though certainly the model is less of a natural fit for this material.

LOOKING AHEAD

The FRBR models are having a profound effect on the way the library community thinks about and constructs its metadata. No model is perfect, and the work that has been done with FRBR since the 1998 publication of the original IFLA report has provided some level of assessment of which features of the model are most useful and which do not function as intended. Additionally, this body of work is contributing to a community understanding of what it truly means to implement FRBR. The work of the V/FRBR project is one step along this path. Taking further steps will require continued reflection and analysis. Library metadata is under continual evolution, and only by asking "why?" at each step can we ensure the specific mechanisms used meet our—and our patrons'—needs.

NOTES

[1] This suite of models is made up of three publications: FRBR, FRAD, and FRSAD, as follows: IFLA Study Group on the Functional Requirements for Bibliographic Records, *Functional Requirements for Bibliographic Records: Final Report* (Munich: K. G. Saur, 1998), http://www.ifla.org/en/publications/functional-requirements-for-bibliographic-records (as amended and corrected through February 2009);

IFLA Working Group on Functional Requirements and Numbering of Authority Records, *Functional Requirements for Authority Data: A Conceptual Model*, ed. Glenn Patton (Munich: K. G. Saur, 2009); IFLA Working Group on Functional Requirements for Subject Authority Records, *Functional Requirements for Subject Authority Data (FRSAD): A Conceptual Model* (Munich: K. G. Saur, 2009), http://www.ifla.org/files/classification-and-indexing/functional-requirements-for-subject-authority-data/frsad-final-report.pdf.

[2] FRBR Review Group, "Discussion Lists," accessed 1 July 2011, http://www.ifla.org/en/node/891.

[3] "The FRBR Blog," accessed 1 July 2011, http://frbr.org.

[4] Arlene G. Taylor, ed., *Understanding FRBR: What It Is and How It Will Affect Our Retrieval Tools* (Westport, Conn.: Libraries Unlimited, 2007); Robert L. Maxwell, *FRBR: A Guide for the Perplexed* (Chicago: American Library Association, 2009); Yin Zhang and Athena Salaba, *Implementing FRBR in Libraries: Key Issues and Future Directions* (New York: Neal-Schuman, 2009).

[5] *Cataloging & Classification Quarterly* 39, no. 3/4 (2005): 1–303. Also published as Patrick LeBoeuf, ed., *Functional Requirements for Bibliographic Records (FRBR): Hype, Or Cure-All?* (Binghamton, NY: Haworth Press, 2005).

[6] Brad Eden, "Functional Requirements of [sic] Bibliographic Records," *Library Technology Reports* 42, no. 6 (November/December 2006): 5–49.

[7] Barbara Tillett, *What is FRBR?* (Washington, D.C.: Library of Congress Cataloging Distribution Service, 2004), http://www.loc.gov/cds/downloads/FRBR.PDF.

[8] Jenn Riley, "FRBR," *TechEssence* (blog), 8 May 2006, http://techessence.info/frbr.

[9] "Back to the Future: Understanding the Functional Requirements of Bibliographic Records Model (FRBR) and Its Impact on Users, OPACS, and Knowledge Organization Preconference." For handouts from the preconference, see "ALCTS, 2004 Annual Conference Events, Presentation Handouts," accessed 1 July 2011, http://www.ala.org/ala/mgrps/divs/alcts/confevents/past/ala/annual/04.

[10] "FRBR Workshop," 2–4 May 2005. See "FRBR Workshop, Program and Proceedings," accessed 1 July 2011, http://www.oclc.org/research/activities/past/orprojects/frbr/frbr-workshop/program.htm.

[11] Joint Steering Committee for Development of RDA, *RDA: Resource Description & Access* (Chicago: American Library Association, 2010).

[12] FRBR Review Group, "FRBR Bibliography," 27 October 2009, http://www.ifla.org/en/node/881.

[13] FRBR, 3.

[14] FRBR, 2.

[15] A. Ralph Papakhian, email to MLA-L mailing list, 14 November 1993, "Re: video me (video who?) ((video you??))," https://listserv.indiana.edu/cgi-bin/wa-iub.exe?A2=ind9311B&L=MLA-L&P=R1741&X=55D3AA4D0D7645AB5C&Y=.

[16] William Denton, "FRBR and the History of Cataloging," in *Understanding FRBR*, 35–58.

[17] Ibid., 35.

[18] International Council of Museums, "The CIDOC Conceptual Reference Model," 10 November 2010, http://cidoc.ics.forth.gr.

[19] "The <in*d*ecs> Metadata Framework: Principles, Model and Data Dictionary," June 2000, http://www.doi.org/topics/indecs/indecs_framework_2000.pdf.

[20] Dublin Core Metadata Initiative, "DCMI Abstract Model," 4 June 2007, http://www.dublincore.org/documents/abstract-model.

[21] Jenn Riley, "Moving from a Locally-Developed Data Model to a Standard Conceptual Model," in *Culture and Identity in Knowledge Organization: Proceedings of the Tenth International ISKO Conference, 5–8 August 2008, Montréal, Canada*, ed. Clément Arsenault and Joseph T. Tennis (Würzburg: Ergon Verlag, 2008), 124–30.

[22] Mikael Nilsson, Pete Johnston, Ambjörn Naeve, and Andy Powell, "Towards an Interoperability Framework for Metadata Standards," in *International Conference on Dublin Core and Metadata Applications, DC-2006—Colima, Mexico Proceedings*, http://dcpapers.dublincore.org/ojs/pubs/article/view/835.

[23] A. Ralph Papakhian, email to MLA-L mailing list, 15 January 1998, "Re: Steve Reich," https://listserv.indiana.edu/cgi-bin/wa-iub.exe?A2=ind9801C&L=MLA-L&P=R749&D=0&X=55D3AA4D0D7645AB5C&Y=.

[24] A. Ralph Papakhian, email to MLA-L mailing list, 11 November 1994, "Re: Generic title, plural or not?," https://listserv.indiana.edu/cgi-bin/wa-iub.exe?A2=ind9411B&L=MLA-L&P=R2891&X=0C8EF815F6877F7362&Y=.

[25] Papakhian was well known to persist with these types of questions, even beyond the subject of cataloging. On MLA-L, for example, he would question the rationale behind maintaining lists of Internet resources related to classical music (A. Ralph Papakhian, email to MLA-L mailing list, 22 August 2007, "Re: DW3 Classical Music Resources," https://listserv.indiana.edu/cgi-bin/wa-iub.exe?A2=ind0708D&L=MLA-L&P=R624&D=0&X=0C8EF815F6877F7362&Y=) and which title to print on the spine of a library-bound volume (A. Ralph Papakhian, email to MLA-L mailing list, 14 November 2003, "Re: spine label titles," https://listserv.indiana.edu/cgi-bin/wa-iub.exe?A2=ind0311B&L=MLA-L&P=R5061&D=0&X=0C8EF815F6877F7362&Y=).

[26] See, for example, from among the dozens of papers on this topic: Martha M. Yee, "FRBRization: A Method for Turning Online Public Finding Lists into Online Public Catalogs," *Information Technology and Libraries* 24, no. 2 (June 2005): 77–95; Zorana Ercegovac, "Multiple-version Resources in Digital Libraries: Towards User-centered Displays," *Journal of the American Society for Information Science and Technology* 57, no. 8 (June 2006): 1023–32.

[27] Smiraglia published widely on this topic, including the monograph Richard P. Smiraglia, *The Nature of "A Work": Implications for the Organization of Knowledge* (Lanham, Md.: Scarecrow Press, 2001).

[28] In this article, all FRBR entities are italicized in order to distinguish them from terms that are used generically.

[29] Harriette Hemmasi, "Why Not MARC?," in *ISMIR 2002 Conference Proceedings* (Paris: IRCAM-Centre Pompidou, 2002), 242–48, http://ismir2002.ismir.net/Proceedings/02-FP08-3.pdf; Jenn Riley, Caitlin Hunter, Chris Colvard, and Alex Berry, "Definition of a FRBR-Based Metadata Model for the Indiana University Variations3 Project," 10 September 2007, http://www.dlib.indiana.edu/projects/variations3/docs/v3FRBRreport.pdf; Sherry L. Vellucci, "FRBR and Music," in *Understanding FRBR*, 131–51.

[30] Mikael Nilsson, Thomas Baker, and Pete Johnston, "The Singapore Framework for Dublin Core Application Profiles," 14 January 2008, http://dublincore.org/documents/singapore-framework. See

also commentary on this approach in Jenn Riley, "Enhancing Interoperability of FRBR-Based Metadata," in *International Conference on Dublin Core and Metadata Applications, DC-2010—Pittsburgh Proceedings*, http://dcpapers.dublincore.org/ojs/pubs/article/view/1037.

31. A. Ralph Papakhian, email to MLA-L mailing list, 18 May 2009, "Re: Sound recording cataloging," https://listserv.indiana.edu/cgi-bin/wa-iub.exe?A2=ind0905C&L=MLA-L&P=R2977&X=08AA665FD9DA07196A&Y=.

32. A. Ralph Papakhian, email to MLA-L mailing list, 18 April 2003, "Re: MCD 25.25A footnote 9," https://listserv.indiana.edu/cgi-bin/wa-iub.exe?A2=ind0304C&L=MLA-L&P=R5246&X=08AA665FD9DA07196A&Y=.

33. FRBR Review Group, "Report of Activities, 2009–2010," 26 July 2010, http://www.ifla.org/files/cataloguing/frbrrg/activities_2009-2010.pdf.

34. Library of Congress Working Group on the Future of Bibliographic Control, "On the Record," 9 January 2008, 33, http://www.loc.gov/bibliographic-future/news/lcwg-ontherecord-jan08-final.pdf.

35. Ibid.

36. "Variations/FRBR: Variations as a Testbed for the FRBR Conceptual Model," 24 October 2010, http://vfrbr.info.

37. Indiana University Digital Library Program, "Variations as a Testbed for the FRBR Conceptual Model," 6, http://www.dlib.indiana.edu/projects/vfrbr/projectDoc/admin/Narrative.pdf.

38. Full MARC FRBRization routines developed for the V/FRBR project are documented in "Variations/FRBR: Spring 2010 Recording FRBRization Specifications," 24 October 2010, http://www.dlib.indiana.edu/projects/vfrbr/projectDoc/metadata/mappings/spring2010/vfrbrSpring2010mappings.shtml.

39. Diane Hillmann, Karen Coyle, Jon Phipps, and Gordon Dunsire, "RDA Vocabularies: Process, Outcome, Use." *D-Lib Magazine* 16, no. 1/2 (January/February 2010), http://www.dlib.org/dlib/january10/hillmann/01hillmann.html.

40. Ibid. See especially the discussion surrounding the figure "The Roles Case: Properties, Subproperties and FRBR Entities."

41. "XML Schema Definitions for FRBR, Version 1.1," 27 October 2010, http://www.dlib.indiana.edu/projects/vfrbr/schemas/1.1.

42. A more detailed explanation of the V/FRBR XML formats may be found in Riley, "Enhancing Interoperability of FRBR-Based Metadata."

43. "XML Data Export Files for Variations FRBR (efrbr), Version 1.1," 18 February 2011, http://www.dlib.indiana.edu/projects/vfrbr/data/1.1.

44. Indiana University Digital Library Program, "Variations as a Testbed," 5.

45. "Cataloging Tool: Design Wireframes," 31 January 2011, http://www.dlib.indiana.edu/projects/vfrbr/projectDoc/metadata/catalogingTool; more details of the planned cataloging process will be shared in other forthcoming publications related to the V/FRBR project.

46. A. Ralph Papakhian, email to MLA-L mailing list, 27 May 2004, "Re: uniform titles for arrangements of improvisations?," https://listserv.indiana.edu/cgi-bin/wa-iub.exe?A2=ind0405D&L=MLA-L&P=R1609&D=0&X=08AA665FD9DA07196A&Y=.

47. Caitlin Hunter, "Addressing Ethnic/World Music in the Variations2 System," 13 July 2006, http://variations2.indiana.edu/metadata/ethnic/EthnicMusic.htm.

EPILOGUE

Arsen Ralph Papakhian

RALPH

A Remembrance

Sue Ellen Stancu

On 15 March 1979, I began my first week as the new sound recordings cataloger in the Technical Services Division of the Music Library at Indiana University. The entire cataloging staff was housed in a small, windowless room in the basement of Sycamore Hall, just a few steps away from the administrative offices and circulation desk. The music collections were housed in multiple locations: books and scores housed in the Sycamore Hall basement, recordings in the basement of Merrill Hall, and the performance materials also in Merrill Hall, on the floor above the Dean's office.

The technical services office contained four desks (one for each of the full-time staff), two or three tables where part-time student assistants worked, and the shelf list cabinets for books, scores, and recordings. On occasions when the entire technical services staff happened to be seated and working at the same time, it was very, very difficult to maneuver through the room. In one corner of the room, on a well-worn study carrel rescued from the public area of the library when reader space was sacrificed to make room for more stacks, sat the single, OCLC dedicated-line terminal. On the wall just beside the operator's chair and at eye level, was posted a "terminal schedule." OCLC terminal access time was precious—full-time staff, student searchers, and inputters had to mark out their hours every week. At that time, catalogers wrote out their cataloging on preprinted paper forms and student employees copied the catalogers' work into OCLC. Beside the terminal schedule, on a piece of silver-coated, thermal printer paper that came in giant rolls, there was taped a pencil drawing of a skeleton figure sitting in front of an OCLC terminal. Down one side of the drawing the words "Retry momentarily" were written a dozen or so times.

There was also an antechamber, probably not quite eight feet by ten feet, which housed the official catalog and two large tables, one for the student cataloger for School of Music performances (a recording of an opera in those days could use between six and eight seven-inch reels), and another for volumes of the *National Union Catalog* and *Music, Books on Music, and Sound Recordings*.

Ralph Papakhian, head of the Music Library Technical Services Division, reigned with great expertise and subtle good humor over this crowded domain of music cataloging. His desk sat almost exactly in the middle of the room and on it rested the only telephone for the entire cataloging section. At least all of us had our own IBM Selectric typewriters (with Library Elite type ball elements—the ones with all of the diacritics) so that we could type our authority cards and cross references for the public catalogs. (Ralph was the only cataloger who also typed his OCLC cataloging workforms. No wonder the student OCLC inputters argued over who was going to input Ralph's catalog copy; it was always readable.) There was no need for electronic mail or text messaging as long as one had a voice capable of being heard above the cacophony of typewriters, chattering students, and the occasional Bruckner symphony being played on an old console stereo.

I remember taking a subject heading question to Ralph shortly after beginning my job in the IU Music Library. I don't remember the exact question, but Ralph was unsure of the usage for the particular heading. What I will never forget is Ralph's response to me: "Hold on—I'll just call Harry Price at the Library of Congress and see what he has to say about this." And Ralph did! At the time, I didn't know it was possible to just pick up the phone and converse with a specialist at LC. I had my answer in a few minutes, after Ralph had talked and laughed and asked how everyone there was doing. I could not anticipate then that I would be so fortunate as to spend the next thirty-one years working with one of the outstanding leaders in the music librarianship profession.

Ralph was born in Detroit on 28 December 1948. He was invited to attend Cass Technical High School in Detroit as a student in the science and arts program and transferred to the music program as soon as possible after enrollment. Cass Tech is one of the few public high schools in the country with a full curriculum in music. Subsequently graduating, summa cum laude, with a B.A. in music history from Western Michigan University in 1971, Ralph went on to obtain a Master of Music degree in musicology and music theory, and a Master of Science in librarianship with an emphasis in cataloging and academic librarianship from the same institution in 1973, both graduate degrees with honors. His instructor for classification and cataloging was John Comaromi, later the head of the Dewey Division at the Library of Congress. Ralph often credited Comaromi for instilling in him his love of cataloging and classification.

From August 1973 to August 1975, Ralph worked as humanities cataloger at the University of Florida Libraries in Gainesville, and in September 1975 he began his thirty-five-year career as a music librarian with the IU Libraries when he accepted the position of head, Music Library Technical Services Division. He received tenure in 1981 and achieved the rank of full librarian in 1985.

Ralph's accomplishments in music librarianship and his contributions to the Music Library Association (MLA) and related organizations will serve as an everlasting legacy to his colleagues in the field and to aspiring students of music librarianship. He served on the board of directors of MLA as assistant fiscal officer and then fiscal officer (1986–88) and as executive secretary (1988–92). He was awarded MLA's Special Achievement Award in 1992 for the co-founding of the listserv for music librarians, MLA-L, which has become the conduit for the exchange of information and ideas for music librarians all over the world. In 2008, Ralph was awarded the MLA Citation (the highest honor awarded by the association) for his dedication and advocacy for the profession of music librarianship in general and music cataloging in particular, and for providing, over the course of thirty-five years, inspiration, instruction, and mentoring to the next generation of music catalogers.

Ralph received two Richard S. Hill Awards for the best article on music librarianship: in 1983, for "Music in the OCLC Online Union Catalog: A Review"[1] (written with Richard Smiraglia) and in 2002 for his article "Cataloging,"[2] published in an issue of *Notes* dedicated to "Music Librarianship at the Turn of the Century." In 1992, Ralph established the MLA Clearinghouse at Indiana University for the purpose of collecting and disseminating miscellaneous MLA documents both electronically and in hard copy.

One of the founding members of the Music OCLC Users Group (MOUG) in 1977, Ralph went on to serve as its vice chair (1978), secretary/newsletter editor (1980–82), and chair (1995–96). Ralph was honored in 2002 by the Steering Committee of the Program for Cooperative Cataloging for coordinating the first NACO funnel project in 1988, known as the NACO Music Project (NMP). The project was funneling contributions from about fifty member institutions which, at the time the award was presented, had completed ninety-four thousand records. Through the end of September 2010, that total had risen to more than three hundred thousand new and changed authority records. Ralph started the NMP-L listserv to facilitate communication among the project's members, and since NMP's creation, trained and reviewed dozens of potential NACO contributors.

Among the accomplishments of which Ralph was most proud was the creation in 1978 of the Music Librarianship Specialization program at Indiana University. Students also have the option of enrolling in a dual-degree program to obtain a master's degree in library science as well as in musicology. Ralph believed very strongly in the necessity for students interested in music librarianship—especially music cataloging—to have practical experience before embarking on their careers. The internships in cataloging and reference required by the specialization program served to meet that need. As a teacher in the specialization program, Ralph is perhaps best known for his work in supervising seventy-four cataloging interns and very often acting as mentor throughout their careers. Ralph had firmly established feelings about the program, since it had become one of only two or three such music-librarianship programs offered in the country. He felt that the Indiana University Music Librarianship Specialization program was in a position to become the principal locus for the training of the next generation of music librarians. Since IU had an established record in that arena for more than thirty years, Ralph believed that accomplishment should be fostered as a matter of responsibility for the future of the profession.

Ralph was instrumental in organizing, and was co-instructor of, IU's Summer Music Cataloging Workshop. The workshop was created with the assistance of the School of Music's Office of Summer Programs. Ralph saw the need for continuing education and had the beginnings of an idea for the workshop before the music library had an appropriate space in which to conduct it. Finally, in January 1996, when the IU Music Library moved to its new facility and became the William and Gayle Cook Music Library, a space to accommodate a cataloging workshop was available in the Technical Services area.

In the summer of 1996, the first of ten Summer Music Cataloging Workshops was offered, with space allowing for an enrollment of ten. With participants coming from throughout the United States as well as Canada and Greece, the workshop was more successful than had been imagined. For each of the following nine workshops, an announcement went out on MLA-L and AUTOCAT, and the enrollment for the workshop was filled within two days, usually with a waiting list. All in all, the ten summer workshops allowed one-hundred additional students of music cataloging the advantage of Ralph's tutelage.

MOUG recognized Ralph's outstanding role in educating and mentoring new music catalogers by presenting him with the Distinguished Service Award in 2005. Acknowledging his hand in sending forth countless people into the profession, the award read, in part, "[The students] have been conditioned to approach work with rigor, curiosity, and creativity; among them are many recognized leaders in music librarianship and in the larger library world. . . . Those persons have come to know that what they do, and how they do it, matters, whatever signals to the contrary may appear. Ralph strives to preserve the best aspects of cataloging while adapting to new rules, new needs, and new technologies. They also know that they have a friend and mentor for their career."

To honor Ralph's service, his many contributions to the Music OCLC Users Group, and his mentoring role in music librarianship, the executive board of MOUG has established the "Ralph Papakhian Travel Grant" in order to support attendance at its annual meeting by newer members of the music librarianship profession, students, and paraprofessionals.

Ralph's dedication to serving Indiana University was remarkable. He demonstrated a fervent commitment to faculty governance evidenced by his participation on the IU Faculty Council and its various committees. He helped to organize a chapter of the American Federation of Teachers on the IU Bloomington campus. Through his activities on behalf of all employees of IU, Ralph facilitated the open faculty salary listings to which we have computer access today. For many years prior to that, he copied the data by hand from a listing in the Dean of Faculties office, organized it, and made it available to anyone who wanted it. He was a lifetime member of the American Association of University Professors. Ralph also served as a member of the IU Bloomington Library Faculty Council, and his leadership role in the Council's various committees throughout his career is a testament to his firm belief in the highest ideals of collegiality in an academic institution.

Ralph was an outspoken advocate for social justice and, in his rational and measured way, was the first to come to the aid of any colleague seeking assistance or advice. In the mid-1980's, during his tenure on the MLA board of directors, Ralph was involved with the anti-apartheid movement in Bloomington. He introduced a resolution, subsequently passed by the MLA Board, to remove any funds that the organization might have in South African–related investments.

I had not realized until a few months ago, while preparing to teach a session on the library catalog to the students in the Music Specialization seminar, that Ralph was also an active member of ALA's Social Responsibilities Roundtable (SRRT) and monitored their listserv

(SRRTAC-L). I wanted to mention Sanford ("Sandy") Berman in the seminar session, so I studied Berman's website in the hope of finding some juicy tidbit that might stimulate the imagination or curiosity of the seminar students. I became mesmerized (as usual) by the information available there about this legendary character. To my surprise, Ralph's e-mail from the SRRTAC-L listserv was included as the first response to Berman's announcement (in late winter 1999) that all was not well in the Hennepin County Library. Ralph was a "Sandynista"?! (I had been lucky enough to hear Berman speak at a conference while in library school in Arizona and have always admired his perseverance; he spoke just before Ben Tucker of the Library of Congress.) I found that Ralph was a contributor to issue number 1, the "Sandy Berman Rocks My Socks" issue, of the zine *Kiss My Filing Indicators*.[3] This particular issue of the zine was dedicated exclusively to showing support for Berman and honoring his work. Ralph wrote these words about Sandy Berman, but for me they describe Ralph as well: "Occasionally someone who is in tune with the people materializes—someone who can be nothing except active in the cause of humanity and humaneness; someone who disregards all received societal boundaries."[4]

Ralph never did anything halfway. He was passionate about everything in which he was involved. He was passionate about his family: his wife Mary, his four lovely children, and five adorable grandchildren. He conversed easily with friends and colleagues alike—not only about work but about their families—and commiserated about problems that they may have shared.

He was passionate about his heritage. I think his must have been the only car in Bloomington with a bumper sticker that read, "I am famous in Yerevan." The subscription to his Armenian newspaper came to him at the music library. Immediately after he was presented with the large red-and-white sign "Parking for Armenians only—all others will be towed," it became a permanent fixture in his office window. Ralph had several nicknames. Back in the days before e-mail, Ralph signed all of his typed or handwritten memos with his initials ("arp"), "Mr. Ralph" (the more formal mode of address originated I think with Becky Dean when she was a student at IU), and "Raffi." Ann Churukian let me know that she had looked up "Raffi" in her dictionary of Armenian names and found three definitions: (1) exalter, (2) flash of lightning, and (3) glorious man.

Of course, Ralph was passionate about his job, music cataloging, and in his quiet and humble way would always let you know exactly what he thought. He was generous with his time, never turning away a question, be it in person or via e-mail. Ralph loved to attend performances by students of the Jacobs School of Music—often many evenings a week, seldom missing a performance by one of his student employees. Sometimes, checking my email messages first thing in the morning, I'd notice a posting from Ralph, sent at some awfully early hour, like 1:30 or 2:00 am, and think to myself: He must have gotten home late from the Philharmonic Orchestra concert last night and sat up, wine glass in hand, catching up on his correspondence.

Ralph enjoyed the company of his students and library colleagues and loved lunching with them at Mother Bear's Pizza. An informal group of librarians was formed shortly after the music library moved into its new quarters in the Simon Library and Recital Hall building in 1996. I'm not sure we ever agreed on a name, but we usually dubbed ourselves the "Southside Catalogers." The group consisted of Ralph, Emma Dederick, and myself from the Cook Music Library; Suzanne Mudge, librarian for the Archives of Traditional Music; Liana Zhou, librarian for the Kinsey Institute; and Elizabeth Johnson, head of technical services for the Lilly Library. The Southside Catalogers met for lunch at Mother Bear's on an irregular basis, or whenever there was some hot library topic to discuss. Sometimes we invited guests from the "Big House," as Ralph called the Wells Library (the main library for the IU Bloomington campus, located on the north side of campus). Suzanne Mudge and Ralph perfected a secret handshake for the group—I've never been able to get the hang of it, but haven't given up yet. The group lunches were a wonderful chance for us to share information about work, families, problems, personal goals and accomplishments, and just about anything else.

The Southside Catalogers—minus one—continue to meet. It was just a few weeks ago, during one of these lunches, that Elizabeth Johnson remembered how excited Ralph used to get in the early days of OCLC when the number of bibliographic records in the database neared another millionth mark. Ralph would encourage everyone throughout the Bloomington catalog departments to save as many records as possible, proofread them, and have them ready to produce. As the magic number drew near, there was a flurry of activity. Catalogers furiously retrieved their records from the save file and pressed the produce key as quickly as possible, repeating the process over and over. Response time slowed, until: too bad, the next OCLC record number assigned was 135 beyond the next million mark. A group groan echoed throughout the technical services office.

Ralph and the rest of the staff in Music Technical Services prepared for this moment every time the possibility of inputting an OCLC gold record approached. Sure enough, it finally paid off. The Indiana University Music Library received not one, but two OCLC Gold Records: the eleven-millionth record on 28 July 1984, and the twenty-one-millionth record on 3 Feburary 1990. At that time, the cataloger who input the gold record got a picture and write-up in the OCLC Newsletter. Ralph was ecstatic!

Ralph always looked for the best in everyone. He was a man without a trace of pretense or guile. He had a brilliant intellect and was friendly, kind and caring, generous, resourceful, down-to-earth, persistent, and patient. Ever the teacher and mentor, his door was always open; he always had time to answer a question. Ralph had a wonderful sense of humor.

During Ralph's last few years, when his illness kept him from coming into the music library on a regular basis, he continued to work from home. The last annual MLA meeting that Ralph attended was the 2006 meeting in Memphis. He dearly missed seeing all of his friends and colleagues.

In October 2009, the MLA Midwest Chapter was scheduled to meet in South Bend, Indiana. It took some convincing, but Ralph finally agreed to attend. The meeting was only a few hours drive away. I know that Ralph had a wonderful time meeting up with chapter friends.

After the meeting, on the drive home to Bloomington, he remarked, "It sure was great to hang out with a bunch of music librarians again."

Ralph died at his home in Bloomington on Thursday morning, 14 January 2010, after a sixteen-year struggle against colorectal cancer.

It is fitting isn't it, that postings on the MLA-L listserv, for which Ralph won a Special Achievement Award, were on that January 14th almost solely devoted to messages and remembrances of Ralph? Ruthann McTyre, then MLA President, encouraged the MLA family to share their memories and stories in celebration of Ralph's life.

One of the messages that was most meaningful to me was that of Dick Griscom. I share it below with Dick's permission.

> In 1981, I was working as a cataloging intern in the IU Music Library. On the bulletin board in technical services, someone had posted a photocopy of a page from AACR2 (this would have been the original orange-covered edition of 1978). It was a page from the section of appendix A that deals with religious names and terms. The first rule instructs the cataloger to "capitalize the names of God, terms referring to the Christian Trinity, and the names of other deities," and it gives examples including Allah, the Almighty, the Father, King of Kings, Lord, Mars, Providence, and Zeus. A bit farther down the page is the instruction to "lowercase most derivative words, both adjectives and nouns." The examples include "godlike," "messianic hope," and "christological." On this photocopy, someone had added other examples, using the "letter gothic" ball on one of the Selectric typewriters in the department: "Ralph" was the example for the first rule, and "ralphlike" for the second. I always thought we could all benefit from being a bit more ralphlike.

NOTES

[1] Richard P. Smiraglia and Arsen R. Papakhian, "Music in the OCLC Online Union Catalog: A Review," *Notes* 38, no. 2 (December 1981): 257–74.

[2] A. Ralph Papakhian, "Cataloging," *Notes* 56, no. 3 (March 2000): 581–90.

[3] Katia Roberto, comp., *Kiss My Filing Indicators #1: The Sandy Berman Rocks My Socks Issue*, accessed 23 May 2011, http://www.sanfordberman.org/zine/zine1.htm.

[4] Ibid., http://www.sanfordberman.org/zine/zine10.htm.

ABOUT THE CONTRIBUTORS

Peter H. Lisius is the music and media catalog librarian and an assistant professor at Kent State University. He has held this position since February 2007. Prior to his employment at Kent State, Lisius was a senior librarian/music cataloger at the New York Public Library from July 2000 through January 2007. He is currently a member of the MLA-BCC Subject Access Subcommittee and is a past member of the MLA-BCC MARC Formats Subcommittee. He is an independent contributor to both the NACO Music and NACO-AV funnels. Lisius led workshops in video-recording cataloging at the 2010 Online Audiovisual Catalogers meeting held in Macon, Georgia, as well as the 2011 meeting of the Council on East Asian Libraries' Committee on Technical Processing held in Honolulu, Hawaii. He has also collaboratively written several articles for *Cataloging and Classification Quarterly*, focusing on authority control and cataloger training in relation to NACO and OCLC Enhance. Lisius would like to thank his colleagues Roman Panchyshyn, who initially suggested the idea of a new volume of essays on music cataloging dedicated to Ralph Papakhian; Gary Mote, who assisted in the taking of digital photographs for "Square Pegs in Round Holes"; and Diane Sperko, who created mockups for the iPod Nano digital pictures for the article. He also thanks Christia Thomason and Leslie Kamtman for permission to cite and discuss their presentation, "The iTunes Project or, We're All Pod People Now." Finally, he would like to thank his coeditor Dick Griscom, whose experience and advice has been invaluable throughout the entire process.

Richard Griscom is head of the Otto E. Albrecht Music Library and the Eugene Ormandy Music and Media Center at the University of Pennsylvania. He is a former editor (1997–2000) of *Notes*, the journal of the Music Library Association, and has held many positions in MLA, including chair of the MARC Formats Subcommittee (1985–88), fiscal officer (1989–90), and executive secretary (1992–96). He is the editor of *Music Librarianship at the Turn of the Century* (2000) and coauthor (with David Lasocki) of *The Recorder: A Research and Information Guide* (2012).

Lisius and Griscom thank D. J. Hoek, Ruthann McTyre, Linda Blotner, and Jerry McBride, without whose support this book would not have been published. They also thank James Zychowicz of A-R Editions for deftly guiding the volume through production.

H. Stephen Wright is a cataloger in the Northern Illinois University Libraries in DeKalb; he was also music librarian at NIU for seventeen years. He was editor of MLA's Technical Reports series from 2000 to 2006 and is also a former chair of the MLA Midwest Chapter and the Music OCLC Users Group. He has written extensively on the topic of music in films. His publications include *Film Music at the Piano* (2003) and *A Research Guide to Film and Television Music in the United States*, with Jeannie Gayle Pool (2011).

Richard P. Smiraglia is professor, Information Organization Research Group, in the School of Information Studies at the University of Wisconsin–Milwaukee. He has defined the meaning of "a work" empirically, and has revealed the ubiquitous phenomenon of instantiation among information objects. Recent work includes empirical analysis of social classification, and epistemological analysis of the role of authorship in bibliographic tradition. His "Idea Collider" research team is working on a unified theory of knowledge. An Honorary Fellow of the Virtual Knowledge Studio, Amsterdam, he is a collaborating member of the Knowledge Space Lab effort to map the evolution of knowledge in Wikipedia. He is editor-in-chief of the journal *Knowledge Organization*.

The Students of the University of Wisconsin–Milwaukee LIS 791 Summer 2010 were Khristi Blocton, Jennifer Bromley, Casey Brough, Victoria Chu, Brian Clark, Sherri Griscavage, Kathleen Harrison, Karla Jurgemeyer, Marianne Kordas, Emma Lawson, Christina Linklater, Kay Lunkenheimer, Shauna Mendez, Emily Miller, Joanne Ratke, and Stuart Simon. LIS 791 Music Cataloging was offered online by the School of Information Studies through the WISE (Web-based Information Science Education) Consortium from 1 June through 6 July 2010. The class members and Richard P. Smiraglia acknowledge the assistance of Edward O'Neill of the OCLC Office of Research with constitution of the random sample and Elizabeth Milonas, doctoral student at Long Island University, with data analysis.

Jay Weitz is senior consulting database specialist at OCLC and was previously assistant catalog librarian at Capital University, Columbus, Ohio. He is the author of *Cataloger's Judgment*, both editions of *Music Coding and Tagging*, and the cataloging Q&A columns of the *Music OCLC Users Group Newsletter* and the *Online Audiovisual Catalogers Newsletter*. He was the recipient of the MOUG Distinguished Service Award in 2004, OLAC's Nancy B. Olson Award in 2005, and for his work on the reimplementation of Duplicate Detection and Resolution software in WorldCat, an OCLC President's Award in 2010. He has been a performing arts critic in public radio, in print, and on the web, and currently serves as theatre and dance writer for the weekly alternative newspaper *Columbus Alive* (http://www.columbusalive.com). Portions of his article have been adapted, updated, and expanded from his "Music and OCLC: Past, Present, Future," delivered at the International Association of Music Libraries, Archives, and Documentation Centres conference in Berkeley, California, 7 August 2002, and Jay Weitz and Neil Hughes, "MOUG Time Line," *MOUG Newsletter*, no. 70 (September 1998): 9–19. He extends additional thanks to Larry Olszewski, director of the OCLC Library, for research assistance.

Damian Iseminger is the technical services librarian at the New England Conservatory of Music in Boston, Massachusetts. He has been a member of the Music Library Association Bibliographic Control Committee (BCC) as Authorities Subcommittee chair since 2009 and has been a member of several BCC task forces and working groups, including the BCC Working Group on Work Records for Music (2008), the BCC Task Force to Develop Draft BIBCO Standard Records for Scores and Sound Recordings (2010), and the BCC Task Force on RDA Best Practice Guidelines for MARC 38X Fields (2010). He also participated in the U.S. National Libraries RDA Test as a member of the joint MLA/OLAC Funnel (2010–11). He is a member of the Music OCLC Users Group, serving as secretary/newsletter editor (2010–12), and is an independent contributor to the NACO Music Project. He wishes to thank Michelle Koth of Yale University for her early contributions to this article, especially as it concerns music uniform titles in AACR2.

Suzanne Mudge has been a cataloger at Indiana University's Archives of Traditional Music since 1994. She would like to thank Jeffrey C. Graf, reference computer coordinator at Indiana University Wells Library, for his keen editorial eye and feedback on an earlier draft of this article and Beth Iseminger, music and media catalog librarian at Harvard University's Loeb Music Library, for her suggestions and review of processes at the Loeb Music Library Archive of World Music. Thank you, Ralph Papakhian, for your leadership, inspiration, and unwavering support.

Beth Iseminger is a music and media catalog librarian at the Eda Kuhn Loeb Music Library of Harvard University, where she catalogs printed and recorded music and ethnomusicological special collections. Prior to working at Harvard, she was a music catalog librarian at Kent State University and at the Oberlin College Conservatory Library. Iseminger is the chair of the Genre/Form Task Force of the Music Library Association's Bibliographic Control Committee and the Technical Services Committee of the New England Chapter of MLA. She is past chair of the MLA-BCC Subject Access Subcommittee and was a member of the BCC Task Force on RDA Best Practice Guidelines for MARC 38X Fields. She has also served on the program committees of both MLA and the Music OCLC Users Group. She thanks all the members of the MLA-BCC Genre/Form Task Force. The work that the task force has done has been highly collaborative, and much of her paper represents the thoughts and discussions of the entire group. She also thanks the LC Music Genre Project Group and especially Geraldine Ostrove, music specialist in the Library of Congress Policy and Standards Division and the driving force behind much of the music genre project. Finally, she thanks Ralph Papakhian: "You continue to inspire and you always will."

Michelle Hahn is the music catalog librarian for Central University Libraries at Southern Methodist University. She received a Master of Library Science degree with a Music Librarianship Specialization from Indiana University and is currently working toward a Master of Music degree in Music Education from SMU. Hahn is a member of both the Music OCLC Users Group and the Music Library Association, for which she served as a member of the Membership Committee, and is co-chair of the Local Arrangements Committee for the 2012 MLA meeting in Dallas, Texas. She has been co-editor-in-chief of *Music Reference Services Quarterly* since 2010, and her research interests include music education literature and music periodical indexing. She is also the 2010–11 recipient of the Outstanding Achievement Award from SMU Libraries. Hahn would like to thank the staff of the William and Gayle Cook Music Library at Indiana University, especially Sue Stancu and Chuck Peters, for their unending friendship and support. She is exceedingly thankful for Ralph Papakhian, who was one of her teachers, employers, and mentors in the field of music librarianship. He, along with the other contributors to this volume, brought her into this profession and raised her with great care to be passionate about serving the materials, the users, and above all, the profession and its people.

Jenn Riley is the head of the Carolina Digital Library and Archives at the University of North Carolina at Chapel Hill. In this position she leads a department that combines digital technologies with library and archival collections to support the work of scholars, students, and librarians at UNC and beyond. In this role, Riley also works to enhance faculty digital research and scholarship, builds partnerships to advance the state of the art in digital libraries, and develops sustainable and streamlined workflows for the publication of digital content. Prior to arriving at the University of North Carolina in 2010, she was the metadata librarian with the Indiana University Digital Library Program, and in this capacity worked on a wide variety of music digital library initiatives. She brings a digital and technical perspective to her work with music collections, and looks for opportunities to leverage her music background in support of her digital library work. Her music cataloging internship and subsequent discussions about library metadata with Ralph Papakhian have profoundly influenced her thinking in this area. Words cannot express her gratitude and respect for Ralph and his legacy.

Sue Ellen Stancu has been a cataloger in the Technical Services Division of the William and Gayle Cook Music Library at Indiana University since 1979. Prior to that she worked as a library assistant in the music library at Arizona State University. Stancu received her Master of Library Science degree from the University of Arizona where she studied cataloging and classification with Dr. Margaret F. Maxwell. She would like to thank the following people: Elizabeth Johnson for her encouragement and support, and Therese Zoski Dickman, who interviewed Ralph on 18 March 1999 as part of the Music Library Association's Oral History Project. (Full text of the interview appears in *Midwest Notebook* 19, no. 1 [May 2010]: 11–24, available on the MLA Midwest Chapter website at http://www.mlamidwest.org/documents/notebook/19_1.pdf.) Special thanks and appreciation go to Ralph Papakhian for his mentoring role over the course of thirty-one years, his steadfast commitment to excellence, and his refusal to settle for "good enough."

INDEX

A

AACR2. See *Anglo-American Cataloguing Rules*
AACR3, 50
Acker, Robert, 37
American Library Association, Committee on Cataloging: Description and Access, 16
AMIM. See *Archival Moving Image Materials*
Anglo-American Cataloguing Rules, changes to headings required by, viii, 20, 22, 31, 33; description and access using, 44–45; use for digital music metadata, 111–38; use with ethnographic field recordings, 90, 91; history, 15, 16; principles underlying, 140; enduring value of, 80
Apple Inc., 112, 123
APPM. See *Archives, Personal Papers, and Manuscripts*
Archival Moving Image Materials (AMIM), 91
archival recordings. See ethnographic field recordings
Archive of World Music (Harvard University). See Harvard University
Archives of Traditional Music (Indiana University). See Indiana University
Archives, Personal Papers, and Manuscripts (APPM), 91
Arnold, Donna, 36
ARP. See Papakhian, Ralph
Associated Music Libraries Group, 34
Association of Research Libraries, 16
Ausdal, Karl van. See Van Ausdal, Karl

B

Bach, Johann Sebastian, ix; uniform titles for works by, 31, 32
Bade, David, 38
Baker & Taylor, vendor records supplied by, 7
Barnhart, Linda, 33
Bartl, Joe, 36
A Basic Music Library, 4, 5
Bauer, Sally, 38
Baunach, Kerri Scannell, 35, 37
BCC. See Music Library Association
Bendig, Deborah, 33, 36, 37

Berman, Sanford, 161
The Best of MOUG, 32, 36
Bibliographic Control Committee (BCC). See Music Library Association
Borgman, C. L., 17
Bowen, Jennifer, 34
Bucknum, Mary Russell, 89, 91, 93
Burnett, Kathryn E., 36
Busselen, Catherine Gick, 38
Buth, Olga, 28, 29

C

Caldwell, Ann McCollough, 32, 33, 37
Cass Technical High School (Detroit, Mich.), 158
cataloger envy, ix, 35
Cataloger's Judgment (Weitz), 34
cataloging, as a public good, xi
Cataloging Unpublished Nonprint Materials, 91
Cauthen, Paul, 37
Caw, Tom, 38
CCDA. See American Library Association, Committee on Cataloging: Description and Access
Cherubini, Tim, 34
Children's music, subject access to, 70
Churukian, Ann, 34
CIDOC Conceptual Reference Model, 140
Clarke, Arthur C., ix
Classification and Index of the World's Languages (Voegelin), 101
Colby, Michael, 34
Comaromi, John, 158
Coral, Lenore, 28
Corwin, Dean, 32, 33
Coyle, Karen, 148
Cunningham, Robert, 29, 30, 31
Cutter, Charles Ammi, 140

D

DACS. See *Describing Archives*
DCMI. See *Dublin Core Metadata Initiative*
De Sellem, Phillip, 35

Dederick, Emma, 162
Delsey, Tom, 49, 50
Denison, Barbara, 28
Denton, William, 140
Describing Archives: A Content Standard (DACS), 90
Describing Music Materials (Smiraglia), 90, 92, 113
digital music, use of AACR2 access points with, 111–38
Dublin Core Metadata Initiative (DCMI), 140
Dunsire, Gordon, 148

E
Eastman School of Music, Sibley Library, 3
Eden, Brad, 35
envy, cataloger, ix, 35
ethnographic field recordings, description of, 91–100; access points for, 100–101; subject access to, 101–2
Ethnologue: Languages of the World (ed. Lewis), 101
Evans, Bruce, 37

F
Feldt, Candice, 33, 36
Fling, Robert Michael, 4
Flood, Beth. *See* Iseminger, Beth Flood
form, providing access to, 63–77
Format Variation Working Group. *See* Joint Steering Committee for the Revision of AACR2
FRAD. *See Functional Requirements for Authority Data*
FRBR. *See Functional Requirements for Bibliographic Records*
Freeborn, Robert, 37
FRSAD. *See Functional Requirements for Subject Authority Data*
Funabiki, Ruth Patterson, 31
Functional Requirements for Authority Data, as extension of FRBR, 142; definition of "medium," 66; overview, 47–49
Functional Requirements for Bibliographic Records, speculative catalog based on, 82–84; as foundation for library metadata standards, 139–53; history, 46; and metadata sharing, 148–49; overview, 46–47, 80–81; V/FRBR project, 143–50
Functional Requirements for Subject Authority Data, 142–43

G
Garland, Catherine, 31
The Garland Encyclopedia of World Music, 69, 101

Gardner, Ron, 33
genre, providing access to, 63–77
Gerboth, Walter, 27
Gerhart, Catherine, 37
Gick, Catherine. *See* Busselen, Catherine Gick
Girsberger, Russ, *Practical Guide to Percussion Terminology*, 69
Glennan, Kathy, 37
Godwin, James L., 16, 23
Goldner, Matt, 38
Gorman, Michael, 30
Grandy, Christine, 34
Green, Laura Gayle, 34
Griscom, Richard, 163
Grossi, Henry, 36
Grove Music Online, 69, 101
Gullickson, Lynn, 35

H
Hafner, Joseph, 37
Hagberg, Karen A., 28, 29
Harden, Jean, 35, 36, 37
Hartsock, Ralph, 65; *Notes for Music Catalogers*, 113
Harvard University, Loeb Music Library Archive of World Music, 89–110
Hemmssi, Harriette, *Music Subject Headings*, 69
Herman-Morgan, Debbie, 35
Herrold, Charles, 35, 36
Hess, Ann E., 29
Hill, Janet Swan, 38
Hillmann, Diane, 148
Hixon, Don, 32, 33
Hoerman, Heidi, 38
Howarth, Lynne, 37
Hughes, Helen, 29, 31
Hughes, Neil, 35, 37
Human Relations Area Files, 101
Hunter, Caitlin, 38, 65, 66
Hyde, Thomas, 140

I
IAML. *See* International Association of Music Libraries, Archives, and Documentation Centres
IBM Selectric typewriter, 157–58, 163
indecs, 140
Indiana University, Archives of Traditional Music, ix, 89–110; music cataloging workshop, 159–60; music librarianship specialization program, 159; music library, 3, 4; personal name headings in the music

catalog of, 15–25; Variations project, 64, 69; Variations/FRBR project, 143–50
Inman, Ruth Ann, 35
International Association of Music Libraries, Archives, and Documentation Centres (IAML), lists of medium and genre/form terms, 69
International Standards for Bibliographic Description, 15
Intner, Sheila, 35
ISBD. *See* International Standards for Bibliographic Description
Iseminger, Beth Flood, 37, 65
Iseminger, Damien, 38
iPod Nano, use of AACR2 access points with, 121–23
iTunes, use of AACR2 access points with, 114–21

J
Jaffe, Howard, 37
Jenkins, Martin, 36, 37, 65
Johnson, Elizabeth, 162
Johnson, Bruce, 66
Joint Steering Committee for the Revision of AACR2 (JSC), 16, 49–50; Format Variation Working Group, 50
Jones, Richard E., 30, 32
Jordan, Jay, 37, 38
JSC. *See* Joint Steering Committee for the Revision of AACR2
Juengling, Pam, 33

K
Kaufmann, Walter, *Selected Musical Terms of Non-Western Cultures*, 69
Kaus, Margaret, 32, 35, 36, 37
Kerst, Catherine Hiebert, 90
Kilgour, Frederick G., 27, 29
Kircher, Mela, 37
Kiss My Filing Indicators, 161
Knapp, David, 28, 31
Koth, Michelle, 33, 35, 36
Kruesi, Margaret, 66

L
LaSota, Alice, 35
LCGFT. *See Library of Congress Genre/Form Terms for Library and Archival Materials*
LCRI. *See* Library of Congress: Rule Interpretations
LCSH. *See Library of Congress Subject Headings*
LeSueur, Richard, 37
Levine, Jamie, 29
Lewis, Paul M., *Ethnologue: Languages of the World*, 101
Library of Congress, and the implementation of AACR2, 16; genre projects, 64–65; as the "gold standard" for cataloging, vii; implementation of MARC music format, 29; MARC Development Office, 27, 29; MARC Distribution Service, 4; Program for Cooperative Cataloging, 36; as provider of cataloging, xi; Rule Interpretations, 15; Working Group on the Future of Bibliographic Control, 143
Library of Congress Genre/Form Terms for Library and Archival Materials (LCGFT), 63, 64, 71, 73
Library of Congress Subject Headings (LCSH), 63, 65, 71, 72; western bias of, 101–02
Lippy, Brooke, 65
Littman, Rebecca, 37
Little, Karen, 34, 35, 37
Little, Mary Lou, 27, 28
Lorimer, Nancy, 65
Lotka's Law, 16, 17, 18, 21, 22, 23
Lowell, Kay, 36
Lubetzky, Seymour, 140
Luttmann, Stephen, 36, 37, 38

M
MARC formats, 15; for monographs, 3; for music, 3, 27–28, 29, 81–82
McCallum, Sally H., 16, 17, 23
McCawley, Christina, 30
McCollough, Ann. *See* Caldwell, Ann McCollough
McGreer, Anne, 32
McKnight, Mark, 65
McTyre, Ruthann, 34, 36, 163
medium of performance, providing access to, 63–77
MLA. *See* Music Library Association
Morris, Deborah, 37
Mother Bear's Pizza (Bloomington, Ind.), 161, 162
MOUG. *See* Music OCLC Users Group
Mozart, Wolfgang Amadeus, uniform titles for works by, 31–32
Mudge, Suzanne, 162
Mullin, Casey, 65
Murdoch, George, *Outline of World Cultures*, 93, 101
music, subject access to, 63–77
Music Coding and Tagging (Weitz), 95
Music Genre/Form Project, 63–77
Music Library Association, BCC Genre/Form Task Force, 65, 68–69, 71; BCC Subject Access

Subcommittee, 72; Cataloging Committee, 3; Music Thesaurus Project, 63–64
Music OCLC Users Group, 4, 27–39; archives, 34; Distinguished Service Award, 36; MOUG-L, 35; newsletter, 29; PRISM Review Task Force, 35; Ralph Papakhian Travel Grant, 38; Reference Task Force, 33
Music Subject Headings (Hemmasi), 63–64
Music Thesaurus Project. *See* Music Library Association

N
NACO Music Project (NMP), 33, 34, 36, 43, 159
Napert, Diane, 38
New Grove Dictionary of Music and Musicians, 69
New Grove Dictionary of Musical Instruments, 101
Nilges, Chip, 37
Nilsson, Mikael, 140
Nim, Myrtle, 28
NMP. *See* NACO Music Project
Northwestern University, music library, 3
Notes for Music Catalogers (Hartsock), 113
Nyun, James L. Soe, 37

O
OCLC, viii, ix, 3, 4, 5, 15, 27–39; Enhance Program, 30; EPIC Service, 34; implementation of MARC music format, 27–28; Musical Recordings Analytics Consortium, 30; Office of Research, 6; *Search CD450 Music Library*, 33; Taskforce on the Cataloging of Music Scores and Sound Recordings, 28, 29; WorldCat, coverage of music in, 3–14
OCLC music users group. *See* Music OCLC Users Group
Oglebay Institute on Quality Control, 30
Ohio College Library Center. *See* OCLC
OLAC. *See* Online Audiovisual Catalogers
Olson, Nancy B., 32
On-line Cataloging of Scores, 28
On-line Cataloging of Sound Recordings, 28
Online Computer Library Center. *See* OCLC
Online Audiovisual Catalogers (OLAC), 32, 35
Ostrove, Geraldine, 65, 66
Outline of World Cultures (Murdoch), 93, 101
Oxford Music Online. See *Grove Music Online*

P
Panizzi, Anthony, 140
Papakhian, Arsen Ralph. *See* Papakhian, Ralph
Papakhian, Mary, 161

Papakhian, Ralph, vii–xi, 5, 13, 157–68; article on "cataloger envy," ix, 35; article on name headings, viii, x, 15–25; article on music in OCLC, viii, 4, 30, 159; on cataloging rules, 140; importance of consistency and accuracy to, viii; skepticism about FRBR, 141, 142, 150; service to Indiana University, 160; legacy of, xi; use of language by, 24; participation in MOUG, ix, 29, 30, 32, 33, 34, 35, 36, 38, 159, 160; and the NACO Music Project, 36, 43, 159; opinions about OPACs, ix; as pedagogue and mentor, 159–60; political nature of, viii; questioning nature of, vii, xi, 141; opinion of RDA, x; social activism of, 160–61; on uniform titles, 141
Paris Principles, 140
Patton, Glenn, 30, 31, 32, 37, 38
Pease, Thomas, 65
Penner, Jane Edmister, 35
Petek, Marija, 17
Peters, Karen, 65
Phipps, Jon, 148
Potter, William Gray, 16, 17, 18, 23, 24
Practical Guide to Percussion Terminology (Girsberger), 69
Price, Harry, 158
Procházka, David, 35
Prokofiev, Sergey, uniform titles for works by, 33
psalms, subject access to, 70

R
Raffi. *See* Papakhian, Ralph
ralphlike, 163
Rand, Ayn, xi
Ranganathan, S. R., 140
Rappaport, Ellen, 32
RDA. *See Resource Description & Access*
REMUS. *See* Retrospective Music Project
Research Libraries Information Network. *See* RLIN
Resource Description & Access, creating authorized access points, 55–58; application to archival recordings, 103; core elements, 50–51; use for digital music metadata, 134; identifying *expressions*, 54–55; impact of implementation, 80; history, 49–50; providing access to medium of performance, 72–73; possible solutions to its problems, 58–61; treatment of *works* and *expressions*, 50–61
Retrospective Music Project (REMUS), 30, 33
Ringwood, Alan, 37
RLIN, 3, 9, 15

Robbins, Donald, 28
Robson, Tim, 31, 32
Rudnick, Tracey, 37
Rules for Archival Cataloging of Sound Recordings, 91
Russell, Maureen, 38

S
Sack, Nancy, 37
SACO. *See* Subject Authority Cooperative Program
sacred music, subject access to, 70
Sarmiento, Michael, 38
Savage, Tim, 37
Scharff, Mark, 36
Schipior, Sandra, 38
Schuitema, Joan, 32, 33
Schumann, Robert, uniform titles for works by, 33
Scott, Joseph W., 31
Seibert, Donald, 27
Selected Musical Terms of Non-Western Cultures (Kaufmann), 69
Sellem, Phillip de. *See* De Sellem, Phillip
Shiota, Lisa, 66
Shurk, William, 28
Siegfried, S. L., 17
Sistrunk, Wendy, 38
Smiraglia, Richard P., 16, 17, 19, 20: article on music in OCLC, viii, 4, 30, 159; *Describing Music Materials*, 90, 92, 113; participation in MOUG, 30, 31
Smith-Borne, Holling, 37
Smolko, Tim, 38
Snyder, Laura, 33, 34
Snyder, Tracey, 38
Sony Walkman, use of AACR2 access points with, 134
sound recordings. *See* digital music; ethnographic field recordings
Southside Catalogers, 162
Stancu, Sue, participation in MOUG, 29, 31, 36, 37, 38; memories of Papakhian, 157–68
Starr, Pamela F., 29
Steuermann, Clara, 27
Subject Authority Cooperative Program, 102
Survey of Musical Instruments, 101
Swanekamp, Joan, 31, 32
Sylvester, Anna, 37

T
Taranto, Cheryl, 35
Taylor, Arlene. *See* Taylor Dowell, Arlene

Taylor Dowell, Arlene, 16, 17, 20, 21, 22, 23
Thomas, David, 92
Torres-Blank, Sheila, 65
Tucker, Ben, 161
Tucker, Ruth W., 30, 31
Typewriters, used for catalog cards, 157–58

U
University of California, San Diego, 23
University of Florida, 158
University of Illinois at Urbana–Champaign, music library, 3, 4, 16
University of North Carolina at Chapel Hill, 22, 23

V
Van Ausdal, Karl, 28, 29, 31, 34
Variations Project (Indiana University). *See* Indiana University
Vellucci, Sherry, 16, 19, 35
Vermeij, Hermine, 65
Vigorito, Maarja, 66
Vivaldi, Antonio, uniform titles for works by, 31
Voegelin, C. F. and F. M., *Classification and Index of the World's Languages*, 101

W
Walbridge, Sharon, 29
Weidow, Judy, 32, 34, 36
Weiland, Sue, 34, 35
Weintraub, Tamara S., 17, 22, 23
Weitz, Jay, 31, 34, 36; *Music Coding and Tagging*, 95
Western Michigan University, 158
Windows Media Player, use of AACR2 access points with, 123–27
Withrow, Marty, 35
WorldCat. *See* OCLC
Wortman, Vince, 38
Wright, H. Stephen, 34, 35, 36

Y
Yee, Martha, 35
Young, Janis, 38
Youngholm, Philip, 31
Yusko, Stephen, 66

Z
Zhou, Liana, 162